The V-Spot

The V-Spot: Healing the "V"ulnerable Spot from Emotional Abuse

Joan Lachkar

JASON ARONSON
Lanham • Boulder • New York • Toronto • Plymouth, UK

Published in the United States of America
by Jason Aronson
An imprint of Rowman & Littlefield Publishers, Inc.

A wholly owned subsidiary of
The Rowman & Littlefield Publishing Group, Inc.
4501 Forbes Boulevard, Suite 200, Lanham, Maryland 20706
www.rowmanlittlefield.com

Estover Road
Plymouth PL6 7PY
United Kingdom

British Library Cataloguing in Publication Information Available

Library of Congress Cataloging-in-Publication Data

Lachkar, Joan.
The V-spot : healing the "V"ulnerable spot from emotional abuse / Joan Lachkar.
p. ; cm.
Includes bibliographical references and index.
ISBN-13: 978-0-7657-0391-0 (cloth : alk. paper)
ISBN-10: 0-7657-0391-2 (cloth : alk. paper)
ISBN-13: 978-0-7657-0392-7 (pbk. : alk. paper)
ISBN-10: 0-7657-0392-0 (pbk. : alk. paper)
1. Marital psychotherapy. 2. Psychological abuse. 3. Emotions. 4. Psychoanalysis. I. Title.
[DNLM: 1. Marital Therapy—methods. 2. Spouse Abuse—psychology. 3. Couples Therapy—methods. 4. Personality Disorders—psychology. 5. Personality Disorders—therapy. WM 430.5.M3 L137v 2008]
RC488.5.L3483 2008
616.89'1562—dc22

2007029885

Printed in the United States of America

∞™ The paper used in this publication meets the minimum requirements of American National Standard for Information Sciences—Permanence of Paper for Printed Library Materials, ANSI/NISO Z39.48-1992.

To My Family

Contents

	List of Figures and Tables	ix
	Acknowledgments	xi
	Introduction	1
Chapter 1	The V-Spot and Its Corresponding Concepts	9
Chapter 2	Abusers and Their Enablers	31
Chapter 3	Emotional Abuse and Its Relationship to the V-Spot	51
Chapter 4	Theoretical Considerations	65
Chapter 5	Marital Theatrics	89
Chapter 6	The Internal Abuser	107
Chapter 7	Group Psychology and Cross-Cultural Considerations	123
Chapter 8	Treatment Procedures and Techniques	143
Chapter 9	Final Thoughts	163
	Glossary	167
	References	175
	Index	181
	About the Author	191

~

List of Figures and Tables

Figures

Figure 8.1	Each partner lives emotionally inside the other.	144
Figure 8.2	Boundaries of twoness (ability to move into a new transitional space).	146
Figure 8.3	Boundaries to two separate but bonded, dependent yet interdependent, individuals.	147

Tables

Table 2.1	Different Kinds of Borderlines	38
Table 2.2	Five Types of Abusers and the Types of Enablers That Stay with Them	50
Table 2.3	The Types of Love Bonds That Attract	50
Table 4.1	Chronological Developments of Theorists	68
Table 4.2	Kernberg's (1995) Four Types of Love Relationships	77
Table 5.1	Psychodynamics	103

Acknowledgments

This book is an expansion of my previously published works. Many of the same steadfast friends and colleagues have remained loyal to the continuation of this journey. This book highlights much of the material described in my earlier works but takes on a newer face. The reader of *The V-Spot* may see normal pages, but all I see are endless pages of comments/corrections marked in green, red, and blue, with arrows shooting in every direction. I have a vision of Professor Peter Berton flashing his red editorial pen like a baton with the frenzy and furor of an Arturo Toscanini, shouting, "Repetitious! Stream of consciousness! Make an outline!" I have been extremely remiss in not paying tribute to him in my earlier works in which he also was most instrumental, especially on the chapters on cross-cultural couples. Peter Berton is Distinguished Professor Emeritus at the School of International Relations, University of Southern California and Professor Emeritus at the New Center for Psychoanalysis in Los Angeles. I believe I have learned more about Japanese/Russian/Chinese cultures and politics from him than if I had lived in those countries myself.

Much thanks is due to my former publisher Jason Aronson for his steady encouragement and expansive vision of psychoanalytic theory that extends beyond the consultation room to the political and global arena. It is a great privilege and honor to have worked with him. With his departure, I welcome in a new editorial director, Arthur Pomponio, Ph.D. He has given support and encouragement in the same vein as Dr. Aronson, seeking to explore new territories with the vision of cultural awareness and openness, and also to

Mary Catherine La Mar, editorial assistant, and to all those at Rowman & Littlefield.

There are so many other people to thank for their inspirational help. Special thanks to my personal editor, Haley Grace, for her laser-like eye and insights; to my final editor, Joanne Freeman; to my devoted research assistant, Alexandra Sokhis, for her acuity and never-ending patience; and to my amazing researcher, Shauna Papenbrook, for her remarkable editorial skills and quick eye.

Special thanks to Lloyd de Mause for introducing me to psychohistory. His bountiful knowledge and ongoing influence have encouraged me to continue on this path. I must also pay special tribute to the many mentors who helped guide me through the complex and intricate process of psychoanalysis: Drs. James Grotstein, Peter Loewenberg, Albert Mason, Murray Weiler, Marvin Osman, Robert Kahn, Norman Tabachnick, among others. The master theorists who have helped provide a strong clinical basis for this book include Drs. Otto Kernberg, Wilfred Bion, Melanie Klein, Heinz Kohut, and many others quoted throughout this book.

I am particularly indebted to Dr. Nancy Kobrin, whose corresponding work on suicide bombers added greatly to the chapter on cross-cultural couples. I am also indebted to my good friends and colleagues for their endless patience and critical ears: Dr. Shelley Ventura, for her scrupulous critiquing; Dr. Harvey Martz, for his amazing analytic ear; and Ronit Brautbar and Dr. Orli Peter for their insightful firsthand experiences on the Middle East. I am grateful to my family, particularly my daughters, Sharon Stone, Pamela Brody, and Nicole Raphael, for their encouragement, patience, and sacrifices. I also wish to express special gratitude to the entire staff at the New Center for Psychoanalysis for their continual support and research efforts, with special appreciation of the late Dr. Samuel Eisenstein and Alexander Rogawsky for their amazing encouragement.

In addition to my friends and colleagues from the analytic world, there are those from the dance/artistic world of classical ballet. For years I kept these worlds apart, not knowing how to integrate them until I wrote an article on dance and narcissism published in *The Journal of Dance and Choreography*. I owe much to Bonnie Ota, editor, and dance masters Margaret Hills, Stanley Holden, and the late Carmelita Maracci.

Finally, and most important, I must thank my students, supervisees, and patients with all my heart for their trust and devotion. (They have turned out to be my best supervisors and teachers.)

~

Introduction

Let me not to the marriage of true minds
Admit impediments. Love is not love
Which alters when it alteration finds . . .
Love alters not with his brief hours and weeks,
But bears it out even to the edge of doom.

—William Shakespeare, Sonnet 116

Who knows about love? Does Keats? Shelley? Shakespeare? Freud? The capacity to fall in love is a basic human experience, and when people fall in love, it is felt to be magical (due in part to a high dopamine level). Two people begin their relationship with deep feelings of attraction and longing for each other, but lurking in the shadows is an uncontrollable impulse to destroy, threaten, and sabotage, some kind of primitive idealization that disrupts love because of an unruly past with its archaic memories—known in the psychoanalytic literature as the archaic injury or which I refer to as the "vulnerable spot" (or the V-spot).

This book illustrates how partners who never lay a violent hand on one another can feel just as emotionally violated as those who are physically abused. More important than the damage that occurs psychologically and emotionally is how they protect and heal themselves from the devastation that emotional injuries generate (Lachkar 1998a).

At the core of the emotional pain is an area that has been long neglected in the psychological literature—a raw area of vulnerability. This area gets stirred by the slightest provocation; one wrong move or word and it blows.

This occurs even among couples who are not in emotionally abusive or conflictual relationships. Love relations are not simple; they are complex because they are composed of many interrelated aspects of highly charged emotions (shame, guilt, envy, jealousy, rivalry, control, domination). A man might say, "I don't like it when you wear that tank top and all the other guys are looking at you!" Patients with narcissistic personality and borderline disorders, for example, have a deep desire for intimate relations and present intense erotic venues for finding love. However, with these attachments come disruption and disappointment. Borderline patients particularly "evince a capacity for a primitive kind of falling in love characterized by an unrealistic idealization of the love object" (Kernberg 1995).

This book is a logical development of my earlier works, among them, *The Narcissistic/Borderline Couple* (1992, 2004) and *The Many Faces of Abuse* (1998). In the first book, I describe what happens when a narcissist and a borderline join together in a marital bond or "bind," how each stirs up unresolved conflict in the other, and how the other tends to identify or over-identify with some negative aspect that is being projected (shame, blame, guilt). A person with a borderline character is inclined to attract a narcissistic personality as an object choice. These two personalities then enter into what I refer to as a "dance" that bonds them together and fulfills the conscious and unconscious needs of each partner. In my previous research, I have found that two narcissists or two borderlines cannot "do the dance" because of their dynamics and defenses. However, once paired with an opposing type, a borderline or narcissist appears able to maintain a bond with the opposite.

In the second book, I venture beyond narcissistic and borderline vulnerabilities into emotionally abusive relations, exploring a variety of other dyadic configurations, including how the grandiose self invades and infects other relational love bonds. I explore, for example, what happens when an obsessive-compulsive hooks up with a histrionic, a passive-aggressive with a caretaker, or a schizoid with a borderline/dependent. The goal was to find the unique qualities that make them feel particularly vulnerable to one another. I then highlight these various disorders by noting their distinctive defense mechanisms, psychodynamics, and qualitative differences as symptomatic of the couple's pathological makeup including the unique qualities of the couple that make them vulnerable to one another.

Although I revisit various couples and topics from previous works in this book, I extend these relational love bonds to more specifically pinpoint the exact area or vertex where their archaic injuries meet and interface.

While working on my last manuscript, I tried to shorten the term "the area of vulnerability," which appeared repeatedly throughout the text. The

"V-spot" is the abbreviation I devised to describe the most sensitive area of emotional vulnerability that gets instantly aroused when one's partner hits a raw spot. The term V-spot is more user-friendly than "archaic injury" and somehow says it all. It is the emotional counterpart of the physical G-spot. Whereas the G-spot is pure physical pleasure, the V-spot is pure emotionality that is provoked by even the slightest annoyance. The V-spot is the heart of our most fragile area of emotional sensitivity, known in the literature as the archaic injury, a product of early trauma that one unwittingly holds on to and retains throughout adult life. With arousal of the V-spot comes the loss of sense and sensibility; everything shakes and shifts like in an earthquake (memory, perception, judgment, reality).

In one of my seminars, a student was asked what happens to the patient's thought processes when he or she is in a state of vulnerability. The student contended that when a patient's ego goes into fatal mode, his or her judgment, memory, reality, thinking, cognitive ability, and perception get corrupted by the demons of the past. This showed a deep understanding of how a patient's defense mechanisms, archaic injuries, and injury reactions from the past can severely invade and impair the ego's capacity to function. We must not forget that the therapist's own V-spot can be aroused within the countertransference. The following illustration is an example of this point.

I was very anxious about meeting with Jean and Bob because I knew this was the session in which I would have to confront Jean about her aggression and shame/blame defenses. I had tried my best to be empathic, diplomatic, and in a most caring way to show Jean how her aggression and controlling behaviors pushed her husband away (coerced him into being the cruel and mean husband). Meanwhile, throughout the conjoint treatment, Jean was either attacking her husband or, more recently, turning to me as the object of blame, accusing me of not addressing her husband's aggression and cruelty. "But look what he does to me! Aren't you going to do something or say something?"

In spite of all my efforts, the more empathic and understating I became, the more violent and abusive she became. Jean's traumatic childhood of violence and abuse by her bully father constituted the rationale for her barrage of attacks. "This therapy is not working! You have failed me and are blind to how mean and cruel my husband is to me. Look at the face he is making!" Finally, I mustered up the courage to confront her, all the while knowing I was running the risk of her disrupting the treatment altogether, and said,

> Actually the reason this therapy "isn't working" is because you have been doing nothing but attacking, blaming, yelling, screaming, and interrupting. You blame

> me for not addressing your husband's shortcomings and "cruelty," but actually I have. When he is out of line like forgetting your birthday or anniversary, I do address his passive-aggressive defenses and the inappropriateness of his behavior. But basically, you are the perpetrator! You are the aggressor! You are the one who is cruel, sadistic, controlling, aggressive, and non-appreciative, not even taking a breath to reflect on your own behavior! I thought that if I was empathic and understanding this would help you be more introspective. Ironically, I have not been cruel to you and in return you have done nothing but attack and criticize me.

I thought she was going to storm out of the room; instead she sat there with her mouth open, more pensive than I have ever could have imagined her to be (her husband in a state of shock). Then, like a laser, I went right to her V-spot, and softly, quietly, and ever so gently explained to her,

> As a child no one was there for you or kind to you. You were raised by a bully, a cruel and horrifically mean father, and, even worse, by a mother who sat passively and did nothing to protect you. Now you see me as the ineffective non-protective mother not standing by your side. As these injuries get stirred up here, you are not available to see how I am being the protective mommy trying to help you. Instead you only see me as the unavailable and unprotective parent putting you in harm's way. In the same way, when your husband gets frustrated with you, you distort his image, seeing him only as the mean and cruel father. In reality he is not mean; he is merely frustrated and exasperated. So the way you deal with your aggression is instead of expressing your hurt feelings, you have now become your father, a bully/father. All of this is a very convenient way to avoid the closeness and vulnerability an intimate relationship requires.

Since the V-spot is an essential link between narcissistic injury and vulnerabilities, it is natural that this book should delve deeper into the concept of the archaic injury. Kohut elaborates on this exclusively in his pioneer work *Self Psychology* (1971, 1977) but does not specifically link this concept to the ego and the mechanisms of defense. The archaic injury has a more specific destination. "Tell us what to do? Should we stay? Get a divorce? Have another baby? Have her mother move in with us?" In response, the therapist must go directly to the "zone" rather than the solution. "I suppose if you have spent your entire life being a caretaker feeling responsible for everyone, it would be difficult to make a clear and rational decision and stay focused on your needs." Individuals who cannot tolerate normal consequences of everyday life conflicts, especially around states of confusion and chaos, often feel persecuted by dependency needs, making it impossible to make clear and rational decisions. "It is entirely your fault this is happening!" In my work with couples, I frequently hear that therapists who are aware of this kind of mental state or ego dysfunctionality are in a position to reframe such behaviors and move away from shame/blame attacking defenses. To this the therapist may respond, "To paraphrase Goethe: 'It is difficult to know what to do, especially when so much blaming and attacking is going on.'"

I had some firsthand experience with my own V-spot while writing this book. Inadvertently, I lost two days of work on the computer and, much to my horror, I was unable to retrieve it. My first reaction was panic, along with fear that I would never be able to recover the material. The next reaction was abandonment—that the scholars and colleagues who contributed to it would not be willing to reconstruct the material they had so willingly and generously offered. The end result was that they were most empathic and very helpful in recreating their contributions. I realized that the anxieties that triggered my V-spot were not reality based.

My first influence for this book came from working with couples. Therapists are often frustrated when patients refuse to listen to their "good interpretations" or take their "good advice." It was continually baffling to me why people stay in painful, conflictual relationships that involve destructive, ongoing interactions that go round and round without ever reaching any conflict resolution. Even when peace and harmony are offered, they are rebuffed. Why do people sabotage progress just when they are at the pinnacle of success? Why do they repeat the same traumatic experience again and again without ever learning from experience? Why is it that people who are dominated by primitive defenses and have characterological disorders stay bonded more to pain than pleasure, and remain forever loyal to a bad internal object as they endlessly repeat the same traumatic experience (see chapter 2)? As one man vents his deep frustration with his borderline wife, "I feel as though we are going round and round. She keeps my head spinning. I don't know right from left!"

The other contributions and publications on narcissistic/borderline relationships I have written provided fodder for this work. I have expanded on themes on various relationship bonds to recognize how each dyadic unit or configuration has its own unique formation of dynamics and defense mechanisms, or its own personalized "V-spot." For example, patients more inclined toward narcissistic disorders may withdraw or isolate themselves whenever personally injured or whenever their sense of specialness or entitlement is at risk. In contrast, patients more inclined toward borderline organization may explode whenever issues of abandonment or betrayal are brought up (see chapter 4). Even after divorce or separation, such individuals will continue to sabotage, sacrifice, or inflict pain on themselves or others in order to maintain a bond or achieve some semblance of bonding, even if it is destructive. In essence, the way they see it is that any attachment is better than no attachment at all.

The third influence for this work emanated from the Walter Briehl Human Rights Organization, a group of psychoanalysts dedicated to understanding the minds of terrorists and to the treatment of torture victims. Although most individuals we treat in clinical practice are not full-blown terrorists, understanding terrorism and its aftermath paves the way to understanding the infinite magnitude of the severity of aggression, cruelty, and sadism, specifically in the ability to distinguish the malignant narcissists from the pathological narcissists. Through this, I learned that people who have been tortured require special treatment, a familiarity with their culture, and recognition that a classical model of psychoanalytic technique and principles cannot easily be applied. For example, Japan is a "we-group" society, whereas the West is an "I-me-individual" one. To say you will help an Asian develop a sense of his or her "individual self" would be taken by that person as completely out of line. Thus, therapists treating patients from various countries need to have some familiarity with the customs, traditions, and child-rearing practices of their clientele.

The final influence came from my study on the Middle East and the Arab-Israeli conflict. In my research, I have found its confluence of psychoanalysis and psychohistory has striking similarities to the marital discord that I have observed in my clinical practice (Lachkar 1998, 2004). Cultures/nations (like couples and individuals) also have V-spots and archaic injuries traumatically forged through wars, losses, and a lifetime of governmental violations of human rights. These constantly ignited V-spots keep these nations embroiled in endless battles. Where do culture and pathology meet? Where do the boundaries between aggression, cruelty, and cultural tradition interface? My study of culture became a natural lead-in to my examination of cross-cultural relationships (see chapter 7).

The theoretical material presented in this book is designed to act as a backdrop not only toward understanding the varying psychodynamic structures each couple designs, but the kind of pain couples endure. I explore the clinical manifestations of five kinds of relational bonds, the partner types who choose to stay with one another, and the way in which each stirs up some unresolved archaic or traumatic experience in the other. Each dyad brings its own idiosyncratic experience to the relationship. What a person with a narcissistic personality stirs up in a borderline may be quite different from what an obsessive-compulsive partner stirs up in a histrionic partner.

In my experience, many of these personality types share the common denominator of persecutory anxieties, particularly in relation to dependency needs. It is how these needs are qualitatively experienced and defended that makes this quest unique. It is not uncommon, for example, for the obsessive-compulsive to experience his/her internal needs as "dirty," or for the narcissist to experience neediness as tantamount to weakness and fragility. Each couple has its own "vulnerable spot." A narcissist, for example, feels deeply injured and hurt when not properly mirrored and valued as a special child of God. In contrast, the borderline cares far less about being special than about abandonment and issues of betrayal. This is in opposition to the obsessive-compulsive, who is more concerned about order, cleanliness, and perfectionism. These garden-variety V-spots will be further elaborated in chapter 2.

Recognizing these subjective areas can be most beneficial for treatment. It is always a therapeutic challenge to balance and manage the timing of a patient's rage, aggression, and primitive enactments. The V-spot provides a more precise way to zero in on this internal inferno because it pinpoints the exact area of susceptibility that is ignited when a personal injury occurs. In addition, it has diagnostic value in understanding the disorders of the self. Take for example a patient with a proclivity toward abandonment or paranoid anxiety who immediately gets suspicious when his/her innocent partner is going on a business trip. "Ah, here it is again; you're not seeing your husband as loyal and loving, but now suddenly he is like your father running around having affairs, so you immediately got suspicious." I might tentatively suggest this patient is more inclined toward borderline organization. If on the other hand, the patient gets easily hurt when not constantly praised, acknowledged, or basking in the limelight, I may suggest this person is more inclined toward narcissistic personality organization.

The V-spot also provides a new perspective on countertransference, recognizing the analyst's vulnerability to his or her own "V-spot" reactions. Finally, the V-spot has applicability to all areas of life, not only for couples struggling with issues involving intimacy but for all kinds of couples (happy, dysfunctional, cross-cultural, intercultural/racial, gay/bisexual, and even business partnerships and "political" couples—outlined in chapter 7).

Chapter 1 defines and describes the V-spot as the most sensitive area of emotional vulnerability as it corresponds to the psychoanalytic concept of archaic injury. It reconsiders the importance of the ego as a fundamental component of rational thought, perception, and the capacity for reality testing.

Chapter 2 outlines five kinds of abusers (the narcissist, the borderline, the passive-aggressive, the obsessive-compulsive, and the schizoid) and their enablers, detailing their behaviors, personality traits, and defense mechanisms, as well as the types of partners who choose to bond with them.

Chapter 3 illuminates and describes emotional abuse and how it is inextricably linked to the V-spot, within the scope of early trauma and severe forms of vulnerability.

Chapter 4 covers the theoretical constructs, drawing mainly from classical psychoanalysis, object relations, ego psychology, and self psychology. This includes mainly works from theorists such as Sigmund Freud, Melanie Klein, W. R. D. Fairbairn, Donald Winnicott, Otto Kernberg, John Bowlby, Heinz Hartmann, Heinz Kohut, Wilfred Bion, James Grotstein, and others to provide application to the practice of V-spot theory.

Chapter 5 details the "dance" between partners, including psychodynamics, interactions, and defense mechanisms. It also pinpoints each disorder's specific psychic zone of vulnerability.

Chapter 6 focuses on internal and external objects via their corresponding V-spots, how one partner projects a negative feeling onto the other, and how the other then identifies or over-identifies with that which is being projected. This section makes strong distinctions between a defense and a feeling—e.g., the difference between feeling depressed and becoming the depression.

Chapter 7 defines and reviews group psychology and cross-cultural issues from a psychodynamic and psychohistorical perspective as it delves into the question, "Is there such a thing as a cultural V-spot?"

Chapter 8 expands on treatment procedures and techniques focusing on healing the wounds of emotional abuse. This chapter reexamines three phases of treatment that couples move through: the Phase of Darkness, the Phase of Enlightenment, and the Phase of Reason.

Chapter 9 reflects on psychoanalysis and its ever-changing world, exploring its movement from the domestic to the cultural, racial, and global. Recognizing this diversity leads us to new challenges and perspectives as we prepare to meet the many faces that we see daily in our consultation rooms.

CHAPTER ONE

~

The V-Spot and Its Corresponding Concepts

The V-spot, or the "vulnerable spot," is a unique concept I devised for couple therapy to describe the most sensitive area of emotional vulnerability. The V-spot parallels the G-spot. The difference is that the G-spot is equated with pleasure while the V-spot is equated with pain. It is the raw spot that when aroused triggers a traumatic experience related to painful memory traces of early childhood. It is triggered when someone (especially someone we love) hits our hypersensitive core. It can blow with seemingly the slightest event! One wrong word, one false move, and it's off! The V-spot is another name for the epicenter of our most fragile area, known in psychoanalytic literature as the "archaic injury." It is a product of early trauma that one unwittingly holds on to throughout adult life.

Do various disorders have their own idiosyncratic natures, their own archaic injuries? I believe the answer is yes. For example, the narcissist may blow up when not properly mirrored, the borderline when feeling abandoned or betrayed, the obsessive-compulsive when emotions get out of control, and the passive-aggressive when met with excessive demands.

Heinz Kohut (1971) reminds us of the importance of the patient's ability to maintain a healthy archaic grandiose self. He contrasts this with the psychotic delusions of grandiosity, grandeur, and omnipotence formed by patients with prevailing narcissistic personality disturbances. The archaic injury is linked to an emotional area of overwhelming vulnerability where highly charged emotional feelings and sensitivities originating in infancy and childhood remain raw and unhealed. Often it is heavily imbedded in the deep unconscious, with emotional reactors pre-scripted and pre-programmed to react impulsively without thought or awareness, or what Wilfred Bion might refer to as beta elements (Bion 1959).

As clinicians we are continually baffled as to why our patients repeat the same traumatic injury again and again. Sigmund Freud noticed early on (1923) that patients who progress to the threshold of success frequently sabotage what they have achieved. He observed that there was a certain segment of patients who would become discontent when treatment was progressing. Seinfeld referred to this as a "negative therapeutic reaction" (1990).

What happens when the emotions blow? I liken it to a nuclear reactor: One strike and it is ready to explode. With this explosion comes the loss of sensibility, as well the capacity to think and to make rational decisions. Everything shifts as in an earthquake; memory, perception of reality, and judgment become distorted. When the V-spot is exposed, the ego is stripped of its natural resources and its capacity to function, including the ability to mediate and contain anxiety. Anxiety, which the ego does not initially view as a threat, eventually takes the form of panic when signals from the ego are circumvented.

Getting in contact with our area of vulnerability is the only way to break away from emotional abuse and activate the healing process. In emotionally abusive relationships, the V-spot is stimulated and aroused again and again. Locating the V-spot helps patients find their "powerhouse." It is to the psyche what yoga, Pilates, spinning, kick-boxing, and other power workouts are to our muscles. In yoga the goal is to breathe through space—not to cave into the body of pain but to prepare the body through breathing to slowly stretch into a new space or territory. Finding and making use of the V-spot involves an intense emotional workout that strengthens and emotionally restores the individual. It is the beginning of the healing process. One patient, after she found out how to make contact with her V-spot, expressed her liberation this way:

> I never could make decisions before. I would deliberate and deliberate, ask a ton of people for an opinion and still couldn't make up my mind. I always felt that everything was my fault, that I deserved my husband's criticism and mistreatment. Now all I do is turn to my V-spot, and as soon as I get in contact with it, my thought processes clear up. Even though I may not have the "immediate" answer (the quick fix), at least I know I am on the road to acquiring a solution.

Most clinicians are aware of the impact archaic injury has on the treatment of individuals and couples. To emphasize the importance of the role archaic injury plays in their relationship, the therapist must continually remind patients of the thematic material that repeats again and again, like the leitmotif in music.

Healing is a complex, elaborate procedure and a difficult process to translate into clinical terms. Even many classically trained analysts have difficulty fully comprehending the intricate and idiosyncratic nature of the archaic injury (V-spot) and the corresponding elements that link it not only to early trauma but also to the ego and the mechanism of defense. Healing the self is not a quick fix. We must first "experience" that which lies buried in our childhood before the real healing process can take place.

Certainly, one can be told what to do. For instance, behavioral therapists "teach" patients how to overcome emotional difficulties through homework assignments and special exercises. Although helpful, these assignments unfortunately do not lead to lasting healing results, especially from wounds harking back to early traumatic injury. In treating narcissistic/borderline couples, I have witnessed repeated episodes of violent reactions when these early vulnerabilities are ignited. The therapist must continually demonstrate to the partners how old wounds and injuries cause them to react in the way that they do. This requires sophisticated treatment techniques—e.g., making a distinction between a feeling and a defense. The following illustrates this: A prominent narcissistic artist/sculptor tells me he *must* have two women in his life or he cannot function. He cannot comprehend that these women get upset when he trades off between them, going back and forth (ego failure). He tries to convince me that this is a very strong and powerful need. I let him know it is *not* a need, but rather a defense, that since his father died when he was at such a young age, the thought of loss is more than he can bear. So if he has two women he has a double indemnity policy.

What Triggers the V-Spot?

The "attack" that sets off the V-spot arousal most often comes from an intimate partner or significant other—which is especially hurtful—or anyone with whom one has an emotionally charged relationship (lover, parent, child, relative, or boss). However, it can be triggered by anyone—a stranger, a grocery store checker, a salesperson, a waiter. The V-spot is the core of all our pain, an unhealed wound that contains the very essence of our emotional existence.

It has always been striking that well-educated, intelligent, and successful men and women can function so effectively in the workplace and yet regress in their intimate relationships. The effort here is to recognize these chronic spots that infect and invade the psyche and intercept the patient's potentiality for maintaining healthy object relations. Once the patient is able to identify his or her V-spot, the ego is better equipped to peer through the reality lens. The V-spot concept has forced me to rethink the entire subject of emotional abuse, to treat it not by ridding patients of pain but to first identify the pain and see it as an indicator of some internal part that the patient identifies with rather than something to discard. It reminds me of what gurus in yoga classes insist on: "Work through the pain in your body by stretching it out and breathing, not retreating from it."

Contrary to the stance taken by many other clinicians, the approach in this book does not endorse getting rid of pain as a curative modality. Instead, it seeks to help patients make use of pain in a way that is rarely emphasized in the literature. When the patient is able to access the area of vulnerability and the triggers from the past that inflame it and cause one to overreact with panic or fear, the patient will make use of the V-spot as a roadmap or guideline instead of projecting or externalizing the pain by finding someone to blame, shame, or attack. "I think I overreacted to my friend being late; my feeling abandoned is a complete exaggeration and is unwarranted." Once patients have identified the V-spot, they are in a better position to enjoy the crystal clarity of a reality hitherto obscured and blurred by deep-seated defenses.

There are a few typical mantras that are common to many patients who have not yet learned how to identify their V-spots to help them negotiate emotional difficulties:

> You always act as though your friends are more important than I am.
> That is what my mother always did; my sisters and brothers always came first.
> You're not good enough, not deserving enough, too demanding, etc.

Behind these mantras are experiences that include the parent who abandoned the child at an early age, smothered the child with too much affection, neglected/deprived and never touched or soothed the child, or who was not able to contain or detoxify the infant's rage and anger—what Bion termed "detoxification" (1967). Other sources include a caretaker who repeatedly intimates that a child is incapable, undeserving, and demanding. This could involve an emotionally castrating, controlling, dominating, or overbearing parent that takes over the child's mind and spirit.

The V-spot is our mentor and best communicator. It talks to us all the time, instructing us, guiding us as to what path to take, teaching us not to stray into negative zones. Clinicians often hear patients say, "What should we do? What should we do?" The V-spot urges us to trust our perceptions as opposed to our feelings (often defenses), which can often be fallacious and misleading. These new insights impact all areas of interpersonal life, both at work and in the family. When anxiety and depression threaten, one learns to soothe the self by thinking about the process that has aroused the anxiety. This is quite a challenge, especially when one has been in an emotionally abusive relationship and is used to self-flagellation, blame, pity, persecution, or victimization. The following is an example of how a patient was able to work though anxiety (V-spot reaction) about contacting a professor, realizing that the source stems from the residual effects of a verbally abusive relationship with her mother:

> I couldn't decide if I should call this professor and ask him a question about my career. As soon as I contacted my V-spot, I heard my mother's voice saying, "Stop being a nuisance! You're always such a pest, bothering and burdening people with your problems!" The minute I got in contact with that voice, I immediately knew what to do. I called!

Defining the Ego

The ego is a slippery concept. In short, it is the seat of consciousness, the gateway to memory, thinking, judgment, attention, perception, and the capacity for reality testing. It is the mediating agent that provides entry to the unconscious. Yet it continues to elude; even the most well-seasoned clinicians often lose sight of its significance. They forget the importance of its function and what happens to the power of reasoning when the ego becomes dysfunctional and loses the resiliency necessary to process the data of experience. One task of the ego is to observe the external world and preserve a true picture of the moment by eliminating old memory traces left by earlier impressions and perceptions. Another function of the ego is to represent the external world as a reflection of reality in order to learn from experience, which can ultimately save the individual from calamity. However, all too often we lack the stamina and resources to access the ego and blindly resort to id or superego forces that keep the healthy ego from emerging. The ego is often not user-friendly in that it resists what it "knows." In spite of the "horrors" the ego is commonly thought to impose, it brings with it an entire entourage of reasoning and logic that has a soothing influence. "I felt so relieved after finally calling the IRS only to find they were verifying my change of address!"

The ego advances from the function of perceiving instincts to that of controlling them. We may say that the ego stands for reason and circumspection, while the id stands for untamed passions. The ego absorbs information, integrates it, and learns how to sort out the helpful good from the destructive bad. It has the capacity to seek out the real from the unreal. It contains the vestigial remains of our existence, an entire world of internalized object relations and an integrated sense of self.

When we speak of the ego, whose ego are we referring to? A Freudian ego? A Kleinian ego, a Kernbergian ego, a Hartmannian ego, Kohutian ego (self)? Although many authors offer detailed accounts of ego fragmentation or "ego weakness," Kernberg found Klein's and Fairbairn's theories of primitive defenses and object relations so confusing that it forced him to develop his own "operational definition" of ego organization (1980, 6). Hartmann constructed an entire theory of ego psychology and adaptation (1939). He recognized that such primitive defenses as splitting, projection, and projective identification are designed to protect the patient, but at the expense of weakening the ego's function, thereby minimizing its capacity to act as an adaptive tool. Blackman corroborates Kernberg's ego as it applies to borderline and psychotic conditions, recognizing that affect-tolerance and ego power are nominal (2004).

According to Kernberg, the ego struggles between desire and action, the procrastinating factor of thought, during which it makes use of the residue of experience stored up in memory (1980). In this way, it dethrones the pleasure principle that exerts undisputed sway over the processes in the id, substituting for it the reality principle, which promises greater security and greater success. The tyrants emanating from the external world are often inextricably linked to the intolerance around issues of ambivalence and confusion. In the ego's attempt to mediate between the id and reality, it is often forced to respond to the relentless demands of the id and superego, in turn receiving very poor rewards for its recovery.

Thomas Ogden directly links thinking with the attack on the ego, especially when primitive defenses are operative. He states that the "projector" often fails to learn from the experience, and it is the very nature of projective identification that strips the psyche of all resources and capacity for rational thought (Ogden 1980). Although F. Scott Fitzgerald (*The Crack-Up*) was not an analyst, I think he summarizes it best:

> The test of a first rate intelligence is the ability to hold two opposed ideas in the mind at the same time and still retain the ability to function.

Freud's ego is an intrapsychic one with life and death instincts. It is a biological ego that does not have its own destiny or link to an outer world with a cast of characters that can trigger these emotions (1936). In fact, Freud dismisses the ego as a close cousin to emotions, feelings, and vulnerability. Although he does define the ego as a structure responsible for memory, perception, and judgment, he does not view it as a liaison with external objects.

One of the most valuable concepts Freud offers concerns aggression, which he claims is id oriented. He views aggression as a way to channel murderous, destructive instinctual impulses into more constructive and creative outlets. A good example of this would be Ludwig van Beethoven, who transformed the anguish of his hearing loss into powerful music. The ego's applicability to love relations has great value, particularly in addressing aggression in couples, where aggression can feed on aggression. According to his Freud's biographer, Peter Gay, "Aggression must be nipped in the bud" (1988). Gay reminds us how aggression leads to further aggression, that it feeds upon itself. It is an addictive agent, and people become obsessed with it. An extreme example of this at the global level is terrorism. This is crucial to understanding the early hurt emanating from archaic injuries; when emotions are provoked, people will do anything to find justification for it. In some instances, people will hide behind their religion or "a cause for the greater good" in order to validate their innermost cruelty and aggression.

Reality Testing

Reality testing is a function of the ego that offers a valuable diagnostic tool. It is a key element in differentiating subjective from objective. It is the capacity to distinguish between self and other, and to evaluate one's own affect realistically. I am reminded of a certain narcissistic patient who, when she calls for an appointment, offers times she is not available. "At one p.m. I have a nail appointment, at two p.m. I go to the gym, at three p.m. I have a facial, and at four p.m. I have to meet a friend." When asked what time she is available she says she doesn't know, will have to check her calendar and get back to me. She lacks introspection or the observing ego to note how annoying this can be. Her ego cannot organize the data that a busy therapist does not have as much free time as she does; nor is the therapist at her disposal. Another example is offered by Jerome Blackman, who describes a 40-year-old female high school teacher who was sexually attracted to a 15-year-old female student in one of her classes (2004, 145). This patient was seriously pondering whether or not she should ask the girl out to dinner, rationalizing that the girl might have the same attraction toward her. Blackman's case is indicative of a damaged ego unable to process the consequences of such an event.

Otto Kernberg (1992) distinguishes between psychoses and borderline pathology, pointing out that borderline patients lack the capacity for reality testing and experience severe difficulties in interpersonal relationships and their subjective experience of reality. He states that ego weakness emanates from lack of impulse control, empathy, identity diffusion, and anxiety intolerance. According to his research, a borderline's lack of superego functioning has the effect of continually forcing the patient to rely on the opinions and judgments of others as central resources in their lives.

According to Ogden (1986), people dominated by such primitive defenses as splitting, projection, projective identification, shame/blame, and persecutory anxiety lose contact with their internal resources; instead of learning from experience, they repeat the same destructive behavior again and again. Typically people with pre-oedipal struggles with characterological disorders are often easy victims. Many have been exposed to traumatic experiences, and reality testing does not offer soothing or relief. Often because these individuals feel deserving of the abuse and wrongly imagine that everything is their fault, they are compelled to take on the role of caretakers or parentified children. They are forced in early years to relinquish their childhood and perform adult functions for their parents or siblings. They are the "little adults," the mediators, the children who grew up much too soon (Lachkar 1998, 2004).

I am reminded of a borderline wife married to an extremely narcissistic husband, referred to simply as "Mr. Know-It-All!" Her only recourse was to threaten him with divorce. Although she was bright and well educated, it never occurred to her to establish boundaries. Her response was, "Gee, I never thought of that!" Finally, she was able to tell him, "If you put me down in front of the kids one more time, I am taking them to a hotel room with me. You can spend the time by yourself pondering whether or not you will pursue conjoint treatment with me. It is your choice!" When she returned, he readily agreed to five additional visits, "Okay, have it your way, five visits and that's it!"

The following case is an example of how the ego can become dysfunctional when one is in a vulnerable state, and how one is inclined to distort, confuse, delude, and lose contact with reality. In this case Rebecca becomes completely paralyzed.

Case of Rebecca and Steve: The Waiting Game

Rebecca is a perfect example of someone suffering from V-spot disorder. During the first session she repeatedly said, "I just feel so vulnerable. I start to imagine things. I can't help myself. Whenever I feel my boyfriend isn't there for me, my emotions run wild. I get out of control. At that point, I'm gone!"

Rebecca: There we were, the six of us invited to Steve's house to watch the Wimbledon play-offs and have dinner. The guys brought in take-out food and the girls provided drinks, appetizers, and dessert.

Therapist listens attentively, noticing Rebecca's increasing tension and mounting anxiety as she spoke.

Rebecca: The game started, and that's when I lost it. Steve totally ignored me. I tried to signal him to move closer to me, but he ignored me (tears beginning to mount).

Therapist: I can see you felt ignored by him.

Rebecca: Ignored isn't the word. I felt as if I had disappeared, as though I didn't exist. He was totally engrossed in the game. I really felt bad. Later I scolded him and told him that the other men in the room did not ignore their girlfriends. "Look at Frank, he was engrossed in the game yet still able to sit and be close to his girlfriend."

Therapist: So it was at that moment you felt you were going to lose it?

Rebecca: Yes, that is what scares me. I have in the past sabotaged all my relationships, and I don't want this to happen again. My head was spinning. I couldn't get the thoughts out of my head. "He really doesn't want to be with me. He'd rather be with someone else." I got so panicked I went to the bathroom and started to cry. At that point I had no choice but to leave. I felt terrible after the guys brought such a beautiful dinner (roast, garlic potatoes, pear salad), so I just stormed out of there.

Therapist: So when you felt vulnerable you had feelings you couldn't control.

Rebecca: Right!

Therapist: But you did have a choice.

Rebecca: Choice? What do you mean a choice?

Therapist: Like asking Steve quietly to come and talk to you for a moment to calm and soothe you.

Rebecca: Oh no, not in a million years. I did not want him to know how sick I was. That would have been a disaster.

Therapist: Disaster?

Rebecca: Exactly, but I forgot to tell you one more thing. He did finally come over and give me a hug, but then I just pushed him away and told him to forget it. I was so angry.

Therapist: So you finally got what you wanted, and when you got it you sabotaged it.

Rebecca: That's what I am trying to tell you! That's what my mom would do. She would want something from my dad and when my dad would finally come over and hug her or put his arms around her, she would yell and scream so loud the house would shake. I did the same thing with my dad as well. After a disagreement or something he would come over and give me a hug and I would just pull away.

Therapist: Like your mom, huh?

Rebecca: Yeah, but I don't want to do that anymore. I run away because I'm scared Steve will find out I'm nuts!

Therapist: Crazy?

Rebecca: Yeah, I was hospitalized for a few days, and they put me on medication.

Therapist: (laughing) If that is your definition of "crazy," then three-fourths of the people here in LA are crazy!

Rebecca: (also laughing) I'm confused.

Therapist: Yet you immediately think you were diagnosed with some severe mental illness.

Rebecca: Hmm! That's true. I never thought about it that way.

Therapist: Rebecca, when your V-spot [archaic injury] gets stirred, the first thing that goes is not your emotions, but your reality. You stop functioning. You confuse your mind with someone who gets an anxiety attack, a momentary breakdown with someone who has a severe mental illness.

Rebecca: I guess you're right, but it doesn't feel that way.

Therapist: Well, when you are in that state your feelings are fallacious. Besides, those are defenses.

Rebecca: Are you telling me my feelings are not real! That I am making things up?

Therapist: Rebecca, now your emotions are getting out of control with me. What I'm saying is those are not feelings.

Rebecca: If they are not feelings, then what are they?

Therapist: They are defense mechanisms. When you go into abandonment and neglect mode, paranoid anxiety sets in and you then pull away, withdrawing as a defense against feeling vulnerable.

Rebecca: You're right about that.

Therapist: And when your defenses take over, your perception gets all muddled up, and then you imagine Steve would rather be with someone else.

Rebecca: Then what do I do about it?

Therapist: Now you want to quickly fix it, run away with this new idea rather than taking the time to digest this new way of thinking.

Rebecca: I guess I feel attacked, like I've done something wrong and I better fix it before I get into trouble.

Therapist: Trouble?

Rebecca: My father used to beat me with his belt. I guess I learned that I better do it right or else I will get it.

Therapist: Rebecca, you are experiencing the same feelings here. Unless you get it right and fix it right away, something bad will happen.

Rebecca: Well, I know you won't beat me, but you will get annoyed with me and maybe won't be there for me.

Therapist: That's the same thing that happens with Steve. You confuse your inner state of unworthiness, projecting into Steve that he will not be there for you when in fact he is. When your V-spot gets aroused, you momentarily lose it with me just as you do with Steve when you think he will abandon you and would rather be with someone else.

Rebecca: So, I guess I will have to work hard to stay in the moment and not allow my past to come back to haunt me.

Therapist: Exactly! See what happens when you separate from the past injury, how clear your thinking is?

The Ego and Its Dysfunctionality

The ego is not master in its own house.

—Sigmund Freud

What makes an abusive partner think he or she has a right to be abusive? What makes shopaholics think they can afford to buy the things they purchase? Of course there are many psychological answers and reasons, such as self-image, grandiosity, delusional thinking, and a plethora of defense mechanisms, including environmental and biological factors. In considering these kinds of issues, however, V-spot thinking, or rather non-thinking, takes center stage. Again, it is astonishing how thinking, judgment, perception, memory, functioning, and reality become distorted when the V-spot is activated. I refer to this as ego failure. Wilfred Bion (1967) more eloquently refers to this as "thoughts without a thinker." It helps us understand why people fabricate all kinds of preposterous stories to the exclusion of reality and in the belief that their lies are the truth.

How the V-Spot Affects Thinking, Memory, Perception, Judgment, and Ego Functioning

The best way to understand the deeper meaning of V-spot thinking in relation to the ego is by comparing the neurotic to the psychotic. Here the ego function takes on an entirely different shape. People with these disorders tend to hallucinate, have delusional thoughts, as well as impairments in functioning and reality testing. Ogden (1980) makes the point that in neurosis the patient remains linked to the object world and maintains a connection to the libido. In psychosis and schizophrenia, the linkage to objects is severely cut, and the unleashed cathexis of energy causes the ego to revert back to the stage of early narcissism, driving the person to withdraw from the external world and any relationship to it. Ogden aligns himself with Bion's idea that all psychopathology is a thought disorder. He describes psychotic conflict as a form of pathology that destroys all meaning and the capacity to think in order to create new experience.

To use an analogy, when someone is involved in a car accident, they become momentarily paralyzed and immobilized. They can't think, can't remember the make of their vehicle, can't find their wallet, and forget where they put their insurance card. This is because perception and normal functioning are impaired by the situation. The same impairment occurs when our V-spots are triggered. We react and respond in a similar manner. Our thinking and judgment become clouded, and we are unable to function normally. Suddenly we feel that everything is our fault and thus perception becomes obscured. The following case is another example of an aroused V-spot reaction that, in turn, causes ego dysfunctionality.

Case of Sasha and Jim: Endless Promises

This case illustrates what happens when the V-spot is attacked by the patient's past experiences, creating fusion with the object; destroying all capacity to hold on to one's reality, perception, and judgment; and leading the patient to believe that the partner's lies are the truth.

Sasha: We have been in a relationship for five years. He promised me marriage, a home, and children. I am thirty-nine years old and my biological clock is running out and nothing is happening.

Therapist: But you say in addition to not making a commitment to you, he also fails to follow through on dates, holidays, taking you out.

Sasha: I don't even have the status of being a date. At least with a date there is some kind of commitment. He makes promises, gets me all excited, then suddenly vanishes and I don't hear from him for several days.

Therapist: This is when you panic, isn't it?

Sasha: Panic isn't the word! I get so desperate, I call and call. But he doesn't return my calls; all I get is voice mail.

Therapist: This is when he tells you to wait, be patient, and everything will work out. Isn't this what your mother used to do? Keep you waiting and waiting and waiting?

Sasha: I remember when I was in the fourth grade, school got out at three p.m., and my mother didn't show up until six p.m.

Therapist: Well, what your mother did was very inappropriate, keeping her child waiting. That is totally unacceptable! And now the same inappropriate behavior is enacted/reenacted in your relationship.

Sasha: That's true! That's all I do is wait and wait and wait. I guess he is unpredictable like my mother. Suddenly, he will call around eight or nine o'clock on a Saturday night and say, "Okay, are you ready to go out now?"

Therapist remains silent, listening.

Sasha: I am reeling inside, but I am so desperate after waiting so long.

Therapist: This reminds me of your birthday, how he planned to take you out and then didn't show up because he said he was so tired he fell asleep.

Sasha: I guess you are tired of listening to this (patient projecting her own frustration onto the therapist).

Therapist: I think you are telling me how tired you are (therapist not taking in the patient's projection). In fact, I think that you are exhausted.

Sasha: Then when I call him and do reach him, he offers me no sympathy. He says things like, "What do you want from me? Whatever I give you is never enough? I just took you out last week, what more do you want from me? Come on, Sasha, you know I love you."

Therapist: Ah, now I can understand the confusion. Jim is not only abusive and cruel, but I can also see that he can be seductive.

Sasha: Yes, suddenly he tells me how much he loves me, cares for me, can't live without me, and makes endless promises.

Therapist: And thus the "dance" starts all over again.

Sasha: Yes, it is a dance. We go round and round, endless promises as he keeps me on a hook. And when I call him he tells me he will call back later.

Therapist: And then?

Sasha: I wait and wait, but no call.

Therapist: As a little girl you felt helpless. You were dependent on your mother; you didn't have a car, you didn't have your own phone, and there was not much you could do. But now you are a grown woman and you are still projecting into your current relationship this little helpless, victimized girl.

Sasha: Okay, what should I do about that? I am still hooked.

Therapist: I am not sure what we can do about it, but what I can tell you is that when your V-spot gets stirred up by this abusive mommy/Jim, it's hard to know what to do because the abuse attacks and infects your mind's ability to think clearly.

Sasha: You are right because I keep losing things, I don't remember things, I get into accidents, and my mind is all blurred.

Therapist: But you're also losing time. He is more concerned with controlling you than caring about you and your biological clock, which is a reality.

Sasha: Yes, there is a real clock isn't there?

Therapist: Yes, but your emotional clock is also off. We need to help you understand how it's bad enough to be treated like this, but even worse how the little girl in you tends to identify or over-identify with all the negative stuff he projects into you.

Case of Clara and Michael: The Unavailable Partner

This is another case that illustrates the inherent nature of "the unavailable object." These are people who are always object-seeking but never object finding. Borderline and dependent personality types often attach themselves either consciously or unconsciously to people who are detached, withdrawn, narcissistic, or self-absorbed (emotionally or physically).

Clara: We had a date Saturday night. I kept calling and calling to confirm. He did not return my call.

Therapist: And?

Clara: I began to panic.

Therapist: He has done this before, as I recall last Saturday night as well.

Clara: That's true, but let me finish. I just kept calling and calling and got no response. Finally, at ten minutes to eight he called me on his cell telling me he remembered that he had to go to his best friend's wedding and he was calling from the Bel Air Hotel.

Therapist: Oh my!

Clara: Remember the same thing happened last week. At the last minute he suddenly remembered he had a business meeting with a partner.

Therapist: And the week before he suddenly had to go out of town, and the week before that he had a headache and needed his stupid "space" to catch up.

Clara: But you didn't hear the worst of it.

Therapist listens attentively.

Clara: The week he said he was out of town I drove by his house and found the car of his old girlfriend.

Therapist: You found what?

Clara: Yes, you heard right—his old girlfriend! He just isn't available. He just can't commit to anything. Why do I put up with this?

Therapist: Yet, you do put up with it!

Clara: He keeps telling me he loves me and someday we will get married. I guess I feel I am not deserving of anything better so I keep waiting for him to come through.

Therapist: So not only does he "stand you up," but also you stand yourself up, deny yourself, and not "show up for yourself." You only think you exist when Michael calls you. The rest of the time you feel like a nothing and then just sit and wait and wait.

Clara: If only he would be there for me, then I would get better. I know how I feel when I am with him.

Therapist: Waiting and waiting, huh?

Clara: Yes, what are you getting at?

Therapist: You know.

Clara: I guess you are referring to the time when my mother was hospitalized and I sat by the window as a child waiting and waiting for her to come home.

Therapist: How about the time she went to the hospital and gave birth to your younger brother, and then gave him all the attention to the exclusion of you?

Clara: I guess that is what Michael does, makes everyone and everything seem more important than me. I am then ousted from my position.

Therapist: Yes, but I can understand your confusion, because like your mother he withdraws his love, time, and attention and constantly betrays you.

Clara: That's my V-spot, isn't it? I know what you are getting at.

Therapist: Exactly, the early injury that this relationship stirs up. And when it gets ignited you are unable to see that you are not a helpless child. You have options.

Clara: Options! I don't think I have any choice. I am stuck. When he makes a date with me, I get frozen, paralyzed and this makes me feel crazy. This keeps me waiting and on hold.

Therapist: You may feel frozen, paralyzed, or crazy, but that doesn't mean you are those things. Besides, those are not feelings they are defenses. (Clara holds on to Michael as a defense against rejection/loneliness.)

Clara's case is an example of abandonment anxiety so profound and acute that it acts as a barrier to prevent the light of reality from seeping in. It is an example of how an external object can abandon her while at the same time she internally abandons herself by believing that his lies are the truth, disregarding her mind and what she knows to be truth. The seduction is so pervasive that it strangleholds her to the extent that she can no longer hold on to her reality. In her internal world, "reality" is felt to be so intolerable that instead of facing the idea of separating from her lover, she becomes "stuck." Thus, instead of *feeling* the stuckness, she *becomes* the stuckness.

V-Spot Addictions

Patients with compulsions are the most difficult to treat. It is not enough to say these people lack impulse control, or that they are looking for the "quick fix." The psychological components must certainly not be neglected. One might liken it to the ego's failed capacity to function, ego failure as a psychotic way of soothing the self. Take for example the idea of "comfort food." An obese patient says, "I eat for comfort. I just love to eat! The taste of food on my palate is the most delicious and comforting experience." To this the therapist with V-spot awareness might respond, "Although you say food is comforting, the next day, the irony is, you tell me you can't move, you feel sick, you smell of urine, you have headaches, and you experience torture, pain, and persecution, which are worse than the thing that led you to seek the comfort of food." Thus, even addictions have their delusional qualities. Love can also be an addiction. You say that painful love is comforting? What the patient thinks is "comforting" is in reality discomforting.

Many couples fall so in love that they use this "love" to become one another's addictive agents. There are also some biological/neurological features to be considered. Let us take for a moment Helen Fisher's work *The Anatomy of Love* (1992). Fisher, an anthropologist at Rutgers University, wrote *The Anatomy of Love: A Natural History of Mating, Marriage and Why We Stray*, which included amazing studies on hundreds of couples in love. Scanning their brains by putting them through a "love machine," she found that love was an addiction and that couples in love had very high levels of dopamine and serotonin. She suggests that all the antidepressants people take in today's society may keep millions of Americans from falling madly in love. She says that love is a drive and not a feeling. One can wake up in the morning feeling depressed and later in the day feel angry. When you are in love you wake up in love and by the afternoon you are still in love. On the down side, when the love is rejected or one is dumped, the dopamine level paradoxically rises while the amygdala part of the brain triggers enormous rage and anger.

A lapse in perception occurs when we fall in love. As Freud (1914) writes, the need for the other and the need for love are very powerful emotions, and with them comes an over-flowing of ego libido onto the object. That overflowing mimics a psychotic state or psychotic trance—a reunion between highly charged emotional and bodily experiences.

> We are never so defenseless against suffering as when we love, never so forlornly unhappy as when we have lost our love object or its love.

While people in love are in this state they are blind to reality. They see only what they want to see through their delusional, lovesick, myopic eyes. Consider the patient who said that each time she hangs up the phone after an argument with her fiancé, she imagines the relationship to be over. She panics, yet she knows deep down that he will call because he has always called after a blow-up, a pattern that has been going on for three years. So why would he not call now? This leads us to the point that as painful as the linkages to the V-spot are, they also have dramatic soothing qualities. For example, a patient goes into a complete panic each month his tenant is late paying the rent. The therapist asks if the tenant has ever failed to pay in the past. As soon as the patient realized his anxiety emanated from his early childhood experience with a parent who continually made promises but never followed through, he was immediately relieved and reassured. It is also interesting to note that people with addictions, like lovers, also have a distorted sense of reality (smokers, overeaters, gamblers, drug addicts, alcoholics).

I am reminded of a woman who diligently followed a very restrictive diet. On occasion she would deviate, sending her into a massive depression. It was difficult for her to acknowledge that overeating was not a crime, that she is human and merely had a setback, which does not warrant a depression. This is not a far cry from the alcoholic who has one glass of wine and feels that all is doomed.

Reverse Superego

Many of my patients have what I refer to as a reverse superego. This is a bitter paradox for when the child gets punished for being good and at the same time gets punished for being bad. This creates chaos and confusion; the child grows up not knowing when and how to be rewarded. The superego is designed to provide guidance and moral codes. Freud notes that the superego is the voice of the father, which helps the child differentiate right from wrong (1923). The following case illustrates what happens when the superego goes in the wrong direction.

Case of Alfred

Alfred has had two marriages: one to a porn star and another to what he describes as "some sort of low-life woman." He exhibits a very passive-aggressive personality. It took him a year to buy a pair of shoes, plan a trip, get a new couch, and find employment. Alfred is a highly successful, competent man, working for a stock corporation. The company becomes a reenactment of his dysfunctional family, about which he obsesses.

Alfred: I can't stand Roberto (a stockbroker working in the firm). What's the matter with him? He was supposed to get the inventory report done, and he still hasn't done it. He keeps delaying and delaying.

Therapist: Maybe that reminds you of a part of yourself that procrastinates, puts things off and keeps people forever on hold.

Alfred: Yes, I know I do that myself, and it drives my wife crazy. I delay and delay, put things off. But he really pisses me off. I invited him to our office meeting, but he never showed up. I asked him for the stock reports; he never did them. When I complained to our manager, he got upset because he couldn't tolerate the confrontation and was particularly annoyed when I went to the CEO. At our company meeting I brought up some of the incompetencies in management and asked if anyone else was feeling that way. They all looked at me as though I was from the moon. No one said a word. The room became absolutely silent. I felt like a complete fool.

Therapist: In a way that's good. It gives you time for self-reflection about the need for validation from others. This was a good thing you did. Remember when you were a child? Whenever you did something bad you would get punished, and even when you did something good you would get punished. Just like in this corporation you never get rewarded. I remember you telling me your mother would say, "I don't care if you got all As on your report card. Go clean up your room."

Alfred: I guess that's why I keep everyone on hold and get people angry with me because my whole life was waiting for some recognition or reward, so now you understand why I withhold.

Psychosis

Although the couples we see in marital therapy are not psychotic, it is revealing how often they tend to take on certain psychotic elements and momentary displays of psychosis. The "psychotic" has the tendency to confuse a mental state of mind by *becoming* it instead of *feeling* it. This has relevance here because often patients with primitive disorders confuse a state of being with a state of feeling. "I feel depressed therefore I become the depression. I feel paralyzed therefore I become the paralysis." To this, the therapist might respond, "There is a difference between *feeling* paralyzed and *becoming* the paralysis." On the same note, one might address the patient's depression, "It is not that you *feel* depressed, you have *become* the depression. You have had a setback and feel disappointed."

Ogden (1980) describes psychosis as a dichotomy between a wish to maintain a certain psychological state in which meaning can exist and a wish to attack and destroy all meaning. Ogden sees schizophrenia as taking two positions: the wish to maintain a psychological state where meaning can exist and the wish to destroy meaning as a buffer zone against finding new meaning and seeking and learning from experience.

He makes the point that in neurosis the patient remains linked to the object world and maintains a libidinal connection with it. Freud (1924) states that the schizophrenic relinquishes all connection with the object world and turns inward. In so doing he severs his ties to external objects and with reality. In psychosis, object relations deteriorate, and thinking and reality testing are lost to the delusional inner world. Only a fragment of reality remains as attempts are made to restore or find meaning in meaninglessness. Because many borderline patients over-identify with bad internal objects, they actually become the identified bad object (see chapter 6).

For example:

- He makes me feel depressed (like a nothing, worthless, not entitled).
- I feel depressed; therefore I become the depression (self-hatred turned inward).
- I feel like a nothing, therefore I become the nothingness (emptiness).
- I feel scared, therefore I become the fear (paralysis).
- I feel alone, therefore I become the aloneness (isolation).
- I feel empty, therefore I become the consumer (food, alcohol, drugs, gambling).

One must have the capacity to think about a past painful experience in order to derive meaning from it. In other words, one needs the thoughts to think about the unthinkable—like termination of therapy or an ending of a love relationship. Psychotics and schizophrenics attack meaning, erasing all references to knowledge and language as they turn increasingly inward. Sometimes the regression becomes so pervasive it turns into a schizophrenic defeat, a vegetative or peaceful acquiescence (Ogden 1980). In other instances, all meaning becomes the same: night is the same as the day; there is no differentiation. One might assign the same attributes to the schizoid, where there are no emotions or affects attached to objects; everything is felt to be the same.

The Case of Max

We have discussed what occurs when a person gets overly charged by the triggered V-spot. These are excessively sensitive, susceptible people who are highly connected to their traumatic past and archaic injuries. What happens, however, when the person is disconnected from the emotional traumas of the past? These individuals will be referred to as -V ("minus V"), quite similar to Bion's concept of -K (see chapter 4). Following is a case of someone who is disconnected from needs and desires related to early injuries.

Max: Hi!

Therapist: Hope you had a nice birthday.

Max: Yes, it was very nice. We went walking around Hollywood Boulevard and saw a movie called *The Interpreter*.

Therapist: (silent)

Max: I'm very concerned because I have to renew my medical license and take special courses, but I have not done it yet.

Therapist: You don't seem to show much concern that your license is at stake.

Max: And yet I know it is. But why can't I connect to it? I also have not done my taxes, and for some reason do not think that it's that important, although I know that I must do them.

Therapist: I guess these are just more things that you have put aside and have not assigned much value to.

Max: I know.

Therapist: You are putting yourself on the line and are in danger of losing your medical license, something you have worked hard for.

Max: And yet, doctor, it does not seem to have much value.

Therapist: This reminds me of when you were a child, and nothing you did seemed to have any value to your parents.

Max: It's amazing that you say that, because I remember saving money for my first car, a Ford Mustang. The brakes went out soon after I got it, and my father scolded me for buying an American car. Even when I got my medical degree, he didn't come to the graduation, and when I got married, he came late to the wedding.

Therapist: Yes, and you were also telling me that whenever you had a need or desire for a new toy or game, your parents would ridicule you and make you feel as if you were just a silly, ridiculous kid.

Max: That's right, that's right! When I did something good and got good grades, they would not reward me, but would bring up something negative, like why didn't I help my brother with his homework!

Therapist: That's what happens to children when they don't get the proper recognition, acknowledgment, and mirroring for their good deeds. After a while, they just detach and their accomplishments lose their importance and significance.

Max: That's very true!

Therapist: Now I understand why you don't assign any value to such things as your medical license, your taxes, your bills. They lack value to you. They're all interchangeable, just pieces of paper—nothing much.

Max: I never thought about it like that before. Is that why I am having so much trouble buying a new car? Or why I just choose any girlfriend? Because a car is a car and a girlfriend is just a girlfriend?

Therapist: Yes, a car is a car, a girlfriend is a girlfriend, and a piece of paper is a piece of paper—objects that have no meaning or differentiation. Max, there are some people that get very hurt when they think about all the bad things that have been done to them. But instead of feeling the pain, you have undermined and detached, disassociating yourself from the experience by devaluing yourself and things associated with your success.

For the psychotic, perception is meaningful only when one becomes the experience. For example, the psychotic might feel cold and therefore they become the coldness, turning the self into a piece of ice or going into an abrupt catatonic state. This is not a far cry from the borderline patient who feels paralyzed and therefore becomes the paralysis. Another way of finding meaning is through self-mutilation. When a borderline patient mutilates himself, he feels a connection to external objects (a sense of existence). As he induces the pain, he gets a sense of stimulus, a meaningful act. In essence, there is some semblance of aliveness. The psychotic, on the other hand, will detach from his external attachments to the point where he no longer feels pain. In fact, a schizophrenic patient will think that others are going to cut him up, or alternatively, think he is a knife.

Discussion

Now that we have examined the V-spot in relation to the ego and how certain defenses and dynamics can impact its ability to function, we can see that at the core of emotional pain is an area that has been long overlooked in the psychological field. Even though many of our patients are not psychotic, we can see how they display a moment of psychosis when blinded by childhood baggage. In exploring many of the different kinds of pathological love bonds, I have come to experience pervasive patterns, behaviors, interactions, and defense mechanisms occurring repeatedly within a large range of personality disorders. These dynamics—such as shame, blame, envy, jealousy, rivalry, control, and domination—have become replacements for love and intimacy.

In conjoint settings, spouses often feel offended when we lump their emotional pain into a twinship or fusion, not recognizing their distinct emotions. "Oh, you both feel shame whenever you ask for what you need," or "You both feel guilty whenever you feel the other person attacks you!" Getting in contact with each partner's area of anxiety and the unique way he or she experiences vulnerability enables the therapist to be far more precise in recognizing each partner's individuality. The V-spot is like a musical composition; the thematic motif repeats again and again, often in a different key, but the basic theme is heard throughout.

The next chapter outlines five different kinds of abusers and their corresponding enablers, and how each partnership evokes partners' own distinct areas of anxieties.

CHAPTER TWO

~

Abusers and Their Enablers

This chapter outlines and describes five types of personality disorders (the narcissist, the borderline, the passive-aggressive, the obsessive-compulsive, and the schizoid) and the types of people who choose to stay with them. To keep things simple and clear, their respective titles will be "the abuser" and "the enabler." While a male gender pronoun will be used for the perpetrator of abuse, please keep in mind that the abuser can also be female.

The Narcissist

> I try and get him to take me away on vacation, letting him know I'm tired of staying home alone while he travels all over the world. He tells me that he goes on location for filming and that I should understand the nature of a film director's profession. When he returns he shows me pictures of five-star hotels, sunbathing on the Riviera, and copies of menus from the finest restaurants. I tell him I would like to stay in those hotels. He accuses me of being too needy and clingy, that I should understand he needs his space. The worst part of all is that he shows no consideration for my feelings and thinks I should be happy for him.

Defining the Narcissist

The narcissist has a grandiose and exaggerated sense of self, believes the world owes him something, and has excessive and omnipotent entitlement fantasies. The narcissist is the entitlement lover, the special child of God, stuck in constant search for perfect self objects that are solely available to exquisitely mirror his insatiable self. You know when you are around a narcissist because he talks only about himself, lacks compassion for others, and is completely void of empathy. On the surface narcissists appear to have higher than average self-esteem, but, paradoxically, the narcissist's self-esteem is quite low and quite fragile. They are also characterized by a lack of empathy (the inability to be sensitive to the feelings of others). Because narcissists have poor object relations, it is quite frustrating to communicate with them. Not only does everything center around them. No matter what you say, they always bring the attention to themselves.

Person: I am going to Alaska.
Narcissistic: Oh, I just got back from Alaska.
Person: I have a headache.
Narcissist: Oh, I get headaches all the time.
Person: I am so excited. I am going to get married.
Narcissist: Oh, I just got divorced!

The narcissist is overly preoccupied with self and, when not properly admired, appreciated, or given a sufficient amount of attention, will withdraw and isolate the self in a kind of narcissistic retreat. For example, in custody battles, the narcissist expects to have all the visitation rights, the house, all the money, all the furniture. When their personal sense of pride has been threatened, they will respond with narcissistic rage. They value such things as fame, physical beauty, wealth, material possessions, and power. Typically they were mother's special child until their high-chair throne was usurped by another sibling. This is the narcissist's traumatic archaic injury. In an attempt to recreate the early memorable experience of being mother's special child, the narcissist will spend the rest of his life living a kind of "narcissistic nostalgia," yearning to go back to the time when Mommy and baby were one in total symbiotic bliss and harmony. Narcissists cannot tolerate their own dependency needs and unwittingly project this intolerance onto the other (typically a borderline partner).

It is you that are the needy one! Me, I am as perfect as Mother wants me to be!
I don't need you and I don't need this relationship or this treatment!

While narcissists are busy trying to prove a "special" or perfect sense of existence, their borderline partners are busy trying to prove they exist and could not care less about being special (see the following section on the borderline partner). Could this explain why certain borderlines show up for therapy disheveled, unwashed, unkempt, and dressed as though they just rolled off the couch?

The Type of Partner Who Chooses and Stays with the Narcissist

Because the narcissist cannot allow him- or herself the kind of dependency an intimate partner yearns for, narcissists often choose a borderline partner, someone they unconsciously project all their "neediness" into. The borderline partner does not have a sense of self and does not feel entitled, and is easy prey for the narcissist's projections. This arouses V-spot feelings of abandonment, victimization, unworthiness, and shame in the borderline, who already has a thwarted sense of development. People who choose narcissistic partners are generally borderline, with low self-esteem, with a defective sense of self, and living primarily within the domain of persecutory and abandonment anxieties. They feel unworthy of being loved and are easily seduced by the narcissist's omnipotent and grandiose qualities. Borderlines are mesmerized by the narcissist, idealizing him and deluding themselves into thinking that the narcissist is "everything" and they are "nothing." These are the women who attach themselves to the unavailable man. This makes for a perfect fit; the narcissist's inflated sense of self and defenses of withdrawal and isolation make him emotionally and physically unavailable (Lachkar 1992, 1998, 2004).

The cruelest blow delivered by narcissists, who are devoid of feeling or compassion for their partners, is to make others feel highly valued and more important. It is inconceivable to their spouses and others around them how suddenly they can show love, caring, and compassion when they meet others whom they idealize and who match their self-object needs. "How come you're so generous, loving, and kind with everyone else, but not with me or our children?"

On the surface, women think they need these powerful, narcissistic partners to make up for the absent or lost father in early childhood. In their deep unconscious, they turn to "powerful" men to make up for earlier deficits and ward off their fear of being abandoned. One might speculate that Marilyn Monroe may have exhibited many of the traits of a borderline personality. She chose authoritative men like Joe DiMaggio, Arthur Miller, and John F. Kennedy to give her a sense of power and status while at the same time staving off deeply rooted feelings of abandonment from her childhood. Ironically, as soon as these men became available, she left them. Kennedy came along as the final blow, and she could no longer "do the dance." Although there is much controversy over the causes that led to her death, one could speculate that her abandonment issue (V-spot) was so out of control that she could no longer turn to her sexuality and fame as the seductive hook.

Unconsciously, the borderline bonds to pain and, as bad as it is, will choose men who are not available, who recreate the painful scenario of abandonment again and again. Often victims/enablers unconsciously seek pain as a means of honor, "Oh, how I have suffered and endured the pain" and a form of martyrdom. Anything is better than having to face emptiness, the black hole, or the abyss.

Borderlines have been emotionally abandoned in early life by parents who were absent, alcoholic, abusive, or physically or emotionally unavailable. This explains how they fall in with the seduction of narcissists, who thrive on power and success. In order not to feel abandoned, they learn to play into their partner's narcissism, to make him feel as though he is the most perfect, most special man in the world. Because borderline partners are so desperate to bond, they know how to playact, becoming the perfect mirroring object/partner for the narcissist. However, the false self cannot maintain this state because of the lack of impulse control (Lachkar, 1992, 1998, 2004).

Underneath the fantasy is the recreation of the lost or unavailable parents. A narcissistic mate makes his borderline partner feel that she is worthless, undeserving, or not entitled to anything, and should not ask for, need, or want anything. The narcissistic husband complains, "All you do is nag, nag, nag." Not knowing how to legitimately express her "real" needs, the borderline wife continues to nag and demand even more. As she nags, the narcissist withdraws; as he withdraws, she attacks and nags even more. This makes her, the borderline, feel even more worthless, inciting old wounds, resurrecting her bad mother's voice lurking in the shadows, "You're worthless and will never amount to anything." The only recourse is to nag, feign sickness, or attack and demand. When the V-spot takes center stage and the old mantra gets repeated and reenacted in the abusive relationship, one cannot hold on to the positive aspects of the self. "I am a somebody, I have a successful career, and I don't deserve this kind of treatment!"

The Borderline

> When we first met he made me feel like the most beautiful woman in the world. He would do anything and everything for me. He was generous, warm, kind, and very loving. One day my kids missed the bus to camp and he drove them all the way to Malibu. I don't know what happened to him. Suddenly he is selfish, cruel, and sadistic. He said he was married twice before and would

tell me gruesome stories about how critical and attacking his exes were. Now I see he was not talking about them, but instead, was talking about himself! He swears and verbally abuses me, yells at the kids, and demands unrealistic things of them and of me.

Defining the Borderline

Borderlines cannot feel a semblance of aliveness unless they are fused in a dysfunctional and destructive relationship. The borderline abuser is characterized by shame, blame, and attacking behaviors suffered as a result of profound abandonment and persecutory anxieties. Borderlines have defective bonding experiences, and as a consequence, exhibit a lack of impulse control, have a poor grip on reality, and suffer impaired judgment and thought processes. Borderlines often bond with their partners through pain, illness, and victimization, ironically sabotaging anything that offers pleasure or gratification. Unlike the narcissist, they have little self-esteem, do not feel entitled to anything, and will do whatever is necessary to establish some semblance of bonding or relatedness with another to avoid abandonment. As intolerable as a painful relationship may be, it is still preferable to confronting the emptiness, the black hole, the meaninglessness that governs their life.

No matter how loving their relationships may be, borderlines always find a way to sabotage. They live in a constant state of terror, remaining loyal to lost mothers, fathers, and neglectful caretakers. Borderlines frequently perpetuate the cycle of abuse by enacting the role of the enabler. They strive to bond with their partners through pain inflicted on them both by self and other. The inability to face their flaws and their tendency to lay the blame on others for what they hate in themselves keep borderlines from learning from experience.

There is still a great deal of confusion about the borderline in the medical literature. Some believe that the term should still signify patients who are between neurotic and psychotic states. Much of what was previously categorized as schizophrenia is now known as borderline disorder.

I mentioned earlier how Freud noted that a certain segment of patients would behave in a peculiar fashion during analysis. Not yet familiar with the term "borderline," he was baffled and confused that while certain patients progressed in their treatment, they would also massively regress. They become defiant at any attempt at progress, sabotage their progress, and react adversely to any praise of appreciation. In his famous Wolfman case, Freud (1914) extrapolated that these patients had a certain proclivity for punishment that was related to unconscious instinctual drives compelling them toward what he later called the "death instinct." Melanie Klein (1957) related this pathology to the "feeding" experience: as the analyst "feeds" the patient, ironically the patient's intolerable envy takes over, rendering him unable to take in any good the analyst has to offer and destroying that which is enviable, or "the good breast" (1957).

Many borderlines view needs as tantamount to danger because vulnerability has gotten a bad rap (as opposed to obsessive-compulsives who experience inner needs as dirty and disgusting). One borderline spouse confided to a therapist, "I'm so ashamed that I told you in front of my wife that I watch porno sites on the Web." The therapist, who understands the need for detoxification and the need for containment, responded with reassuring words, "Yes, it is hard to ask your wife for what you need, so you find ways to stimulate yourself so that you really don't need her or anyone. You can do it yourself. All you need to do is 'click on.'"

Another striking feature is the borderline's tendency to distort, manipulate, and misperceive reality. When they do something bad, they claim that something bad was done to them. When they lie, they claim others have lied to them. When they betray, they claim others have betrayed them. Borderlines consistently and truly believe in the fictitious promises, viewing themselves as having always been betrayed and forever frozen in a victimized state. Borderline patients often develop a preoccupation with pain as a means of bonding with their objects.

Although they share many traits with schizophrenics, the borderline personality lives within its own domain. Dr. James Grotstein (1986) affirms that the borderline suffers from privation (rather than deprivation), boundary confusion, and the inability to accurately assess the data of the external world. The borderline's splitting mechanisms and tendency to project intolerable affects onto others keep them trapped in eternal states of victimization and shame.

Borderlines will do anything to prove they exist, and when threatened, will lash out against those who doubt or betray them, even to the extent of self-sacrifice or self-mutilation. They form parasitic attachments through seduction, manipulation, victimization, and pain, a constant rehashing of all the bad things that were done to them. This kind of preoccupation with pain forms parasitic attachments as opposed to healthy attachments because borderlines project their victimized selves into others and coerce them to feel pity and sympathy.

> When I burn myself with an iron, or drive like a maniac, or even cut myself up, then I know I'm alive! I exist! Anything is better than abandonment: drugs, alcohol, or addictive relationships.

The borderline is dominated by such defenses as shame/blame; persecutory, abandonment, and annihilation anxieties; depression; omnipotent denial; and magical thinking. "One should just know what I need without having to ask!" The focus for the borderline is primarily on bonding and attachment issues. Because the borderline is lacking in early maternal bonding experiences, he is riddled with paranoia. Any reminder of separation, such as a threat to the bond, will cause him to lash out with relentless rage or acts of revenge, self-deprivation, self-sacrifice, or other acts of destruction—at the expense of self or others. Destruction becomes more pervasive than life itself (addictive relationships, promiscuity, deviant compulsive behaviors/addictions, suicide ideation, and other acts to ward off nameless dread). This probably explains why borderline patients frequently exhibit psychosomatic illnesses, compulsions, addictions, thoughts of suicide, and the tendency to form masochistic or sadomasochistic attachments. They will do anything to divert or assuage feelings of isolation or aloneness.

Borderlines are often, in Helene Deutsch's (1942) terminology, "as if" personalities. Or, in Winnicott's terminology, borderlines are "false self" personalities, pseudo selves that belie or mask the true self (1953, 1965). Because they lack a "real self," they must insert an imaginary one to prevent the sensation of emptiness. Often they are the Don Juans who operate through their seductive charm and charisma. He promises and then lets down. His inflated rhetoric can make even the most emotionally attuned persons initially believe in him.

> I feel so stupid! How could I ever have fallen for a guy like that? When I first met him, he was so charming. He seemed so sincere. He made me feel as though I was the most beautiful woman in the world. "You are the sexiest woman I have ever met." He would call me five and six times a day just to tell me he loved me. Shortly thereafter I was in a bistro for lunch, and there he was drinking wine with another woman, kissing her—kisses were interminable—just as they were with me. I couldn't believe my eyes.

They often have an exquisitely formed false self. "I'll be whatever you want me to be." One woman told a man that she loved the music of Gustav Mahler. After he took her to several Mahler symphonies she thought she would die of migraine headaches. Her pretense was so realistic that he never knew how she despised the dissonance. Borderlines are often very seductive and persuasive, especially in their stance as a "victim" needing to be rescued. They delude themselves into thinking if they can get other people to feel sorry for them, they will be liked. In reality, it is the opposite; in general, most people get easily frustrated and fed up.

Table 2.1. Different Kinds of Borderlines

Borderline	Borderlines suffer from privation rather than deprivation, and illusions rather than delusions or hallucinations. Their internal conflicts center primarily around shame, bonding, and attachment. Borderlines are often "as if" personalities and operate through an exquisitely formed "false self." Their inability to deal with loss and face internal deficits, as well as their tendency to blame/shame, keep them in an endless state of impoverishment. In an attempt to defend against shame, they turn to substance abuse, addictive relationships, promiscuity, deviant/compulsive behaviors, suicide ideation, victimization, and self-sacrifice.
Histrionic Borderline	Histrionic borderlines exaggerate, cry easily, have excessive and parasitic dependency needs, and display excessive emotionalism and exhibitionistic qualities. They often use their sexuality to seduce and entice partners. In some instances, the histrionic may appear very narcissistic (e.g., need to be the center of attention); on the other hand, their clinging behaviors and seductive, provocative sexuality exhibit very strong borderline characteristics.
Passive-Aggressive Borderline	Although the passive-aggressive personality type no longer exists in the psychoanalytic literature as a separate category, I have resurrected it for the purposes of couple therapy. These are the couch-potato husbands and the forgetful wives. "I'll do it later; I'll do it tomorrow; I was going to do it today, but the car broke down." They forget, delay, avoid, cajole, and make an endless barrage of excuses—in short, do anything to protect the good little child from the screaming mommy. The passive-aggressive's primary aim is to unconsciously coerce a partner to behave in a certain way to recreate the parent-child dyad.
Obsessive-Compulsive Borderline	Compared to other borderline personalities, the obsessive-compulsive has a more developed and well-integrated ego, has a better tolerance for anxiety and impulse control, as well as a harshly strict but well-integrated superego. At the lower level of functioning, obsessive-compulsives are obsessed with orderliness, cleanliness, and perfectionism; are devoid of feelings; are workaholics; and invariably shame their partners for having emotional needs or desires. They keep their partners on hold and never have enough time for them. Because obsessive-compulsives confuse needs and desires with dirt and disgust, they will find justification to work, work, work under the guise of efficiency or the "good cause." They will also do anything to avoid intimacy. These are the pack rats, the clutterers who can't throw anything away.

Schizoid Borderline	The primary defense of the schizoid personality is a pervasive pattern of detachment; they have few close friends and appear indifferent to the praise or criticism of others. Unlike the narcissist, who withdraws, the schizoid has retreated from external objects and has developed an unconscious attachment to his internal objects. The attachment to his inner world becomes so intense that it completely overshadows reality, blocking involvement with external objects and keeping new experiences from emerging. Continuation on this path can lead to schizophrenia and loss of linkage to the ego, leaving the schizoid borderline trapped and empty (Ogden 1989).
Paranoid Borderline	The paranoid suffers from suspiciousness, lack of trust, and inability to believe he can be loved. "You don't really love me; you are just using me!" The attempt to sabotage is impulsive and precipitous; before the ego has the ability to organize the data of experience, the paranoid borderline jumps to immediate conclusions. A woman tells her husband, "I just know you are having an affair; you have been coming home later and later."
Cultural Borderline	The cultural borderline will do anything to hold on to his nationalistic pride and resist vehemently any adaptation to his new country. Not only a person but an entire array of cultural traditions and ideologies comes with him. On a more global level, some will rebel/retaliate, and at the extreme level, become a freedom fighter, a terrorist, a suicide bomber, or do anything to maintain a cult-like mentality or the group's collective identity.

There are several subcategories of the borderline personality, which are briefly summarized in table 2.1.

The Type of Partner Who Chooses and Stays with the Borderline

What kind of person chooses a borderline partner? Typically it's a narcissist, someone who is in need of constant admiration and excessive mirroring. This attracts them to the seductive and provocative powers of the borderline. The borderline will often promise the world, only to bring disappointment and emotional pain in the end. Because the narcissist equates needs as degrading, small, and equivalent to impotency, he projects his needy self into the borderline, while simultaneously and brilliantly tapping into the borderline's V-spot: the deep reservoir of unrequited love. The borderline is already pre-programmed and pre-scripted to identify with these negative projections (dual projective identification), ready to respond and act a certain way. First, the borderline complies, submits, gets depressed, then apologizes, giving way to the submissive victimized self. In other cases, the borderline will retaliate, seek revenge, and then betray. Whatever the case may be, the inflated ego and grandiose qualities of the narcissist stir up old wounds from the past. "You are everything and I am a nothing!" The following is an example of this kind of projection.

> He gets so easily injured; one wrong move and he's gone. When I didn't respond to his immediate needs he stormed out the house and didn't return until the next morning. He wanted to have sex, and all I said was wait a minute. I first needed to go to the bathroom!

At the beginning of the relationship, the narcissistic partner is often duped by the borderline's masked personality. At first, narcissists do not recognize that the borderline's intentions are false and self-serving, and in turn fall prey to the borderline's seductive and seemingly compliant self. Narcissists are susceptible to these charms because they are in constant need of adulation, admiration, and recognition, relentlessly out to prove their sense of specialness. It almost seems as if the borderline has a kind of built-in radar system or narcissistic surrender that hooks precisely into the narcissist's voracious hunger for attention and endless need for the perfect self object. Borderline women, on the other hand, will often attach themselves to narcissistic, self-absorbed, powerful men, whom they later perceive as selfish, sadistic, and arrogant. In some cases, when they do feel love, they get bored and move on. Marilyn Monroe again is a good example. As soon as she found the love she was searching for from Arthur Miller, she moved on to a more exciting object: John Kennedy.

In business, frustration occurs for many who deal with borderlines because at the beginning of employment, in order to appear compliant and willing to cooperate, they agree to almost anything. However, in the long run, these same people will turn around and destroy/sabotage/lie, doing just the opposite of what they originally promised, claiming that something bad had been done to them. They are the con artists, sociopaths, rule breakers, and contract breakers. Beware therapists and lawyers: contracts, separate property, custody agreements, normal procedures, and sets of rules all become meaningless through the distorted lenses of the borderline. Paradoxically, borderlines will accuse their partners of doing the very thing they are guilty of. "You are the one who broke our agreement; you are the one who betrayed and lied to me! I don't give a shit about your lawyer and your stupid trusts, wills, and separate property!"

The Passive-Aggressive—
The "Poor Me, the Victim"

> He is always sleeping. I ask him why he sleeps, he tells me he's tired. Then I ask him to go to the market. When he returns he tells me the market is closed. I get mad and frustrated so I go myself. I get enraged, and then he accuses me of always being angry when he is such a "nice guy." When I return he is asleep again. I ask him if he got the car fixed; he says he couldn't find the keys, but that he will do it tomorrow. Tomorrow never comes.

Defining the Passive-Aggressive

Passive-aggressives resist responsibility and show it through their behavior rather than open expression of their feelings. The passive-aggressive is often dominated by behaviors such as procrastination, inefficiency, forgetfulness, and avoidance. The most annoying feature is the need for constant reminders and continually to be told what to do by others. They present a sweet innocence and a willingness to comply, but when the time comes they disappoint, frustrate, and fail to follow through with what was requested of them. If they do follow through, it is often in a way that sabotages and creates anger and frustration in the other person. "I thought you were going to come home to feed the dog. The dog was not fed, and I had to drive all the way back home just to do what you promised to do but didn't. The dog was starving, and I was really pissed off!"

What's it like to be involved with a passive-aggressive partner? Passive-aggressives are difficult to treat because they are always trying to recreate the parent/child dyad. Passive-aggressives are the couch-husbands/wives, the forgetful ones, the excuse-makers. They repeat the same patterns of behavior in the most obsequious and insidious way. "I'll do it later, I'll do it tomorrow, the car broke down, I forgot, I lost the keys/the checkbook, I couldn't go to the market, the store was closed, I couldn't do the taxes because the accountant's number got lost. I tried to make the therapy appointment but couldn't find the address." He forgets, delays, avoids, cajoles, and offers an endless barrage of excuses. Passive-aggressives persuade their partners into enacting the role of the bad, punitive parent. "I'm really the good little husband and you are the bad, attacking mommy, always finding fault with me." Typically they hook up with caretaker types who perpetuate the passivity, evoking rage in the enabler's inflamed V-spot. In this way, the partner is predetermined to take on the role of caretaker, doing it all and being everything to everybody.

In chapter 3, we will examine in more detail how emotionally abusive women fall into the role of caretakers. These women have played the role of caretakers or parentified children their entire lives, grew up much too early and much too soon—often as caretakers to their own parents and siblings. They often act precipitously, taking over the role, functions, and obligations that the passive-aggressive fails to meet.

The Type of Partner Who Chooses and Stays with the Passive-Aggressive

Typically the passive-aggressive's partner choice is an obsessive-compulsive personality or a caretaker type. Obsessive-compulsives are individuals who are compulsively striving for perfection. Because they have an uncontrollable urge to take charge and can't tolerate "a mess," they tend to relieve or take over the passive-aggressive's responsibility.

The following cases show how passive-aggressives not only covertly express their concealed resentments and anger toward their partner, but also how they unconsciously coerce their partner into taking on split-off resentments and rage. They are what I refer to as the "silent abuser." In their dance or through their mutual projective identifications, the negligence and forgetfulness of the passive-aggressive forces the other (the caretaker) to take on an undue amount of responsibility. "If I don't pay the taxes, pay all the bills, drive the kids to schools, who will, while you just lay around? Who will?"

Case of the Sleeper and the Nag

Anna: He never listens or hears me.

Therapist: How can he? He's sleeping.

Bill: She's just jealous. I like to sleep and she can't.

Therapist: Are you sleepy now?

Anna: This really infuriates me!

Bill: Doctor! See how easily she blows up?

Therapist: I guess you feel you're not doing anything wrong.

Bill: No way! I'm just minding my own business.

Anna: But, our home and our family is your business and you expect me to do it all!

Bill: I'm not just lying around. I am thinking of projects and things to do. Why don't you leave me be?

Therapist: I think you are awake now because you feel stimulated, involved, and included.

Bill: That's not the way I feel with her and her family.

Therapist: How do you feel with her family?

Bill: They always exclude me.

Therapist: So instead of expressing how you feel or finding a way to help out in the family you sleep so you don't need to express your feelings of being excluded!

Bill: Why should I? No one will listen to me anyway.

Therapist: They don't listen because you have withdrawn and people don't take you seriously.

Anna: That's right, no one respects him. So that's what he does, he sleeps!

Bill: That's what I feel like doing.

Therapist: But that's not a feeling.

Bill: If that's not a feeling, then what is it?

Therapist: It is a defense. You feel vulnerable and not part of the group, so instead of expressing your anger or frustration you go to sleep.

Bill: Maybe that's what I do when she nags and nags.

Anna: He never listens to me so I nag.

Bill: It's easier for me to lie down on the couch and take a nap.

Therapist: But there is another part of you that has gone to sleep.

Bill: What are you talking about?

Therapist: The part of you that has given up. It's much easier to sleep than have to deal with the real feelings and issues that you have difficulty expressing directly.

Anna: I think you're right, Doctor.

Bill: I'm getting annoyed. I don't think either of you are listening or paying any attention to how I feel!

Therapist: Hey, we are making progress. You are getting angry with us. Now I know you are awake. At least you are more direct!

Case of the Barking Dogs

Diana: We were at a dinner party when a potential client of mine mentioned he was going away for a few days and asked, since we were dog lovers, if we would mind stopping by his house to feed the dogs and take them for a walk. Before I had a chance to respond or say anything, my husband volunteered and said he would gladly do it. I later asked Adam, "Do you know where the house is?"

Adam: I told her I did remember where the house is and that I would stop by around lunchtime and feed the dogs.

Diana: Well, guess what? I called Adam at noon, at one p.m., and at three p.m. Each time Adam had an excuse and said he would do it later. I knew he didn't go because he didn't stop at home to pick up the key.

Adam: I told you I would do it, if only you'd stop bugging me.

Diana: I had to restrain myself from going to the house myself because I know this would be another way of enabling Adam, relieving my anxiety, and then I'd be right back into my caretaking role each time Adam screws up.

Therapist: Then what happened?

Diana: This is the best. Late at night Adam said he did go, but he went to the wrong house. I said, "Adam, how could you do that?"

Adam: It was dark. I couldn't see so good.

Diana: That's why you were supposed to go during the day.

Adam: Look I did the best I could; besides, I forgot the key.

Diana: How can you not have any compassion for the dogs? You didn't even stop by our house to get the key! So of course you knew I'd do it! As exhausted as I was, I got in my car, went over to the house and fed the dogs, didn't walk them because I was just too tired.

Therapist: Diana, at least you held out and tried not to relieve him of his responsibilities and commitments. You did the right thing. You couldn't let the dogs down, let alone your client.

Diana: Maybe I should have at the time told the client we couldn't do it.

Therapist: But as caretaker and the one responsible for everything and everyone, that is hard for you to refuse.

Diana: Not anymore. I've had it!

Adam: What about me and my pressure?

Therapist: Adam, you took on a responsibility and, like a child, you set up your mommy/wife to take over your responsibility.

Adam: I'm really pissed. Neither of you understand that I tried my best.

Diana: Yeah! Sure!

Therapist: Even though you're pissed, at least you are being direct here about your anger and not putting your "piss" into Diane. Yet, you've been pissing all over her all these years and now you wonder why you feel pressure! But at least you are expressing yourself directly and this is far better than doing it indirectly.

Adam: I resent that!

Therapist: What you feel inside is not piss; rather it is real and genuine emotion. You may resent what I'm saying, but at least you are being direct and straightforward with me. I think you worry that if you get angry or resentful you will sound like a barking dog!

Adam: Hmmm.

Therapist: Same for you, Diana. Being able to refuse is not piss. It is a genuine reality check on what you can realistically do and cannot do.

Diana: Interesting!

Therapist: Good we are making some progress.

Anna, in the first case, is a medical technician, very meticulous and organized. She cannot tolerate putting things off or waiting. Because she must attend to things right away and turns to the quick fix, she gets very anxious holding on to the boundaries long enough to convey to her partner the message that she is no longer going to take over his responsibilities. Bill, her passive-aggressive husband, unconsciously knows how to stir up Anna's V-spot. He knows that if he denies his responsibility, she will not be able to withstand the chaos and will be forced to "clean up after him." A therapist may say to the passive-aggressive partner, "This can be very frustrating for your wife. She expects you to do things you promise and never follow through. Then you wonder why she is always angry with you."

The same holds true for the case of Diana and Adam. Should Diana have gone to feed the dogs, or should she have allowed the dogs to go hungry and upset her client? These are the kinds of struggles that occur in passive-aggressive relationships, and their solutions are not simple. When the V-spot is alarmed and the ego gets infected with an undue amount of guilt, it becomes difficult to make appropriate decisions. Analytic work helps make these decisions possible.

The Obsessive-Compulsive

> We were about ready to go back East for the Christmas holiday. As usual, we were late for the airport. We were all waiting in the car when Jeff decides he'd better go back in to check to see if he turned off the computer and mailed off all the briefs. He comes back out and then goes in and out three or four times to check and recheck the doors, the locks, and make sure he packed all his work. I couldn't get the airplane tickets because he would not allow me to touch things on his desk. By the time he got in to start the car we were late, the kids were hot and tired; he forgot the airplane tickets, and we missed the plane!

Defining the Obsessive-Compulsive

The obsessive-compulsive constantly tries to control and dominate. He is overly preoccupied with cleanliness and perfection, is devoid of feelings, a workaholic, and invariably puts down his partner for having needs or desires. He is preprogrammed to withhold affection and support from his partner, always making his work come first. He keeps his partner on hold, waiting, because he never has enough time for her. He is the one who will be able to talk as soon as he's "finished" working, cleaning, fixing, or doing whatever he is preoccupied with.

In order to assuage his guilt over not meeting and matching the needs of others, he will hide under the banner of efficiency to find justification to work, work, work. He lives by the motto, "I'm doing it for the greater cause!" In some instances the obsessive-compulsive may cheat, scheme, abuse, deceive, or manipulate, do anything to avoid facing his emotional or vulnerable self. For partners who stay with obsessive-compulsives, this is a familiar theme. Often it is a reminder of an unavailable father, or someone in the past who always kept the child on hold, endlessly waiting, and was never emotionally available. These stirred-up old feelings of resentment and unworthiness ignite the V-spot in the partners, who already exhibit lack of self-esteem.

A conflict with an obsessive-compulsive mate often involves a woman with histrionic features or, to be more precise, a histrionic with borderline and dependent features. These are women who cry easily, are easily offended (V-spots skyrocket), exhibit excessive parasitic dependency needs, and display excessive emotionalism and exhibitionist qualities. Marilyn Monroe once again fits this clinical picture.

The Type of Partner Who Chooses and Stays with the Obsessive-Compulsive

Often histrionic women attach themselves to obsessive-compulsive abusers, and as their self-esteem starts to diminish, they fall even farther prey to the obsessive-compulsive's dark and anal world. In 1959, Martin Bird wrote an article about the "love-sick" wife and the "cold-sick" husband, one of the first descriptions of the histrionic/obsessive-compulsive couple. Together they form a collusive bond or "*folie à deux*." The obsessive-compulsive appears cold, distant, and inconsiderate of his partner's desires, projecting into her a part of himself that he has long abandoned—his own repressed needs that are felt to be dirty and disgusting. He may be the child of an overly protective mother obsessed with orderliness, while she is the product of a home characterized by chaos and confusion. She may need some of his orderliness and he some of her outgoing free-for-all ways. Ironically, the obsessive-compulsive is never compulsive enough; they are so busy being perfect that they ruin any chance of maintaining intimate connections.

Initially, the obsessive-compulsive may be attracted to her warm, outgoing personality, her laid-back, *mañana* attitude, while she is compelled by his order and cleanliness. Because of their own chaotic lives and exhibitionistic and seductive qualities, histrionic women search for men who offer the promise of structure, stability, strength, and security, but who are in reality overly structured. In time, he gradually becomes more irritated by her neglectful and procrastinating ways and begins to attack and criticize her. "I don't understand! Why do I stay with a woman who's always late, can't find her stuff, takes two hours to put on her makeup!" He gradually comes to see her as messy and dirty and begins to detach himself from her by becoming indifferent and not allowing her to touch his things (or even him). "It is money, time, and order that count."

Often histrionic women fall prey to their obsessive-compulsive abusers, and their self-esteem starts to diminish further as they fall prey to the obsessive-compulsive's anal world. As a result, the histronic begins to identify with the conviction/projection that her needs are disgusting and frivolous. To this the therapist might respond, "It is not your needs that are disgusting; they are healthy and normal. It is your hysteria and manic expression that are out of line."

It has been suggested that these women are often a female version of Don Juan. They feel inadequate about their sexuality and femininity and thus develop manic defenses by exploiting their sexuality to the fullest. Otto Kernberg (1980, 286) refers to this as the Don Juan syndrome. He finds this syndrome typical in men, but sees similarities to promiscuity in women, with the causes ranging from severe narcissistic defects in early childhood to a deficiency in identification with the opposite-sex parent.

In treatment, understanding the collusion of this couple—how each desires some aspect in the other—can forge a closer bond and become the replacement for the sadistic qualities in the husband and the masochistic qualities in the wife. As the couple improves, they begin to see that the other possesses the qualities they have long abandoned or never acquired in the early stages of their development. In this way, they have less need to destroy that which is enviable or desirable. "Now I actually appreciate my husband's orderliness. I am in school and have learned a lot about keeping my files straight."

The Schizoid

> I feel like an object on a shelf, like a piece of fine china, just a thing. My mother would take me off the shelf to show me off to her friends, to satisfy her own narcissistic self. But as soon as they would leave she would put me back. "Oh, look at my son, how handsome and bright he is." As soon as the guest would leave, she would ignore me. I felt as though I was a robot. Gee, we were having such a good time.

Defining the Schizoid

The schizoid and the narcissistic personality have many similarities. The schizoid can be very charming, seductive, and appears quite sexual at the onset of the relationship. It is only later that we find out how frightened and vulnerable he is. These are the hollow iceberg men who are cold, aloof, and indifferent. The schizoid abuser is a misogynist, preprogrammed to fear intimacy. He often feels suffocated and engulfed as soon as the dance of intimacy begins.

He maintains a fragile emotional equilibrium by avoiding intimate personal contact, thereby minimizing conflict that he tolerates poorly. Schizoids are often described, even by their nearest and dearest, in terms of automata ("robots"). They are uninterested in social relationships or interactions and have a very limited emotional repertoire. It is not that they do not have emotions; rather they express them poorly and intermittently. Schizoids appear cold and stunted, flat, and zombie-like, are anhedonic (find nothing pleasurable and attractive), but not necessarily dysphoric (sad or depressed). They pretend to be indifferent to praise, criticism, disagreement, and corrective advice, although deep inside they are not. They are creatures of habit, frequently succumbing to rigidity and predictability, and have very narrow interests.

The bitter paradox is that as the schizoid exhibits an overwhelming fear of engulfment, he is at the same time desperate for attachment and emotional involvements with others (which is often experienced as too taxing on his psyche) (McCormack 2000; Lachkar 2004). Both the schizoid and the narcissist fail at interacting on the interpersonal level; while the narcissist will "perform" when there is the potential of mirroring by self objects, the schizoid will remain uninterested and indifferent. Both lack the capacity for empathy. In his or her early informative years, the schizoid individual may have experienced two extremes: severe rejection and humiliation, or an undue amount of over-protectiveness and intrusiveness from early caretakers. "My mother was always breathing down my neck, never gave me a moment. Where were you? Why didn't you call? I've been worried sick all day!" According to McCormack, the schizoid enters a relationship already prescripted to be antagonistic to his needs and feelings. As a result, he disconnects from others and is never able to make true commitments. Unconsciously, he is protecting the other from himself and his aggression. McCormack states it best, "In terms of the borderline and schizoid marriage, we may say that the borderline spouse is unable to be alone, so the schizoid spouse is unable to be with others" (2000, 45).

The Type of Partner Who Chooses and Stays with the Schizoid

The schizoid projects into the dependent that she is too emotional, too impulsive, and too demanding. He, like the obsessive-compulsive, is often repulsed by her neediness and inability to "give him space." "Just let me be! Stop always touching me! I just want my space!" To this one patient replied to her schizoid husband, "What are you an astronaut?" As each one enters into the *folie à deux* (or complicity of their dance), she needs to attach and cling, while he needs to isolate and alienate himself from his love object. As she clings, he not only withdraws (like the narcissist), but completely detaches himself from a partner who already has a weak sense of self, creating even more abandonment anxiety. Typically when intimacy is offered, he backs off, exacerbating in his partner even further into affective states of rejection, humiliation, and unworthiness. Eventually she does attempt to give him space at the heavy price of aloneness and isolation. For the schizoid, his relief is only momentary as he runs away from his internal smothering, suffocating mother.

Case of Alan and Rose

> When I first met Alan, he seemed like a really nice guy. I was so pleased to finally find a stable man who had substance, a good position in life. It was such a relief to know that I finally stopped bonding to abusive, non-available, and depriving men. Jeff was substantial, successful, and well-to-do. He was a surgeon, and I really like that he had status and a good position in life. Jeff was so gentle, kind, understanding and really had a way of listening to me. Finally we made love. This is when everything became "nutsy." He would talk in prose like "porno verses," phrases he must have retrieved from porno sites on the Internet. When he was about ready to penetrate me, he suddenly withdrew, only to tell me he really doesn't care for intercourse but prefers that we each please or masturbate ourselves. I knew this was really crazy but not wanting to lose him, I complied. All the while, he recited these verses, and not once made absolute reference to us or to our intimacy. Also, what was crazy was the way he suddenly jumped out of bed, put his trousers on, and said he had to be on his way. I tried to hug him, and he abruptly told me he does not like to be touched. He had some awareness of his mental condition, and did share that he has a problem with intimacy because his mother smothered and suffocated him his entire life.

In treatment Rose was quite relieved to learn that Alan's behavior had nothing to do with her. She had not known him long enough to show her clingy or needy side. His behavior (as she later supported) was consistent with all women, not just with her. Rose and I proceeded to delve into ways certain men trigger her already existing fear of abandonment. Because of early loss and separation, men like Alan easily set off her "V-spot" alarm.

Discussion

A bizarre thing happens to many couples exhibiting characterological disorders dominated by primitive defenses, as outlined in this chapter. They share the normal desires and wishes that most intimate relationships require, but when that which is desired is offered it is refuted, and often is sabotaged and

Table 2.2. Five Types of Abusers and the Types of Enablers That Stay with Them

Five Types of Abusers	*Types of Enablers Who Stay with Them*
The Narcissistic Abuser	Borderline Personality
The Borderline Abuser	Narcissistic Personality
The Passive-Aggressive Abuser	Caretaker or Obsessive-Compulsive Personality
The Obsessive-Compulsive Abuser	Histrionic Personality
The Schizoid Abuser	Dependent or Histrionic Personality

Table 2.3. The Types of Love Bonds That Attract

The Narcissist (specialness)	and	The Borderline (pain/victimization)
The Passive-Aggressive (forgetfulness)	and	The Caretaker (rage)
The Obsessive-Compulsive (messiness)	and	The Histrionic (excessive emotion)
The Schizoid (aloofness)	and	The Dependent (clingy-ness)

rejected. A common denominator is the inability to tolerate and contain the feelings of intimacy and dependency. Instead of the love being the dominant theme, it gets transformed into hatred, jealousy, envy, rivalry, control, and domination (see Pathological Love in chapter 4).

Tables 2.2 and 2.3 are a simplified reference of the material presented in this chapter, useful in tying these concepts together.

CHAPTER THREE

Emotional Abuse and Its Relationship to the V-Spot

> Men are not gentle creatures who want to be loved. . . . Their neighbor is for them . . . someone who tempts them to satisfy their aggressiveness on him, to exploit his capacity for work without compensation, to use him sexually without his consent . . . to humiliate him . . . to torture and kill him.
>
> —Sigmund Freud, *Civilization and Its Discontents*

Since writing *The Many Faces of Abuse: Treating the Emotional Abuse of High-Functioning Women* (1998a), I have been amazed by how women from all parts of the world have contacted me and shamelessly admitted that they are victims of emotional abuse. Oprah Winfrey (2004) was so startled to discover that many of the women on her television program were victims of emotional abuse that she published a review of my book on the subject, "Women Who Become Undone" (Ball 301–5, 327–30). She noted that many high-functioning women also become the targets of human rights violations and men's aggression.

Recent surveys report that men are more often the perpetrators, and women more often succumb to forms of psychological domination. According to Otto Kernberg (1992), women are more masochistic and men more sadistic. Unless someone is beaten, raped, or physically assaulted, it is difficult for most women (particularly the high-functioning one), as well as some men, to admit or even realize they are being abused, especially when they identify with the abuse or feel "deserving" of it.

Although this book focuses primarily on aggression toward women, one must understand that men can also be the victims of verbal or physical abuse or "enablers." They can be subject to malicious, drawn-out custody battles; excessive alimony payments; psychosomatic illnesses; infidelity; and shopaholic/alcoholic/drug addictions. Until now, the term "enabler" has been used instead of "victim." Enabler implies that the person has recourse, the opportunity to "do" something about it. This does not in any way imply that there is justification for the mistreatment. The term "victim" suggests that the person has no recourse, as with people who live in fundamental dictatorships, totalitarian governments, or militant Islamic regimes where people/women have no choice other than death or being maimed (see chapter 7 on cross-cultural differences). Although the couples we see in clinical practice are not full-blown terrorists or violent perpetrators, it is important to acknowledge how aggression and rage at any level can impact a relationship. For example:

> I can't believe that a smart man like me would allow himself to get into such a mess. I met a woman who begged me to move to Italy with her and her three kids. I was so smitten and excited by her that I divorced my wife, left my kids, and moved to Italy. At first everything was wonderful. I gave Sophia everything, took care of her kids, bought a small villa, until finally one day I caught her having an affair with her boss. I called her on it, and all she did was lie. Even then I could not tear myself away from her. I kept trying to buy her, hoping she would return to me. She sure stirred up my V-spot. My father left us when I was two years old. He made promises, he lied to us, and yet we always wanted to believe in him. I guess Sophia stirred up those same wishes.

Many middle-class women today are not only the mothers in their households but at the same time the breadwinners and significant financial contributors. Often these women—as well as stay-at-home wives and mothers—complain of being overworked and exhausted because they have to bear the brunt of the responsibility for housework, shopping, child care, school involvement, tutoring, carpooling, and the like. "When I come home I see my husband spread out on the couch; the dog's barking, the children aren't fed, and they're screaming and fighting with one another. He promised to stop and buy milk on the way home, but, of course, typically he 'forgot.' I then had to go all the way back through tons of traffic to pick up what we needed and again take up the slack for his neglect." Some women are abandoned by their spouse, do not receive child support, and are the sole bearers of responsibility. "I don't know how he gets away with it but my ex-husband has not contributed one penny toward child support, nor has he seen the children for several years." Another patient is shocked that the state officials cannot help with child support claims because the husband has moved out of the country.

One cannot talk about the V-spot without addressing the subject matter of emotional abuse and how it is directly associated with early trauma and severe forms of vulnerability. Earlier I described five kinds of abusers and the typologies of those who choose to stay with them. I detailed their corresponding dynamics and defense mechanisms to illustrate how each of these pathologies hook into their enabler's unresolved unconscious issues. According to Loring (1994), emotional abuse is just as devastating as physical abuse. Women—particularly women who have been violated and emotionally abused—tend to identify with the negativity of the other person or persons involved. In addition, they are inclined to over-identify with labels and unwarranted treatment that are given to them by others. They often feel that everything is their fault and that they are deserving of the abuse heaped on them. Helping patients to get in contact with their V-spot will facilitate their knowing when to take responsibility for an action and, more important, when not to.

This section is devoted to a segment of women who have not been given much attention in psychological literature. I refer to them as the high-functioning women (HFWs). These women are successful, and because they are successful, they are envied, idealized, and tend to attract less sympathy from others. They are often ridiculed. "What! You! A lawyer, a judge, a corporate executive, and YOU allow yourself to be betrayed? Abused! You of all people . . . you should know better" (Lachkar 1998). A woman who may be outraged to find Internet messages to her husband from another woman may feel too much shame to admit that her marriage is going through a crisis and her life is less than perfect.

In Richard Tuch's book *The Single Woman–Married Man Syndrome* (2000), he offers in-depth understanding into the plight of one specific kind of abusive relationship: the married man and the single woman. It is a beautifully written volume by a respected and renowned psychoanalyst that offers deep understanding of narcissistic men who claim psychological bondage from single women. He explains two types of narcissistic men: the Don Juan, who merely wants to conquer women in order to dominate and control them, and the narcissistic man, who seeks the other woman to fulfill and make up for a missing part of himself. Both these men use and manipulate women for their own self-serving interest. Tuch offers a comprehensive approach to the pain and abuses these women experience. For example, the married man will have two or more women pining over him, while the single woman will only have a fraction of a man. Although Tuch's book does not zero in on the woman's unconscious participation in the abuse by exposing her most sensitive area of emotional vulnerability, it does make the point that people get duped and sucked into pathological love bonds.

Understanding the V-spot is a lifelong process, but once discovered, it can deeply enhance the therapeutic experience. For example, the V-spot theory pinpointed the area of pain and conflict in a patient struggling through a severely abusive relationship. She was in love with a man who was arrogant, selfish, and overly concerned with himself. Immediately we focused on the ego, the blind spots she was failing to see. The realization hit me after she kept saying, "But I love this man. I have never been so in love in my life!" I confronted her with the brutal reality that she was not "in love" but, rather, she was preoccupied with the pain, bonded to the pain and the old injuries that this relationship stirred up. Pain became the replacement for "love," transposed into eroticism because it is highly charged. This confusion between love and pain and self-masochism goes back to childhood, to a father who "loved" her but also left her as a baby. She simply couldn't get how a man who "loves" her so much could be so insensitive, distant, and disrespectful. As the woman becomes more aware and can zone into V-spot territory, she will begin to experience a sense of enlightenment, an inner sense of vitality, and no longer will be frightened of her power.

> There we were at a family gathering. It was the first time he had met my parents. Suddenly he completely dominated the conversation, brought up some very highly charged topics that generally end in bitter battles, like money/politics. Yet, he never gave anyone a chance to speak. I signaled to him to "cool it," but he was relentless. Afterwards I told him how shocked and surprised I was at his behavior. I don't understand why he is so arrogant. Even with people who agree with him he continues to barrage them with a series of assaults, attacks, and acts like Mr. Know-It-All. My family thinks I'm crazy to stay with a man so narcissistically absorbed and controlling.

I immediately let her know that she was not crazy for staying in the relationship. She was just confusing love with pain. Quite surprisingly, she admitted that she was more in love with the conflict than anything else. It was clear that she was reenacting a highly unresolved traumatic experience with a mother who always had to be right, knew it all, was intrusive, and never allowed her to have her own thoughts or opinions. The V-spot theory was remarkably helpful in getting immediate contact with the anxiety zone that gravitates such a person to an abusive object. Each time her lover "became" her narcissistic/controlling/invasive mother, the zone of confusion replaced reality. Moreover, bonding with a familiar internal mother who was highly sexualized led to the pain and ambivalence becoming eroticized. "Yes, yes, I think you're right! I am in love with the conflict, not with him."

Defining Emotional Abuse

Emotional abuse is an ongoing process, differing from physical abuse in that one person, either consciously or unconsciously, psychologically attempts to destroy the will, needs, desires, or perceptions of the other. Although both physical and emotional abuse epitomize aggression and pent-up rage, they embody different elements. Emotional abuse is insidious, lingering, and often covert. It can be just as harmful as physical abuse, and in some cases even more harmful (Lachkar 1998).

The most salient feature of emotional abuse is its insidious nature. It is about power, domination, control, and, thus, is harder to identify. Emotional abuse over time brainwashes a normal woman and transforms her into an enabler. It is quite common for the woman (or man) to believe that he or she is responsible for the abuse and consequently adapt and adjust to it. Instead of leaving, she strives to modify her behavior with the hope of de-escalating the aggression. According to Loring (1994), there are two types of psychological abuse: overt and covert. Overt abuse is openly demeaning and defacing (e.g., verbal remarks, put-downs, constant criticisms); covert abuse is more subtle, hidden, but no less devastating. Psychological abuse includes verbal and behavioral means to undermine someone's sense of self, resorting to such tactics as ridiculing, shaming, blaming, criticizing, threatening, and neglecting the partner's emotional needs (Lachkar 1998). It is subtler than physical abuse because there are no obvious signs like broken bones, scars, or bruises; however, the emotional scars it leaves are just as devastating. Physical abuse is generally cyclical and intermittent, whereas emotional abuse often follows a predictable, ongoing pattern. Even though episodes of emotional abuse may be followed by pleas for forgiveness and remorse, as tension builds, promises are replaced by threats and the assaults escalate once again.

Emotional abuse has some roots in cultures where women are taught that true love means pleasing men and caring for them even at the sacrifice of the self. This can be seen more prevalently in Asian and Middle Eastern societies as opposed to Western cultures (see chapter 7 on cross-cultural differences). Another strong factor that enables emotional abuse is the belief that any relationship, abusive or otherwise, is better than being alone, alienated, and outcast as a single woman. In this way, women come to associate even an abusive marriage with status and stability.

The following are common fears expressed by women about leaving an emotionally abusive situation:

- Fear that the rage will escalate and move into physical danger to herself and her children if they try to leave.
- Fear that leaving will result in something worse.
- Fear of losing economic support for her and the children.
- Fear of being alone, alienated, isolated by society.
- Fear that she can't cope with home and family on her own.
- Fear that the children will feel abandoned.
- Fear of losing custody battles and long, drawn-out court battles.
- Fear of finding (or not finding) work, housing, and child care.
- Fear of recrimination from friends, family, and social community.
- Fear that reporting severe emotional abuse could result in a police report that will bring shame to the family and hinder future employment.

The fears described above most often involve women who may not have the means to care for themselves if they decide to leave. However, there is another segment of the population that may feel just as fearful and violated despite having other recourses. I refer to these distinct types as the "higher level" and "lower level" HFW (Lachkar 1998).

Defining the Higher Level High-Functioning Woman

Not every emotionally abused high-functioning woman exhibits the same level of early trauma or proclivity toward trauma and developmental arrest. The level of functioning is based on the level of splitting or regressive defense mechanisms, ranging from the degree of impulse control, acting out, addictive or compulsive behaviors, capacity for reality testing, and the structure and level of defense mechanisms.

The higher level HFW exhibits more advanced ego functioning. She has an intact ego, is aware that she is being abused while not feeling deserving of it, and has a certain amount of resiliency that enables her to keep her marriage intact. Even though she may have been exposed to early trauma, she is able to self-soothe by turning to "reality" (intact ego). When the abuser arouses her V-spot, she does not explode; instead, she rationally and logically calms herself down. Reality offers her relief because she is not dominated by primitive defenses; her judgment is not obscured or impaired. But even though this woman may be high functioning, she may feel too embarrassed or ashamed to admit that she is being abused. If she does admit the abuse, she is ridiculed, shamed, or disbelieved. "No wonder you don't want to seek help; no one would believe a person like you could let herself be abused and mistreated the way you've been. After all, you are a counselor and you should know better!" In her external life, the abused woman often reveals a highly motivated, energetic, well-educated, career-oriented, and successful persona. She is a highly competent, efficient woman in the workplace—decisive, comfortable with her autonomy, and extremely talented at making decisions and fulfilling responsibilities. But in her personal and family life, she may operate at many different levels of ego functioning (Lachkar 1998, 2004). Most people would be horrified that a woman of this caliber could put up with the same kind of abuse and treatment as her fellow "lower level HFWs." In fact, many of these women were surprised to find that the shelters they called were filled with women from various socio-economic classes. In fact, one shelter reported to me that they rent out and reserve rooms and suites in first-class hotels (like the Ritz-Carlton) to ensure not only the privacy and protection of these women, but to gain their trust and respect.

Defining the Lower Level High-Functioning Woman

The lower level high-functioning woman hypothetically operates at a more primitive level of ego and superego functioning, and is characterized by many unresolved pre-oedipal struggles. She is dominated by such primitive defenses as splitting, projection, projective identification, envy, shame/blame, magical thinking, omnipotent denial, and persecutory anxieties. Unlike the HFW, this woman has been exposed to early traumatic experiences, and reality testing does not offer soothing or emotional relief (ego failure). Instead, what seems to be a relatively harmless statement quickly escalates into an out-of-control experience.

Seeking to "relieve" themselves of anxiety states, these women turn to all kinds of behaviors and defenses to protect themselves from fragmentation (blaming/shaming, yelling, screaming, attacking, drugs, alcohol, addictions, etc.). The lower functioning HFW is more susceptible to V-spot flare-ups, which can lead to symptoms such as depression, psychosomatic illness, or victimization. These are the women who feel deserving of and identify with the abuse. The ensuing depression and emotional paralysis is followed by a descent into major regression, with the women believing everything is their fault. "Is this really happening to me or am I imagining it?" They do not see themselves as enablers, but as victims of abuse with no way out.

Furthermore, because these women were themselves the product of abuse or grew up without discipline, structure, or boundaries, therapists are often horrified when they attempt to help them apply boundaries. The women respond by asking, "What is a boundary? Many of these women have been preprogrammed and prescripted to play the role of caretakers or parentified children who in their early years had to relinquish their childhood because of family crises and performed adult functions for their parents or siblings. Thus, they feel an undue responsibility to take in all the negative reactions from others. "It is up to me to fix it!" They confuse submission with discipline and boundary setting (Lachkar 1992, 1997, 1998).

The following example involves an emotionally abused man, but it could easily be a woman speaking:

> I couldn't sleep, eat, or work. I cried all the time, was lethargic, and was a textbook model of depression. Was so low, and Sophia offered no caring or sympathy. We were having major financial difficulties, so instead of being a partner and discussing with me what we could do she went to New York and went wild shopping. Never a concern about me! She was only concerned with her own image, trips, clothes.

Many clinicians have witnessed repeated episodes of violent reactions when these early vulnerabilities are ignited. Let us look for a moment at the impact a pathological liar has on the partner's psyche. One woman imagined she had a relationship with a man who promised that someday he would get his act together and they would become a "real" couple. She waited and waited as endless days and weekends would go by with nothing more than an XOXO e-mail. When she called, she would discover he was out of town, usually with another woman, whom he claimed meant nothing to him. The woman was paralyzed and could not move out of her house. Reality was not soothing, and the more reality she was faced with, the more she moved into denial.

> I know it happened. I saw it happen but still when he tells me his lies for some reason I lose my reality. I knew he was staying at the Ritz-Carlton Hotel. I could not help myself and was determined to enter his room. I begged the housekeeper to let me in under the guise of forgetting my key. When I entered I was in complete shock. There on the bed lay a black negligee, Victoria's Secret underwear, and two bottles of Cabernet Sauvignon with used wine glasses. When I confronted him, he said, "It's not true. You are imagining things again!"

People who are particularly vulnerable to abandonment, anxiety, and depression need constant reassurance from the therapist to remind them of the "reality." The patient will take great satisfaction in learning to evaluate his or her own perceptions by constantly referring back to experience, replaying it again and again.

Case of Sandra

Sandra had been involved in a 10-year relationship with a man who promised her the world but never came through and was a pathological liar. She was obsessed with trying to figure out why he "does these bad things to her," why he treated other people with care and consideration, but not her. She was not allowed to come over to his house; he claimed that all she did was make trouble (looked through his things, found notes, cards, lingerie). She looked through his things because she didn't trust him. After a major confrontation as a result of finding him in bed with another woman, she asked him, "How come she gets to come over and I don't?" Trying to defend himself, he said, "She doesn't go looking through my things like you do!" She says, "Well, she has nothing to find because nothing of mine is in your house. If you want to screw me, you come over to my place, or if I come to yours, it is only for a short time and then you make sure all of my stuff is gone!"

Sandra: (enters very distraught shaking and sobbing)

Therapist: What's the matter?

Sandra: You won't believe what happened!

Therapist: (Silent)

Sandra: I couldn't sleep. It was a three-day weekend. I hadn't heard a word from Sam. I got up at five in the morning and drove to his house as I have in the past. I saw Laura's car there. Just as I suspected, it was her birthday. He promised he would not see her and that he would not take her out for her birthday. Remember how he did not take me out for my birthday?

Therapist: Yes, I do!

Sandra: Well, I slightly pushed the door and it was open. I entered. I heard their voices in the bedroom. I did not know what to do. Suddenly Sam came out. He was in shock. I started screaming at him. He told me to be quiet and to get the hell out, that I had no right to barge in. I was hysterical. I told him that he had been lying to me. He pushed me into my car. I hit him; he hit me back. I slapped him. She came running out. I said to him, "Get in my car! Get in my car!"

Therapist: And then?

Sandra: He got into my car and said he would call me later. Suddenly she pulled up in her car next to us. He threatened me, telling me I dare not say anything to her. I then rolled down my window and said, "Look, I guess he has been lying to both of us." She looked pissed and drove away.

Therapist: This was a major confrontation. I guess you had to see what was going on to really believe what you already knew because you couldn't trust your mind.

Sandra: I then said, "Well, guess I ruined her birthday!"

Therapist: Wanting to get even for how he ruined your birthday, all the years of lies, betrayal, and unmet promises.

Sandra: Not only that, he was supposed to send me money, but obviously I don't think he will.

Therapist: I have a feeling he will, probably feeling guilty enough.

Sandra: You think so?

Therapist: A good chance. Yes, if you can trust your mind, there is a good chance he will, because, as you say, he always has in the past.

Sandra: He does feel guilty; he got caught and cannot wiggle his way out of this one.

Therapist: But maybe you're feeling guilty!

Sandra: I guess I shouldn't have entered?

Therapist: No, not a good idea. But at least it brought some clarity to the confusion going on all these years.

Sandra: It did, but then he started to attack me, telling me if I weren't such a wild and intrusive woman we would have had a relationship, that it is all my fault.

Therapist: He sounds like your father, always finding a way to blame you for everything, not taking any responsibility.

Sandra: I think I will go to bed and take a Xanax.

Therapist: I think you should go out and celebrate!

One can always question how one sets limits with a severe pathological liar. But one can also see how Sandra's submission put her in the role of an enabler. This case presents a typical scenario of how a pathological liar operates and how someone as vulnerable as Sandra, desperately fearful of abandonment, can get sucked into delusions, lies, and manipulations. Pathological liars are often skillfully deceptive and very convincing. They easily divert themselves from accountability by making up new lies when questioned. Even when caught in the lie, they can make the other person feel as though they have imagined it all. Sandra was always amazed that the more questions she asked, the more she invited new lies. From a legal, moral, and ethical point of view, Sandra did the wrong thing. From a psychological point of view, she did what she "needed" to do in order to catch the liar in the act. Seeing him "in my face" was what she really needed to finally realize the truth.

Case of Kathy and Tim

One of my first high-functioning women was Kathy, who contacted me in June 1977 while living in Alabama. Her concerns were about severe depression and anxiety, exacerbated by a painful and abusive relationship with Tim, a gang member. She complained that her relationship was tumultuous and combative, enormously wild and intense. Tim would replay her worst nightmare of an unavailable/betraying father by making plans on major holidays and birthdays, and then at the last minute not show up and go out drinking beer with the guys. When she first contacted me, she was in the process of completing her residency in neurology at a very prestigious medical school.

Kathy was an unusually attractive, bright young woman with a great scientific and analytic mind. She had an aversion to perfunctory forms of therapy such as those she had encountered in prior treatment. One therapist advised her to simply break up with Tim. Another offered hypnotherapy. Another terminated her on the basis that she was "resisting therapy." Another claimed it all had to do with repressed memories. Another said she didn't need treatment; she just needed a new boyfriend. None of them seemed to recognize that Kathy required a highly specialized form of therapy.

Kathy first met Tim at a bar in her hometown. He was covered with tattoos, piercings, and chains. She recalled that he was, "Not my usual type of a guy, but there was something mesmerizing about him. It was love at first sight." They lived together for the first couple of months. Tim was held on robbery and drug charges while she was doing her residency. Later, Tim was in jail for auto theft. As time went by, Kathy became more withdrawn, depressed, and shamed. "What would happen if my friends/colleagues/interns found out about him?" I let her know it was hard for her to imagine that intuitively people would understand her dilemma, that love is a powerful force and anyone can fall into the private madness of a love bond. While Tim was in jail, they continued their relationship through correspondence, but prior to his release, they broke up.

Her father, who left home when Kathy was two years old, always canceled plans because he had to be with his girlfriends. Her mother was depressed, drinking, and sexually abused Kathy when she was seven years old (asked to tickle her nipples). She went to her father's house only to find him in bed with two lesbians. Meanwhile, Kathy excelled in school, was a straight-A student, and performed extremely well in all other areas of her life.

Eventually she developed a new relationship with Mark, a man she met in the cafeteria at the hospital in which she worked. He was a surgeon, a marked improvement over Tim, but still exhibited many of the same characteristics (always working, unavailable, and unwilling to commit). One could interpret that even though Kathy was in another "abusive" relationship (the unavailable man syndrome), Mark served as a healthy transitional object, helping her move away from the destructive and shameful one.

It was surprising to me that other therapists who had seen Kathy during her relationship with Tim never helped her understand that she really was not "in love" with Tim. Rather, Kathy was addicted to an obsessive relationship that served to mask things she had avoided in her life—moving forward in her own career, isolation, making new social contacts, etc. Furthermore, these therapists failed to recognize Kathy's ego deficits (poor judgment, confusion, ambivalence, non-rational thinking). They offered "advice" but failed to offer a transitional space to help her deal with her shame and enactments of early trauma.

We proceeded with telephone sessions on a twice-a-week basis. What was it about Tim that stirred Kathy's V-spot, and how did my approach differ from that of others? I explained to Kathy that, unlike many other forms of treatment, my focus was not primarily on the relationship; rather, it focused on the developmental needs that the relationship aroused. Not only was Kathy pleased to work within this mode, but it relieved her to understand that there could be a healthy component attached. At work Kathy's functioning was phenomenal, but as soon as she was in the presence of Tim she would suddenly regress. It is amazing that such a bright, intelligent woman was not able to clearly see the destructive and abusive nature of her boyfriend. This inability in itself indicated a defective ego.

Warning Signs of Emotional Violations

What constitutes emotional abuse? Let us look at some warning signs of emotional abuse offered by Peace at Home (1997), a human rights agency that addresses not only the severity of domestic violence but the warning signs of abuse. In addition to Peace at Home, I have included warning signs from other groups and organizations specializing in emotional abuse. Some signs are blatant and obvious indicators of abuse; others are of a more covert, subtle nature. What follows is a modified list from *The Many Faces of Abuse* (Lachkar 1998a).

The abusive partner:

- Rarely or never attempts to understand or hear your point of view.
- Dismisses your concerns as unimportant or an overreaction.
- Always puts his needs first.
- Expects you to perform tasks that you find unpleasant or degrading.
- Makes you feel like you have to "walk on eggshells" in an effort not to upset him or her: "Watch out for his V-spots!"

- Makes fun of logic or any effort to make sense of things. Instead, he manipulates you into feeling guilty for things that have nothing to do with you.
- Belittles any outside contact, activities, or external support that helps you maintain control.
- Blames you for everything, for any ill-fated event in his life.
- Makes you feel guilty by enacting the role of self-sacrificer or martyr as a means to obtain constant pity or attention. "I'm doing this all for your sake!"
- Engages in destructive criticism/verbal abuse: name-calling; mocking, accusing, blaming, shaming, ridiculing, stonewalling.
- Uses pressure tactics: rushing partner to make decisions and/or blaming; yelling, swearing, and making humiliating remarks or gestures; "guilt-tripping" and other forms of intimidation; sulking; being moody; threatening to withhold money/sex; manipulating the children; telling partner what to do.
- Abuses authority: always claims to be right (insists statements are "the truth"); makes decisions without consulting partner; uses "logic" against partner for one's own gain.
- Breaks promises: doesn't follow through, refuses to help with child care or housework.
- Teases: keeps the other person on hold, waiting endlessly.
- Withholds emotions: does not express feelings; gives no support, attention, or compliments.
- Does not respect feelings, rights, or opinions of others.
- Exerts economic control: interferes with partner's work or does not let partner work; withholds or uses money as a means o control.
- Intimidates: Makes angry or threatening gestures; stands in the doorway during arguments; shouts at partner; drives recklessly.
- Disavows the other person's perceptions, making her feel as though she is crazy.

Discussion

Typically people with pre-oedipal struggles or characterological disorders are easy victims. They are dominated by such primitive defenses as splitting, projection, projective identification, envy, shame/blame, magical thinking, omnipotent denial, and persecutory anxieties. People with narcissistic, borderline, and obsessive personality disorders are often like handicapped partners, with immobilized capacity for healthy human interchange. Many have been exposed to traumatic experiences, and thus reality testing does not offer relief. These are often individuals who feel deserving of the abuse, imagine everything is their fault, have masochistic tendencies, and are more susceptible to bonding with the pain.

It is quite striking how the subject of emotional abuse takes on far greater meaning when we help the woman (or man) zone in on the exact area that arouses the pain. Take the plight of the abused woman: When she is in the heat of the verbal and manipulative assaults of an aggressive and abusive partner, everything goes—her mind, her reasoning, her logic. She regresses and cannot think of any resources or alternatives. Sometimes the idea of boundaries is so foreign that she has to be guided and taught how to set limits.

Again, it must be emphasized that although the woman may be an enabler, nothing justifies the abuse. These women need special forms of treatment. The self-psychology model can be most effective in mirroring the "enabler" and her experience and providing empathy, but not to the extent of joining the complicity or *folie à deux* of the couple. The perpetrator responds best to containment with effective therapeutic limits and boundaries.

Chapter 4 details the various theoretical perspectives to offer an in-depth understanding of how these theories have applicability to patients with various disorders.

CHAPTER FOUR

~

Theoretical Considerations

Two roads diverged in a yellow wood,
And sorry I could not travel both
And be one traveler, long I stood
And looked down one as far as I could
. . .
Two roads diverged in a wood, and I—
I took the one less traveled by,
And that has made all the difference.

—"The Road Not Taken" by Robert Frost

Divergent Paths

In reviewing the literature, the most inspiring material for me oddly enough came from non-conjoint therapists. It was instead mainly classical psychoanalysis, the British school of psychoanalysis, and self psychology. Behaviorists are too directive, ask too many questions, and focus too much on the relationship and not the individual issues. The self-psychologist is too empathic and too focused on the external world (self objects and faulty mirroring from early caretakers). The object relationist is perhaps too confrontational, relies too much on the internal world (patient's distortions/denials/projections) and may lack empathic tools. I have not found anything too innovative in the psychological literature. However, in *The Disordered Couple* (1998), Jon Carlson and Len Sperry made some major headway in expanding certain types of relationships into many different kinds of attachments (passive-aggressive couples, psychotic couples, dependent/narcissistic couples, eating-disorder couples).

One of my great concerns is the lack of integration and the cult-like mentality of clinicians grabbing onto one theory or school of thought, believing that only theirs can provide a mutative or curative experience. Unlike "the traveler," who must choose one road, therapists have the privilege of choosing from many paths. My work as a couple therapist has been a marvelous journey, exploring not only the study of various theoretical perspectives, but insights taken from the arts.

Bion's concept or projective identification viewed as a positive unconscious form of communication. This is distinct from Klein's concept of projective identification that connotes envy and hostility. Anna Freud, on the other hand, was particularly critical of Heinz Kohut's new school of self psychology. Kohut, in a critical letter to Anna Freud, claimed that the intrapsychic model results in nothing more than guilt, stereotypical responses, and boredom (Cocks 1994, 172). Whereas, he claims the self-psychological model concerns itself more with the "Tragic Man," a product of an unempathetic mother and absent father. Kohut further protests that the intrapsychic approach stresses pathology and conflict, offering very little room for growth and progress.

Anna Freud again strikes back at Kohut, claiming there is no such thing as a narcissistic self, the idealized object, that the Freudian "self" is a highly charged libidinal zone that is virtually nonexistent in reality. She even goes so far as to offer two identical cases in which both patients had mirroring and supportive mothers and both turned out to have severe narcissistic personality disorders. Kohut politely lashes back, criticizing both Freudian and Kleinian analysis intimating the stereotypical nature, questioning what the outcome would be if we told all our patients that they are depressed because they live in a dark, anal space. Kohut suggests they would be out the door, fleeing from sheer boredom.

Even though Melanie Klein's work was an extension of and inspired by Freud's theories, her work split the British community and was denounced by many authors in the mid-1920s as distorting and betraying the basic principles of classical psychoanalysis; for example, conflict was viewed as emanating from the patient's internal world and an array of infantile fantasies, projections, and distortions. John Bowlby's stance on Klein is that the importance of the child's attachment to the mother is missed (1969).

The difference between the psychoanalytic/psychodynamic model and the cognitive approach is that the cognitive approach regards the relationship to be the number one priority, while the psychodynamic approach deems the individual to be number one. So we question who the patient is: the relationship or the individual? My approach begins with the relationship as the patient and then gradually weans the couple away from the relationship to self-development (see chapter 8).

The trend today leans less toward singling out one theory than toward integrating many. Freud's interpretation of the unconscious and Kohut's intrasubjective experience as a representation between the interaction of self and object are not oppositional but complementary ways of understanding the human condition (Benjamin 1988). From a marital therapist's point of view, the end goal is to help patients face their own wrongdoings and shortcomings and to move away from shame and blame to come to terms with guilt and mourning (see chapter 8 on Treatment Phases). In the case of Maureen and Tony, described later in this chapter, I offer an illustration of how these various theoretical perspectives can work together. First let us begin with a brief review.

As a marital therapist engaged in individual, couple, and group therapy, I draw mainly from classical psychoanalysis (Freud), ego psychology (Hartmann, Mahler, Bowlby, Kernberg), object relations (Klein, Winnicott, Fairbairn, Bion), and self psychology (Kohut). This book emphasizes and leans more toward the perspective of ego psychology. This is particularly important in reference to the V-spot model, which is inextricably linked to the ego and its dysfunctionality. There are various theoretical perspectives on the ego, starting with the movement from classical psychoanalytic theory to ego psychology, to object relations, and self psychology (see table 4.1). While ego functions remain basically the same, the ever-evolving meaning and influences are infinite when we consider emotional injuries resulting from early trauma and emotional injury.

Classical Psychoanalysis

Freud did not discuss emotional pain as linked to archaic injury or specific areas of vulnerabilities emanating from childhood. Instead, he offered the term cathexis, a highly charged connection to another person or object. Freud wrote that the need for the other and the need for love involve very powerful emotions and an overflowing of ego libido to the object (1936). In this way, love mimics a psychotic state, a union between highly charged emotional and bodily experiences. Freud also was the first to introduce us to the narcissistic personality disorder in "His Majesty the Narcissist" (*On Narcissism* 1914, 9). He initially referred to narcissism as the state of self-directed

Table 4.1. Chronological Developments of Theorists

Sigmund Freud (1856–1939)	Oedipus; drive/defense; aggression/instincts
Heinz Hartmann (1894–1970) **John Bowlby (1907–1990)** **Margaret Mahler (1897–1985)**	Ego psychology; introducing the environment and adaptation
Melanie Klein (1882–1960)	Object relations; splitting, projection, projective identification (importance of internal world)
Heinz Kohut (1913–1981)	Self psychology; need for self/mirroring objects
Otto Kernberg (1928–)	Importance of aggression to drive/defense; describes four different kinds of relationships
W. R. D. Fairbairn (1889–1964)	Attachments to bad internal objects
D. W. Winnicott (1896–1971)	Transitional objects; different kinds of mothering experiences; environmental/background/holding mother
Wilfred Bion (1897–1979)	Attacks on thinking/linking; therapist as the thinker, container, detoxifying mother
Thomas Ogden (1972–)	Psychosis and schizophrenia

libido, coined after the Greek legend of Narcissus, who fell in love with his own image, an admired infant part of himself. Freud claims that this type of person becomes libidinally cathected to someone who has qualities that he or she wishes to have, or that he or she had but no longer possesses, such as beauty, fame, success, wealth, brilliance, or power. The narcissist then embarks on a lifelong journey of trying to own or possess these qualities through guilt and envy, a defense against the need for object love. However, while Freud was the first to introduce the concept, it must be mentioned that his theory is in sharp contrast to that of the Kohutian model. The Kohutian model of narcissism depicts a more highly developed narcissist, one whose primary and normal narcissistic phases are virtually unattended to at the normal phase-appropriate time (1971, 1977).

Freud's theory is intrapsychic, whereby the individual is driven by instincts emanating from id, ego, and superego. Gradually, Freud recognized the need for external objects when he introduced the notion of transference, yet yielded no further. Slowly, psychoanalytic theory moved away from drives and instincts and the intrapsychic to the interpersonal and the ego, making a separate entity. Freud's ego is a mediator, a structure that negotiates between the id and superego. His primary concern is instinctual drives, making conscious that which is unconscious to effectuate a structural change (Blanck and Blanck, 1974, 9). Freud's method is dictated by the intrapsychic process, not interpersonal, environmental, or cultural influences. Although Freud did not attach external events and objects to narcissism, he held the perception of a person's vulnerability when he introduced the concept of narcissism.

Primary and Secondary Narcissism

Freud's distinction between primary and secondary narcissism is relevant here. In primary narcissism, the child places all libidinal efforts into himself, a state of object love in which the world revolves primarily around the child. In secondary narcissism, the person projects an ego ideal, the substitute for that which was lost in childhood. Thus, that person is left with expectations others cannot meet. People preoccupied with work, art, writing, or music are always craving this kind of atonement through perfectionism. The individual creates an ideal ego against which the real ego is measured, interfacing with the superego and creating continual conflict. One can easily see how such a person can arouse intense feelings of anxiety. "I feel like I don't even exist. The same way my mother treated me."

One of the crucial points that Freud makes in his discussion of narcissism is the lack of need for the object. He refers to primary narcissism as a state in which the infant does not associate needs with external sources for pleasure; rather, it is an omnipotent state in which the cathexis of energy is directed toward self. In secondary narcissism, Freud noted that the need for the love object becomes a very powerful emotion, causing an over-flowing of ego libido to the object, which must be defended against. How then would a Freudian respond to an archaic injury? To the patient who comes into our office in deep emotional pain? "You may be confusing the pain you have with the power of love, and because the feelings are so intense, you find defensive ways to guard against it."

Ego Psychology

Heinz Hartmann (1958), the legendary pioneer of modern psychology, was one of the first to redefine Freud's view of the ego. Hartmann modified and moved the ego away from drives to a separate apparatus, incorporating the importance of the ego as having inborn adaptive functions. Hartmann discusses the role of endowment in relation to adaptation, taking into consideration the environment, the interpersonal, and the ego's adaptive capacity. Hartmann's ego is an entity that maturates and functions independently of the id and superego, with a capacity to adapt within an acceptable environment. In essence, his concepts reflect a major shift away from the intrapsychic, which he refers to as the primarily reciprocal relationship between the person and the environment. Hartmann greatly influenced thinking about the ego in a new way, in that psychological development is not simply a result of movement back and forth between instinctual drives. The ego has its own life, its own determination, and its own destiny.

According to Blanck and Blanck (1974, 7), the classical approach is not designed to treat the "unanalyzable patient"—that is, a patient with impaired ego functioning (e.g., decision making, judgment, perception). This goes beyond the classical approach, which merely interprets resistance. Ego psychology is designed to treat those with more primitive disorders and offer a new "corrective emotional experience" (Alexander, French, et al., 1946).

Hartmann confirms Klein's view of the importance of the mother (1958). This has revolutionized psychoanalysis by turning our attention to the importance of the mother and the baby ("the good/bad breast") and away from the father (penis envy, castration anxieties). The significance of this infant/mother bonding relationship was brought to the forefront of psychoanalysis. Hartmann extends this importance to the environment and adaptation that leads to a new format of ego functioning. According to Kohut, children who have not received the necessary emotional echo or approval from the mother must now give in and indulge the mother to create some semblance of emotional connectedness (1971, 1977). In other words, Hartmann believes the child needs to learn to adapt, whereas Kohut believes the mother must cave in by providing new self-object experiences.

Ego psychology departs from classical psychoanalysis and incorporates the methods of Heinz Hartmann, Otto Kernberg, Margaret Mahler, Rene Spitz, Edith Jacobson, and John Bowlby, among others—all of whom recognize the centrality, as well as the limitations, of the intrapsychic approach. Even though ego psychologists believe in the effectiveness of short-term psychotherapy, they do not believe in the goal of making the unconscious conscious. This requires time to adapt, taking into consideration the interpersonal, the environment, and the culture.

Ego psychology also parts company with classical psychoanalysis in its belief that psychoanalysis does not have the tools to service those with more severe pathology. Ego psychology is broader in depth and scope, more eclectic, and serves those who have impaired functioning (difficulty in judgment, decision making), going far beyond the concept of resistance. Ego psychology, on a personal level, has been a much more workable approach for behavior that is not altered merely by structural changes but also by the environmental and behavioral reinforcements society provides in order to effectuate a new corrective emotional experience (Alexander, French, et al. 1946). In today's ever-changing world, we might ask ourselves, "What do I do to adapt?" And how do we transform violence, emotional/physical/sexual abuse, governmental violations, or racial discrimination to adaptation? This idea takes on more relevance when we consider the treatment of cross-cultural couples (see chapter 7). The important point remains that when the ego is fragmented, it impairs the ability to adapt to a new environment especially when in culture shock.

Attachment Theory

John Bowlby's work draws our attention to the most profound aspect of human development, human attachment, by detecting early vulnerabilities during the crucial early bonding/attachment years (1969). He describes children who cry endlessly until they finally detach out of despair from lack of response from the absent mother. Bowlby's contribution is important because much of his work focuses on the pain surrounding the bonding and attachment experiences as they intersect the separation-individuation process (1969). In this way, Bowlby's work appears to blend well with Klein's, since both have subjects that suffer from early attachment defects.

How might an attachment theorist intervene with a person deeply embedded in emotional pain? How might an involvement with someone aloof, distant, and disconnected from his or her emotions be dissolved? It seems logical that the working-through process would focus primarily on the partner who has the capacity to flee and express deep emotion, in essence the "healthier" one. "Even though you are in pain and your partner makes you feel completely non-existent when he detaches from you, at least you have the capacity and the mental health to stay connected to your feelings, affects, and emotions. What a treasure!"

Object Relations

Melanie Klein (1957), the pioneer of object relations, offers many invaluable and innovative concepts that help couples who face internal deficits, distortions, and projections. Her most effective concept is that of the introjective/projective process, or projective identification. Projective identification is a procedure that translocates and splits off unwanted parts of the self and unwittingly places them onto the other. This process elucidates movements back and forth as a mode of connecting the most troublesome areas of conflict within the dyadic love bond. This priceless model helps us understand the tangled web of the couple's beleaguered relations, or what I refer to as "the dance." Moreover, it sheds light on how one partner projects a negative feeling into the other, and how the other then tends to identify or over-identify with that negative projection. These interactions are confusing to most therapists because while couples are in the blame/shame mode, the ego is so fragmented that much of the dialogue becomes irrational, defying all logic and reason.

The recurrent behaviors and defenses that block true intimacy at the expense of rational thought are inaccessible to the ego. In turn, they cause a distortion in one's current perspectives on reality. In conjoint treatment, we see how certain dynamic mechanisms, such as projection, splitting, projective identification, grandiosity, entitlement, shame, guilt, and persecutory anxieties can destroy the ego's capacity to function and make rational decisions. Object relations theory differs from Freudian theory in that it is interpersonal, which helps explain why people cannot adapt even when the environment is nurturing. Klein, more than any of her followers, understood the primary importance of the mother and the breast. According to Klein, if the child views the mother as a "good breast," the child will grow up thinking the world is a good place (1957). If, on the other hand, the infant experiences the mother as a "bad breast," the child will experience the world as bad, attacking, and persecutory.

Although faithful to Freud's biological theory, Klein goes beyond neurotic defenses to that of primitive defense mechanisms (1921). Her well-known positions include the paranoid-schizoid and the depressive who exhibit more severe pathology and primitive defense mechanisms. The object relation theory is the only psychodynamic theory I know of that shows movement back and forth between self and object or the dynamics that occur in relationships. This theorizes unconscious internal objects, which compel one to form a specific dynamic attachment through the projected lenses of the child's internal experience, which Klein refers to as projective identification (1921). The introjective/projective processes and projective identification are valuable constructs in understanding how one person can project a negative feeling into another, who then tends to identify or overidentify with the projection. How one relates and interacts with others in the external world—taking into consideration infantile fantasies as a template for viewing the external world—is a fine therapeutic measurement and diagnostic tool. It was these "movements" that inspired my use of the metaphor of "the dance."

How might an object-relational theorist respond to a patient whose V-spot is highly charged? Klein might view the highly elevated raw emotion as persecutory anxiety and/or as a projection with which one identifies or overidentifies. "When your partner abandons you, of course it is painful, but there is also a part of you that abandons yourself whenever you avoid or split off taking care of your own needs."

Self Psychology

Heinz Kohut's pioneering theory of self psychology originated primarily for the narcissistic personality. It started as a developmental theory that stressed the importance of the lifelong need for self objects, mirroring, and empathic responses (1971, 1977). Later, it would become applicable to all disorders of the self. Moving away from classical Freudian psychoanalysis—whose theory of an id and superego was more restrictive and relied less on responses from the external world—Kohut significantly transformed the meaning of the ego from a driver or mediator between id and superego into a separate entity that he refers to as the self (1971, 1977).

The work of Heinz Kohut is of eminent importance in defining the narcissistic personality disorder (1971, 1977). Fundamentally, he believed narcissism was not a pathological disorder but instead traced a line of development from healthy narcissism to a state of maturity. Kohut considered grandiosity and idealization as positive childhood development mechanisms. Kohut did not consider even their reappearance in transference to be a pathological narcissistic regression.

Kohut claims the "mature self" is a product of an empathic caretaker's directive into realistic capacities and limitations (Cocks 1994, 18). He parts from Klein in that he does not believe it is enough to confront the narcissist with all his distortions and delusions about his omnipotent and grandiose self. Instead, he believes that the therapist must first assuage anxiety through soothing and empathic responses, mirroring, and providing self-object functions. I believe this is fundamental in conjoint treatment, particularly when a narcissistic partner is involved. Therapeutic bonding is of primary importance, but not to the exclusion of confronting the pathological nature of the grandiose self. To a self-absorbed actor striving to become successful, one might say, "If you want to be a great actor, you cannot get rid of your feelings thinking they make you look too vulnerable. An actor must be vulnerable."

How might Kohut and his cohorts interpret someone's emotional pain emanating from early archaic injuries? For these theorists, working through would mean providing new self-object experiences by mirroring and empathizing with the archaic injuries without addressing the patient's distortions, illusions, and projections. It is noteworthy at this point to mention that many therapists misinterpret Kohut's work and have confused empathy with collusion or fusion. It is essential that as therapists we be empathic to the vulnerability but not the aggression. "No, you are not allowed to beat your wife, but I can understand how you feel that way because that is the way you were treated as a child."

Self Psychology versus Object Relations

This brings us to the contrast between self psychology and the object relations school. The difference lies mainly in the way each gathers data and formulates truth, mostly via vicarious introspection (empathy/mirroring). The self psychologist becomes immersed in the subjective experience of the patient, believing that the patient's truth is the truth. The object relationist, on the other hand, is on the lookout for the patient's distortions, delusions, and projections.

Many have found object relations and self psychology to be incompatible theories—an "odd couple." However, I have found them to make a "perfect marriage." Both can be extremely helpful in searching through the vast terrain of V-spot discovery. I have suggested that self psychology, with its mirroring and empathy techniques, is more suitable for spotting archaic injuries in the narcissist and meeting the narcissist's self-object needs. Object relations, in my opinion, is more suitable for spotting abandonment anxiety and meeting the borderline's containment needs. However, object relations is extremely effective in helping patients (especially couples) face internal deficits, distortions, and projections. This is especially true for the more pathologically disturbed individual, one who is more inclined to misperceive or distort the therapist's empathic stance as weakness or too kind/unduly understanding.

Self psychology does not emphasize the internal world, nor does it assume the patient is distorting. If disturbances do occur, it usually is because of an arrested development or disruption between self and the self-object tie, and not because of patients' projections, distortions, or delusions. Both self psychology and object relations have different ways of finding truth. The self-psychologist strives to understand the subjective experience by putting aside "the reality." In object relations, the patient's distortions, projections, and misperceptions are considered at face value. So whose truth do we listen to? The self-psychologists say we find truth through the subjective experience, the Kleinians through interpreting the patient's distortions (Lachkar 1998, 2004). It is immensely important to note that all of these factors must be taken into account in order to focus on the importance of primary therapeutic bonding (Lachkar 1998, 2004).

Projective Identification: Wilfred Bion

Bion is another prominent figure within the object relational triangle. A mathematician as well as a psychoanalyst, he stresses the importance of rational thought to the extent of even developing a grid to track the patient's rational or irrational thought processes. His work underlies much of the basic premise of the V-spot paradigm (e.g., when the V-spot is aroused, the mind ceases to function). Bion's most crucial ideas center around projective identification, developing the capacity to link, and the -K ("minus K") and K links, which are discussed in the next section. As mentioned earlier, Bion significantly expands our understanding of projective identification. He provides a platform for transformation. When the object is contained, thoughts become accessible for and suitable for rational thought and reasoning; when not contained, intolerable feelings get projected and translocated into the other. Bion emphasizes that this is an unconscious mechanism in which the person has to control the object as a defense against external persecutory anxiety (fear of dependency, being taken advantage of, fear of vulnerability). This can be easily transformed into a defense against the V-spot.

Bion has described projective identification and the splitting processes as major factors in disorganization of rational thinking and the thought processes that lead to a "general impoverishment of reality testing." According to Ogden, it is the nature of projective identification to weaken the psyche and strip the self of all resources (1986). This is the entire basis of V-spot thinking (or not thinking—"minus-thinking"). It hinders the couple from learning from experience and forces them to repeat the same misfortune again and again, what Freud previously referred to as repetitive compulsion.

I cannot resist applying Wilfred Bion's (1967) concept about thinking to couple therapy, for which it has profound applicability. Bion helps us explore not who is right or wrong but the way of deriving "truth." Until now, we have been discussing what occurs when a person gets overly charged by the arousal of the V-spot. These are people who are deeply connected to their traumatic past and whose archaic injuries render them highly susceptible and overly sensitive. Kohut's remedy is empathy and introspection, while Bion's show of empathy is through containment, reverie, and detoxification. For Bion, the "breast" acts as a container to help in thinking and nourishing the mind while detoxifying the bad thoughts and bad feelings. Bion explains that when the object is not contained, thoughts become suitable only for evacuation. Couples who exhibit these kinds of primitive defenses tend to repeat the same mistake over and over again because they lack the containment that would allow them to learn from their mistakes.

Search for Truth and Knowledge— The -K and K Links

The -K and K links are critical to Bion's examination of one's capacity to think and learn from experience. The K link typifies the individual who tries to find truth through introspection and psychoanalytic inquiry (knowledge), and -K suggests the reverse, the avoidance of truth and knowledge. For Bion, the worst crime is the avoidance of truth, knowledge, and curiosity. Bion most admires the critical thinker who does not go along with the group. His innovative construct uses the letter 'K' (as in knowledge) to describe an emotional link between people.

This leads us to Bion's concepts of alpha and beta elements. Alpha elements are the ability to think about a thought, to contain and hold the thought, which can be useful for communication, thinking, and learning. Beta elements are unborn thoughts or preconceptions of thoughts; they often are undigested, intolerable affects suitable only for evacuation via projective identification. Would it be fair to say that when one is in a highly vulnerable state, the level of communication remains at the beta level? This is quite in keeping with the borderline, whose disintegration of self and ego impairment preoccupy him with blaming and shaming so that he can never learn from the experience.

Aggression and Attachment: Otto Kernberg

Kernberg (1992) delves deeply into the complexity of the love bond. Kernberg's primary focus is on how people form attachments through the use or misuse of aggression. Kernberg contrasts his view of aggression with self psychology, suggesting that aggression is all bad but that healthy aggression can be used in the service of the ego. In this way, aggression can be seen as addictive and exciting. Once it starts, it is difficult to stop; people get hooked (Gay 1986).

Otto Kernberg's understanding of the use and misuse of aggression provides a valuable guideline to understanding different kinds of regressive love bonds (1992). Kernberg's explanation of narcissistic pathology in relationship to love object bonds is in part gender related. He states that women have a masochistic tendency to attach themselves to unsatisfactory men who cannot sustain a full and intimate relationship with them. Jessica Benjamin notes that masochism in women can be seen as a means for escaping loneliness by allowing the other to be in control (1988). Kernberg claims that men will often attach themselves to unsatisfactory women for fear and insecurity,

Table 4.2. Kernberg's (1995) Four Types of Love Relationships

Normal	Relationship more important; love takes over conflict
Pathological	Part object functioning; conflict takes over relationship
Perverse	Search for excitement; partners reverse good and bad
Mature	Whole object functioning; relationship is goal/task oriented

which take the form of hostility and resentment toward them—"envy of the pregenital mother" (Kernberg 1995, 56).

Different Kinds of Love Bonds

In *Aggression in Personality Disorders and Perversions*, Kernberg reminds us of the complexities of relationships as he distinguishes between four different kinds of love relationships: (1) normal, (2) pathological, (3) perverse, and (4) mature. (See table 4.2 for a capsulated explanation.) Kernberg's descriptions are both provocative and extremely useful in the treatment of couples. He examines the success and failure of love, taking into consideration the role of narcissism, masochism, and aggression (1995). His premise is that even though couples may fight, abuse, and hate each other, if the desire to maintain a loving relationship is the ultimate goal, the partnership is considered healthy.

Normal Love

In normal love, "love conquers all." The desire to love and have a loving relationship overcomes conflict. Internal strivings and aggression do not interfere with the capacity to maintain a long-range, intimate, passionate, loving relationship. In a normal relationship, individuals are able to face reality. They do not live in denial and are not threatened by the other person's emotions or truth. Erotic desire is linked to the oedipal object and is not obliterated by the failing of internal objects. One has a strong desire for symbiotic fusion with one's mate. Normal love means the relinquishing of oedipal rivals to the realization that one can settle down with one's partner. The desire to love one's sexual partner becomes more pervasive than the desire to possess or control the oedipal/rival object. One now can live side by side with "father" without having to compete with him. Couples who experience a problem within a normal love relationship will benefit from short-term psychotherapy.

Example: A man and his wife from a small farm town in Nebraska entered couple therapy presenting the problem that the husband had a peculiar habit of cutting off heads in photos of family members and gluing them onto porno figures. This enraged his wife. As bizarre as this may seem, their relationship still remained in the realm of normalcy. The couple was very much in love, had great capacity for erotic intimacy, and shared common values. This strange fetish did not interfere with the couple's capacity to maintain a close and intimate relationship. The treatment consisted mainly of helping the man sort out the difference between fantasy life and reality: It is okay to fantasize but it is not okay to act on these fantasies.

Pathological Love

In pathological love, conflict overcomes the desire to love or to have an intimate relationship. Pathological relations encourage the tendency to repeat the trauma again and again. This is also known as "traumatic bonding" (Dutton 1998). In this relationship, aggression and internal conflicts interfere with the desire to maintain a loving relationship. In pathological love, emotions run high. The relationship is steamy, explosive, and alters and falters between states of distress and discontinuity to moments of harmony and bliss. It is a part object tie, in which such primitive defenses as envy, control, sadomasochism, aggression, and cruelty fester. We see this in obsessive love, addictive love, and love that goes in the wrong direction. In severe pathological relations, love gets directed to sadomasochism and perversion, envy, greed, control, domination, and self-destruction. Reality testing does not offer relief; instead, reality is denied, split off, and projected. Couples in pathological love relationships are in need of more intensive psychotherapy.

Examples: A borderline husband falls in love with a narcissistic, histrionic woman who has beautiful breasts. Only later does he feel compelled to kill any man who looks at her. Or a borderline husband unconsciously pushes his narcissistic wife to have affairs with other men, then berates her for having betrayed and abandoned him. In this way, the borderline husband recreates the idealized unavailable woman/mother who died when he was in early infancy, unconsciously recreating the fantasy with the lost object.

Perverse Love

In perverse love, excitement becomes the replacement for love. Because pain is often linked to the love object, the relationship becomes highly charged and eroticized. Many narcissistic/borderline relationships teeter on the fringes of perversity, using excitement and eroticism as surrogates for a loving relationship. Many of these couples cannot tolerate true intimacy and instead turn to excitement. What kills or destroys a perverse relationship is, in fact, love itself. It is the confusion between good and bad that is used as an effort to shield oneself from getting too close to the good thing. Perversion goes beyond whips and chains. It connotes confusion around one's symbolic love objects. For example, a breast may be viewed as bad because it represents a hunger, whereas an anus is viewed as good because it represents withholding qualities (the unavailable object highly charged with libidinal energy). Eroticism then becomes the emotional insurance policy against vulnerability.

Example: A man might rationalize, "Even though I know this woman isn't right for me, I feel excited! I'm with a woman who torments me, a woman who is unavailable just like my mother." Or, he might think, "Why do I stay with a woman who torments me, someone I wouldn't wish on my worst enemy? She is exactly like my mother. She is like an albatross around my neck" (See the case of Maureen and Tony later in this chapter).

Mature Love

In this situation, partners share common goals, values, and traditions. They are aware of each other's vulnerabilities and share a willingness to work things through. Mature love implies a total commitment within the province of sex, emotions, and shared couple values (Kernberg 1995). The desire for erotic and emotional attachment is not obliterated by the world of internal objects. Desire is an outcome of need fulfillment and does not result from part-object erotic desires or oedipal conflict. The following example encompasses many of the theoretical perspectives outlined above. A couple may not have the same passion as they once shared, but the desire for harmony, mutuality, common interest, raising a family, compassion, and being part of a community becomes the predominate feature of their relationship. "Our lives are not terribly exciting but we have a great deal of harmony in our relationship. We enjoy being with our grandchildren, taking them places, traveling, being with our friends."

Putting Theories into Practice

The following case illustrates the projective/identification process or what I have described as dual projective identification. Maureen projects feelings of shame into Tony for abandoning her, and Tony projects into Maureen the role of the "suffocating mommy," the mother who holds him back from developing his career. Even though Maureen's untamed aggression does recreate the suffocating mommy syndrome in Tony, we see how Tony identifies with Maureen's projections that hold him back from self-development (play, fun, adventure, risk taking).

Using the metaphor of the golf game (competition/rivalry) and the "open house" offers the therapist an opportunity to tap into the real needs of the couple. The metaphor "open house" becomes the thematic motif of the entire relationship, the desire to move into new transitional space in which to work and play. In Kernberg's terms, this would be viewed as a pathological relationship, in which primitive defenses—such as money, control, abandonment, and domination—take over the relationship and become more important than the desire to maintain an intimate love bond. Where is the love? (See Kernberg's four various kinds of relationships, table 4.1.)

Case of Maureen and Tony:
"The Persecutor and the Loser"—Part A

The following cases are about a couple that I have been treating for eight months. They have been married for about eleven years and have two small children. They are also known to people in my supervision group as "the couple from hell." Maureen is a Jewish woman from the Bronx, whose father was a meatpacker. She is athletic, overweight, and is probably one of the most orally aggressive, domineering, controlling women I have ever experienced. Tony is from the Midwest, appears to be a nice, clean-cut guy, and somewhat "nerdy" in a passive-aggressive way. He works hard to please his wife, yet whatever he does never seems to be enough. Her anger and demands are interminable and insatiable. To assuage his rage, he gets back at her in the most insidious ways (avoids her birthday, Mother's Day, Valentine's Day, and makes excuses or buys some perfunctory gift, e.g., a sports bag).

Maureen brings to the relationship a traumatic background of abuse, deprivation, and neglect. Tony brings to the relationship a little boy robbed of a childhood, with a father who always made him feel like a failure, "my wanna-be son!" Tony never had to work; he has an extraordinarily wealthy mother. However, he has now reached a point in his life where he wants to prove he can be a man, stand on his own two feet, start his own venture capital business, and eventually sell shares on the New York Stock Exchange. Whenever he ventures out to create a new business, his wife berates and viciously attacks him: "You had two corporations that you started with our 'start up' money and they both failed, and now you want to fail again!" or, "You're a loser, Tony. You have already started two corporations that failed, bought all the wrong stocks, and now you want to start another one. You don't know what the hell you're doing!"

Both Tony and Maureen are struggling with issues around bonding and separation individuation. For Maureen, Tony's venturing out into a new business represents profound issues around separation and uncontrollable dependency needs to an object she forever clings to. "You can't leave me alone! Don't you dare go away without me!" For Tony, venturing out means separating from his father, proving he can be a man not locked in with a suffocating wife/mother, and showing mastery over his oedipal rivals.

One of the dilemmas in treating this couple is getting caught in their delusional system and the difficulty surrounding separating what is real from what isn't. For example, there is conflict around Tony's separate property, the money he inherited before he was married, and the idea that it is his money to do with whatever he wishes. Yet, his wife feels that she is an equal partner, and he must consult with her about his every move, regardless of the legalities. "I don't give a crap about your separate property. We're married, and you need to consult with me before you make any more business decisions."

To what degree does Tony have to take into consideration his wife's wishes? And to what degree is he entitled to act autonomously with "his own money"? This is not an easy dilemma to sort out, and this conflict occurs quite frequently in conjoint and family treatment. Is Tony free to do what he wants with his money without having to consult his wife? My attitude was a somewhat risky one. After giving it much thought and consideration, and knowing full well that it would make Maureen's V-spot explode, I came to what I thought was a compromise. In reality it is Tony's money, but Tony should take Maureen's needs, views, and opinions into consideration. As expected, this started an entire bombardment of attacks upon me. She claimed I showed no consideration or empathy for her, that I was taking Tony's side, was weak like her mother, and was not able to stand up or defend her against her cruel and selfish husband. I felt that I was thrown right into the couple transference. For her I was the weak, incompetent parent who was not able to stand up against her abusive father, and for him I was destroying his capacity to separate from his wife by not having to run to her for approving his every move. At every turn, Maureen would threaten the marriage and the treatment. "That's it. I'm leaving. I will check myself into a hospital, kill myself, because life isn't worth living."

This really stirred up my own V-spot. I found myself becoming very aggressive and forceful (beyond my normal personality trait), and very firmly had to put down the ground rule. "Just as you both need to feel safe and not threaten each other with divorce, you must not threaten or sabotage our space here. We all need to feel safe!" One of the turning points occurred at the end of a session when Maureen approached me as she was going down the stairs, and began to cry. I was touched by her momentary state of vulnerability. I pointed out how this was the healthy part of her and how hard it was to allow herself to show these feelings in the sessions. She suddenly dashed off and yelled out that the reason she can't be vulnerable is because her husband is mean, unsupportive, and a loser.

Case of Tony and Maureen: The Tennis Match Tit for Tat, or The Open House—Part B

Maureen and Tony: Hi!

Therapist: Hi! Who would like to start?

Maureen: Go ahead, you start, Tony.

Tony: No, Maureen, you go ahead and start.

Maureen: No, you start! Well, Tony went out with the guys Saturday night and left me home with the kids.

Tony: No, that's not what happened. You went out with the girls Tuesday night, and we agreed that Saturday night would be my turn.

Maureen: That's not true, you said that you didn't care if I went out.

Tony: But then it was my turn.

Therapist: Don't you usually like to go out Saturday night together?

Tony: Yes, but Maureen doesn't want to get a babysitter.

Therapist remains silent.

Maureen: But that's not the point. Sunday, we had plans, we had a full day, suddenly he wanted to go and see an open house.

Tony: No, that is not what happened.

Maureen: Yes, it was!

Tony: Shut up, Maureen! This is what happened. We always have a tight schedule. Sunday, Maureen was playing golf. We also had plans to play bridge with another couple, but luckily they canceled, so I said, "Good, now I can go see the open house."

Maureen: That's ridiculous, first of all we don't need another house, and secondly, I didn't want him to leave me with the kids, since I was stuck with them all weekend while he went to the horse races with his friends. Now listen to this! I hear he's going to go to a football game with his friend and leave me home again with the kids. He knows how much I love sports, and he's not taking me.

Tony: That's not true, Maureen. Let me talk! (His face gets redder and redder, his veins almost popping out of his eyelids.) My friend called me and invited me, not Maureen. It's the guys' night out.

Maureen: So what am I supposed to do? Not go?

Therapist: It sounds to me that this relationship is more like a sports match or a baseball game. Who's on first, who's on second, a tit for tat? This is fine on the golf course or a baseball field, but it doesn't work in a relationship. I don't hear anything about desires or needs!

Maureen: That's an interesting way of putting it.

Therapist: Furthermore, I think you are telling me you are here because you would like this to be an "open house." You are both living in a very tight, small, and constricted space.

Maureen: I guess I'm very anal and need to have everything very structured.

Therapist: Not too much room then for an "open space" for spontaneity!

Tony: That's true!

Therapist: For you, Maureen, I can understand the need for structure because as a child you could not count on or depend on anyone. You felt very abused and deprived because of your stepfather. Tony, you felt you didn't have much of a childhood; having no father around, you had to be the responsible one. Now it's Maureen that holds you back from playing, from being a little boy and having fun.

Maureen: You couldn't have said it better.

Tony: The idea of the "open house" really nails it. I feel suffocated.

Therapist: You mean I made a "slam dunk"! That was nice, thank you, but I'm not really interested in getting into a match here, because my goal is to help you get in contact with needs, not a competition. Here we're not looking for a winner.

Maureen: Thanks, doctor, see you next week.

Therapist: Have a good week.

Maureen: Go ahead, Tony. You go out first.

Tony: No, you go first.

Therapist: (smiles knowingly as both get the message) "Here we go again!"

Attachment: Bonding versus Separation-Individuation, and Aggression Run Amok

The following case was prompted by a supervisee asking how we know which theory to apply since there are so many. How do we know when we are in Freud, Klein, Bowlby, Mahler, Kernberg, Fairbairn, Winnicott, or Bion mode? This is a concern to many therapists, especially when various theoretical perspectives overlap and more than one theory is operative. In the following case, Maureen, the borderline wife, is in dire need of containment, mirroring, and empathy. But when empathy (Kohutian style) is offered, it is rebuffed; instead she resorts to such primitive defenses as splitting, projection, and projective identification. When the therapist does interpret her defense mechanism, Maureen strikes back, "Well, he does the same to me. He does it too! How come you pick on me?" One might say that at that moment Maureen is in Kleinian mode; she needs to evacuate by translocating her bad self into the object.

One clinician may say Maureen's issues have to do with separation-individuation. Another may ask how it could be separation when she never bonded with the object in the first place. In this case I find myself moving toward attachment theory because it is particularly helpful in understanding her basic issues that center around deprivation with the early mother, making her a perfect "Bowlby" baby. At another time, she becomes a Winnicottian baby, the abandoned baby with no one to "hold" her (Winnicott's environment/background/holding mother). After an outburst of reeling and raging, she becomes a Kohutian baby, the baby that needs empathy and mirroring. Yet when she finally gets the empathy she needs, she thinks it is phony and can't believe anyone could ever care about her. This moves to Bion's and Klein's concept of containment, the lack of mother's reverie, the psyche that cannot "hold" or contain because it has not experienced the "good breast." This case reflects the various movements between the dynamics of the couple and the theories that support them.

The case of Maureen and Tony also demonstrates how easy it is for the therapist to get lost in the projections and private madness of the couple. It is also easy (especially for female therapists) to get duped into the victimization pleas of the borderline. In this way, there must be an effort made to break through Maureen's aggression and oral rage by introducing her to the vulnerable self, long ago abandoned and now using the therapist as a transitional and new self object. For Maureen, it is helping her get in contact with real needs and feelings of vulnerability, weaning her away from her testy aggression, competition, and rivalry. For some time, the therapist has to wear two hats, helping Tony separate while at the same time showing sensitivity and caring by not withdrawing from the relationship. It also clearly illustrates how each partner's early archaic injury becomes profoundly aroused when the therapist attempts to break through any defenses.

Confronting the Aggression: Maureen and Tony—Part C

Tony was very upset that Maureen doesn't allow him any space. Each time he tells her he has to go away (business trip, football game, out with the guys), she begins an onslaught of attacks. In this session, I made up my mind to confront Maureen for her aggression and for breaking the rules of the therapeutic boundaries (attacks, interrupting, yelling, name calling). I try to empathize with Maureen's pain while at the same time show her how her assaults and attacks are inextricably linked to her issues around separation anxiety and pathological dependency. Tony complains that she has withdrawn sex, and she complains that he does not offer her the support and empathy she needs. She does, however, recognize how her behavior depletes and strips from him the potential capacity for empathy. He, on the other hand, does not see how the more he withholds his support the more he fuels her aggression. She is repeatedly reminded throughout the course of the conjoint treatment that she can express how she feels but cannot act out her aggression and rage.

Maureen: Tony is going out of town again. He just went away, and now he is going away again.

Tony: But it's only for a two-day business trip. Last time it was to go to my mother's funeral.

Maureen: It doesn't matter! I won't let you go! You cannot leave me alone with the kids and the dogs. I will not allow it.

Therapist: But you have full-time help around the clock!

Maureen: Joan! You don't understand the nannies are useless. I caught one with Xanax in her suitcase.

Tony: This is what I get all the time. My [individual] therapist thinks she's paranoid.

Therapist: Sounds to me the issues are more around separation anxiety abandonment.

Maureen: How could I separate? My mother constantly left me alone, had affairs, traveled all the time, and left me with neighbors and relatives.

Therapist: So, Maureen, this makes it even harder to adapt to Tony's going away when you yourself were abandoned as a child. So now instead of telling us how you feel when you are alone, instead you attack and try to control Tony.

Maureen: But when I do, he just gets very mean and offers me no support.

Tony: My [individual] analyst says this is not my problem. I need a wife, not a patient. I can't sit there all day and coddle her.

Maureen: I'm not asking you to coddle me. You're just mean. I have two small children, and I need some support and empathy from you.

Therapist: That sounds legitimate. Now you are telling us about your real needs.

Maureen: Why should I bother? He doesn't care!

Tony: I can't do it. There is nothing left of me to give.

Maureen: See what I mean? But, Tony! I need it and can't survive without it!

Therapist (internally): At this very moment I decide to confront Maureen's aggression, setting a boundary long overdue. I feel scared. Will she run? Okay, Joan! Go for it!

Therapist: Maureen, I have sat here for months, listening to nothing but a barrage of complaints, attacks, and assaults on your husband. I know he should have consulted with you more before just taking off like this, but where is your empathy for Tony? Even when his mother died, all you could do was think about yourself! You say you want empathy, but where is your empathy? And just a few moments ago, he poured his heart out, and you didn't bat an eyelash.

Tony: Yeah! Where is your empathy for me? I don't even tell you anything like my business deals anymore because I know you will just put me down and attack me. She does what my mother used to do, always makes me feel that I am a nothing. "You'll never amount to anything!"

Maureen: (getting scared knowing that Tony is about to pack up and leave the marriage) Look! Tony! I know I haven't behaved well. I am trying to work on myself. I guess I talk like my abusive stepfather, the only voice I know. I am not aware that I am being attacking. I just want him to listen to me. That's why I talk in this voice!

Therapist: Ah!

Maureen: So what should I do?

Therapist: Right now, nothing. Let me just enjoy the moment. What you have just said is a therapeutic treasure. This helps me understand how you have incorporated the voice of your stepfather—a loud, angry, fierce, destructive voice that attacks and assaults you.

Therapist: So, Tony, are you saying you cannot offer her any support?

Tony: Why should I? She never gives me sex. I just want out. My therapist tells me to hold on to my boundaries (*sounds more like manic defense to me than boundaries*). After being treated this way, why should I offer her anything?

Therapist: Simple, because you're married. Here we go again with the competition. She doesn't give you sex, and you are not going to give support and empathy, yet you are still in the marriage (have two babies, go on trips, sleep in same bed). You can't be in and out of the marriage at the same time (splitting).

Tony: No, I'm not going to give her anything unless she gives me sex. Because it's too late. I've had it.

Maureen: So what should we do about that?

Therapist: Well, it obviously is not too late, if you felt that way you wouldn't be here. Nor would you each be working in your own individual therapies. As far as what should we do? We're doing it! See you both next week!

Maureen and Tony: Bye.

Discussion

Tony projects into Maureen that she is not worthy of his empathy, and she projects into Tony that, if he acts independent of her, he is bad and must be punished. She unconsciously coerces Tony into being the abandoning mother and the abusive father, while he coerces her into becoming the suffocating mother and the nonsupportive parent keeping his playful free self forever trapped. This is a very familiar scenario, illustrating what occurs when primitive defenses overrule and dominate the relationship. At this juncture it is important to focus more on the needs of the couple rather than who has more and who has less. "Let us take into consideration your wife's mental state, given the fact that she does get depressed and is very vulnerable. And let us see if together we can realistically discover what the real needs are. From here we will get a chance to see the 'real relationship,' as opposed to the fantasized one."

This approach brings up the therapeutic question and challenge: How do couples relate to one another after so much injury has occurred? I argue that while they are in the marriage they must behave with some civility. The case above illustrates the complexity of coordinating many different theoretical perspectives—a crossover between classical psychoanalysis, object relations, ego psychology, self psychology, etc. When do we contain? When do we mirror? Confront? Break through the defenses/the aggression? The main thrust is that of a Kleinian model, how each partner projects a feeling of negativity into the other (persecutory anxiety, guilt, shame, unworthiness), and how the other tends to identify with the negative projection. The challenge for the therapist was not to give way to the patient's aggression or collude with the husband's way of caving, a kind of masochistic surrender. We are empathic to the vulnerability, not to the aggression. The patient needs soothing but at the same time containment. All therapists weave in and out of this mode because it is impossible to maintain the position of breaking through the defenses without the patient going into complete fragmentation. In these moments, thank God for Kohut! When in doubt, mirror!

In chapter 5 we will examine what happens when certain personality types hook up with various oppositional partners, and the V-spot around which each relationship centers.

CHAPTER FIVE

~

Marital Theatrics

> Benedick: But it is certain I am loved of all ladies, only you excepted. And I would I could find in my heart that I had not a hard heart, for truly I love none.
> Beatrice: A dear happiness to women. They would else have been troubled with a pernicious suitor. I thank God and my cold blood I am of your humour for that. I had rather hear my dog bark at a crow than a man swear he loves me.
>
> —William Shakespeare, *Much Ado about Nothing*

One of the most baffling relationships I have ever encountered is that of Beatrice and Benedick in Shakespeare's *Much Ado about Nothing.* These characters offer a prime example of how two people can deny the love they have for one another, and, instead of openly displaying that love, get caught up in the idea that they hate one another. It is only by the persuasiveness of outside players that they are finally able to come to terms with the deep love and passion they feel for one another.

What better way is there to get in contact with one's own conflicting issues or V-spot than a relationship? The very nature of an intimate partnership stirs up many unconscious wishes, yearnings, and strivings. Today, people are obsessed with talking about their relationships because they're not simple and each couple has its own "private madness" (Kernberg 1990). Let us look further at *folie à deux.*

Folie à deux

Few authors have made reference to the concept of *folie à deux* in the psychoanalytic literature. Authors have expressed *folie à deux* in such terms as couples in collusion, oppositional couples, the private madness of the couple, triangulation, or my concept, "the dance." Yet, no one does it so eloquently as Henry Dicks in *Marital Tensions* (1967) and Albert Mason in *Quick Otto and Slow Leopold* (1994). Each describes the *folie à deux* relationship between Wilhelm Fliess and Sigmund Freud, who was mesmerized by Fliess into believing in numerology.

In general terms, *folie à deux* refers to a pair wrapped up in a shared delusional fantasy such as "we both stick together, and our opinions are always right." But there is also a specific use of the term for oppositional couples—couples who appear as though they are at opposite poles but through their projections join up in a collusive bond. Triangulation is a three-part relationship whereby two people form a covert or overt bond against another member, for example, the child and the mother against the father (Maggie Scharf 1987).

Folie à deux is a term that extends Melanie Klein's notion of projective identification, whereby two people project their delusional fantasies back and forth and engage in a foolish "dance for two" (Dicks 1967). It is an example of a perverse relationship, an emotional involvement with a delusional partner (an abusive partner, a teacher, a cult leader, a terrorist) who contaminates the other (usually a person of a dependent or passive nature) and makes them momentarily lose their mind or go "insane," especially when in a state of idealization.

This happened in Freud's relationship with Fliess, a very strange occurrence for two highly trained and sophisticated medical doctors (Mason 1994). It illustrates how even someone like Freud can get duped into something like numerology, which he later abandoned as being relatively unscientific. The dangers of loving and being loved can be very confusing, more so when one yearns for love while at the same time sabotaging it. According to Dicks, the only safe thing is to drive the object away before it destroys or devours (1967). In effect, Dicks equates this with hating, while the object is simultaneously craving dependence and infantile love.

Going beyond the domestic level to the global, this term easily applies to groups, nations, and even political couples. It refers to people who identify with group leaders that perpetuate certain collective delusional fantasies and manipulate or coerce their people through fear and terror to adhere to their delusional myths and grandiose schemes. To give a dramatic example at the global level, I describe a *folie à deux* relationship between the Milosevics and the Serbian people in "Slobodan and Mirjana Milosevic: The Dysfunctional Couple that Destroyed the Balkans" (unpublished paper, 2000). Slobodan (Slobo) Milosevic, president of Serbia and Yugoslavia, died in 2006. He was a ruthless tyrannical leader intoxicated with power and was known as the butcher of the Balkans (Doder 1999), a man brutally invested in killing and mass destruction.

A Political Couple and *Folie à deux*

In April 1987, Slobodan Milosevic faced a crowd of angry, abused Serbs in a suburb of Pristina, the capital of Kosovo. Standing on a balcony, he declared dramatically, "No one will ever dare to beat you again!" The crowd responded ecstatically, "Slobo, Slobo!" and in a fervor of nationalistic pride one could hear echoes, "Serbia at any cost!" Serb victimization was so deeply embedded in Serb nationalism that any reminder stirred up enormous emotions. The impact was mesmerizing. Suddenly, Milosevic became the provider, the longed-for "caretaker" for starving, deprived Serb "babies."

Thus, the depressed, powerless, and helpless Slobodan became a powerful father icon, the omnipotent, all-encompassing father under the guise of "the caretaker." One might interpret that he became his own protective father by learning how to manipulate people, becoming the savior for the victimized Serbs. By relinquishing his own victimized self to the Serbs, he projected and gave up the most vulnerable part of himself: "I'm no longer the needy little depressed boy; I am all powerful!" Power then became the antigen against depression: "Never again will I feel dead. Now I am alive and rejoined with my family of Serbs!" Slobodan learned well the powerful forces behind the group's vulnerabilities, and discovered how to play out the unconscious fantasies of the group's mythology.

As for Slobodan Milosevic's wife, Mira, after the death of her mother, her father—like Slobodan's father—abandoned her and formed a new family of his own. Being rejected by her father caused her to cling even more fiercely to the memory of her late mother, whom she believed was a victim of the party to which she was forever devoted. Mira then stayed with her grandparents, where she spent most of her time caring for them. Aside from teaching and being Slobodan's supportive and devoted political partner, Mira spent most of her life preoccupied with trying to clear her mother's name. One wonders how a woman in the Balkans could take on such a strong role. One explanation might be that women in Serbia had to do men's work. Homemaking and domesticity were considered not only fruitless and useless tasks for women, but ridiculous ones as well (Puhar 1993, 1994). For Mira, identifying with a male figure served to disguise her hatred of men. After having been betrayed by a father who abandoned her, her regression to her mother's icon triggered paranoid delusions. Mrs. Milosevic fits the model of a paranoid borderline personality who is not heavily grounded but who instead magnificently enacts a "false self" (the self that belies the "true self") and will do anything to get back at the father. Through this "false self," she insidiously used her husband as an instrument to play out her most virile, aggressive fantasies.

In their delusional system, or in their narcissistic/borderline dance, Slobo and Mira Milosevic played into each other's conscious and unconscious repressed fantasies as they assigned themselves to "caretaker roles" and embarked upon ways to capitalize on their own victimized selves. Products of unhappy families and brutal child-rearing, both were depressed, lonely children. They created their own singular world. Slobo's grandiose, narcissistic self parading as the newly found messianic leader fed into Mira's vengeful plight. In return, her rage fed into his national and political self-serving interests. Many Serbs felt that it was Mira, inflamed by her own bitterness and revengeful self, who pushed Slobo toward the pinnacle of power. Those who knew Mira personally suggested that she would drive her husband, using whatever malignant and absolute influence she had over him, to take the entire country over the cliff (much akin to the borderline personality who will do anything to get back or get even).

There is a *folie à deux* between Mira and Slobo, but there is also a *folie à deux* between them and their culture. For Slobo, it was the shame of a deprived and depressive childhood, reinforced by a culture that discouraged maternal affection. For Mira, it was the bitterness of early maternal deprivation and loss, reinforced by a society that ignored women's vulnerabilities and dependency needs while stressing predominantly "male" traits. Mira crusaded in support of her husband's relentless quest for power, fueling his split-off, deprived, and dependent self. In return, Slobo's grandiose self and ruthless aggression ignited her victimized and retaliatory self.

Case of Mr. and Mrs. Milosevic: A Fantasy Analysis

Now for the imagination. What follows is a "fantasy case." What would happen if Mr. and Mrs. Milosevic came for conjoint therapy? What would happen if the therapist expressed the unspoken words (of course, not to the patients but to you, the reader)? This will show what the therapist endures and experiences, and how the therapist is able to transform negative feelings into something meaningful that the patient can digest. What comes to mind is

Bion's (1977) concept of transformation and detoxification. This process involves the therapist's ability to take the toxins or poisons out of the patient's internal world and convert them into a more digestible form, suitable for thinking about and understanding.

In this "session," the therapist is very confrontational. It is not a display of the therapist's technique because, in reality, no therapist would respond this way. The main point is to bring to life the *folie à deux*, as the drama of the private madness unfolds.

Therapist: Tell me what brings you here.

Mrs. Milosevic: We feel depressed. Our people are turning against us.

Mr. Milosevic: Not only that. We feel betrayed; we are angry. After all we did for our people, they are beginning to doubt our integrity.

Therapist: What did you do for your people?

Mrs. Milosevic: What did we do? We protected them, we provided for them, we gave them everything.

Mr. Milosevic: When I heard about all the wrongdoings to the Serbs, I was stunned. I stood out on my porch facing a crowd of Serbs and declared, "No one will ever dare to beat you again!" At that moment I felt I was master. The crowd began to cheer and roar.

Therapist: You became the fantasized protective daddy for them, the messianic leader/savior?

Mr. Milosevic: What do you mean "fantasized"? I *am* the protective leader!

Mrs. Milosevic: He's right. The crowd hailed him, "Slobo, Slobo!" with a fervor of intense nationalistic pride.

Mr. Milosevic: We could hear the echoes, "Serbia, Serbia at any cost!" The impact was mesmerizing.

Therapist: Isn't that the same thing that occurred in Egypt when Nasser declared that all the Jews should be driven into the Red Sea? Didn't he become a nationalistic hero?

Mr. Milosevic: Not at all. You don't understand. This is unique to us.

Therapist: Sounds like mass hysteria to me—a mania in which the group bonds to ward off feelings of dependency and helplessness.

Mrs. Milosevic: What do you mean "mania"? Even the most conservative statesmen are entranced by and in awe of my husband.

Therapist: But with all due respect to you, Mrs. Milosevic, your husband is also known to be a pathological liar who commits atrocities, never keeps promises, and will do anything to maintain power.

Mrs. Milosevic: My husband is a very charming, honorable man. He mesmerizes even American congressmen. Whoever meets my husband and looks him in the eye becomes totally smitten.

Therapist: But your husband has slaughtered thousands of Kosovars, and hundreds of thousands were expelled or fled Kosovo.

Mrs. Milosevic: This doesn't matter. Many returned after the peacekeeping forces arrived.

Therapist: So you are saying your husband has a way of manipulating and seducing people by projecting into them some vulnerable part of himself, which you then confuse with honesty and integrity?

Mrs. Milosevic: How dare you suggest my husband is a manipulator?

Therapist: Your husband is a very clever man. He knows how to hook into the unconscious collective group fantasies and myths of the people!

Mrs. Milosevic: You don't know what you're talking about. They are not fantasies. They are realities. After losing thirteen wars, his approval ratings soared.

Therapist: No wonder you feel confused and betrayed.

Mr. Milosevic: All this doesn't matter. I will do anything to help my country regain power. I'm proud to protect the Serbs.

Therapist: Even if it means a continuation of mass murders?

Mrs. Milosevic: How dare you?

Therapist: To meet these unconscious fantasies, the two of you have joined in a collusive bond, a *folie à deux*, marching hand in hand to the tune of your own private madness.

Mr. Milosevic: I don't know why I sit here and listen to your insults.

Therapist: I think this madness is linked to your vulnerability and the need to ward off feelings of helplessness you both experienced in childhood. Now you think you are protecting the Serbs, as you wish *you* had been protected. Now the *Kosovars* are the victims, and *you* are big and omnipotent.

Mrs. Milosevic: "Madness"? It is not madness I equate with helplessness. I have had my share of feeling helpless. My mother died for nationalistic causes. I had to care for my grandparents. I never had a childhood. I was always the caretaker. But without your "madness," I feel dead inside.

Mr. Milosevic: I agree. We need the excitement. It is this excitement that keeps us alive.

Therapist: So there is some kind of erotic excitement in being the all-powerful leaders?

Mrs. Milosevic: (sitting erect and suddenly coming to life) Yes, that's right! That's right! That's what we do, so we don't feel dead inside. Now we know we are alive!

Therapist: So you are aroused by your husband's aggression. Is this why you go along with his destructive acts?

Mrs. Milosevic: (self-righteously) What you call aggression, I call courage. Yes, it does excite me. I encouraged my husband to do things, to be an architect, to go into politics. But I'm the one who really should be in politics.

Therapist: So you live through him?

Mrs. Milosevic: I don't live through him. I *am* him. We are *one*.

Therapist: Let me conclude today's session. You both share a delusional system joined at the borders of victimization and denial. You are inseparable, each one living emotionally inside the psychic space of the other, without any ego boundaries. You are both depressed, have had morbid childhoods, have endured many losses. You have assigned yourselves to caretaker roles. Not having "good enough" parenting, you have become your own "good" parents. You, Mr. Milosevic, had a later loss of your parents. Mrs. Milosevic, you suffered an earlier loss, and you avenge the death of your mother through your husband's aggression. But both of you have capitalized on your victimized childhoods. You both were lonely children, products of unhappy families, and you have now created your own singular world. In order to offset the emptiness in your lives, it is better to kill, mutilate, slaughter, and destroy.

This fantasy analysis was based on a real political couple to elucidate how the dynamics of their relationship parallel the dramatic and traumatic events in the Balkans. It examined the personalities of the Serbian first couple, the interaction between them, and the dynamics of the relationship between them and the Serb masses against the background of the culture's child-rearing practices and treatment of women. After discussing theorists, psychodynamics, culture, and our Balkan couple, where does this all lead? The answer is as simple as it is complex.

In the following case, the therapist is very confrontational in order to bring out the drama of the *folie à deux*. The session is an example of how each partner provokes the other into being abusive while remaining unaware how each is responsible for provoking the abuse.

Case of Maureen and Tony: Unspoken Words

Therapist: Hi!

Maureen: We're on time today.

Therapist: Yes, I see that!

Maureen: We're supposed to go on vacation to Cabo San Lucas, but I don't want to go.

Tony: She doesn't want to go because she knows she will be expected to have sex with me.

Therapist: What's wrong with sex?

Maureen: Nothing, but if I have sex with him, I know he will end up being cruel and mean to me.

Tony: How will I be cruel?

Maureen: You're always cruel and mean to me after we have sex.

Tony: I was cruel because you kept calling me a loser, criticizing me, attacking me, telling me I don't do enough for you, buy you the right gifts, that I don't act like the other husbands.

Maureen: (interrupts) I did not. You are a fucking liar! You use these as excuses so you can be mean to me. What am I supposed to do? Make love to a man who is sadistic? Look at his face. Look at him! He is turning red, and his eyes are popping out of his head. You don't call that mean?

Therapist (internally): I wish you'd be quiet for just a minute and let him talk. You keep attacking and interrupting. It makes it impossible for me to think. Oh my God, I'm lost. Now where do I go with this?

Therapist: But you haven't had sex with your husband since you were in Mexico four months ago.

Maureen: That's right. Why should I?

Therapist (internally): Because you're married, and you have made a commitment to be a wife. You expect him to supply you with things when he is mad! Don't you get it? Why should he support you, buy you gifts, when all you do is put him down and then accuse him of being cruel?

Maureen: I want support from Tony. I want him to get me coffee in the morning. Sometimes I wake up with migraine headaches. All he does is go into the shower, turns on the TV, and runs to the computer, and boom he's out the door. No good-bye, nothing.

Therapist (internally): If I acted the way you acted, I'd have headaches as well. No wonder he runs out of the house. And you complain he is mean to you. How do I deal with this distortion? What do I do now? Do I empathize, or confront, or just sit and listen?

Tony: You have headaches because you scream, demand, and yell all day. Anybody would get a headache.

Maureen: Shut up, Tony! See? All he does is criticize and attack me. The other day I went out of my way to get my sister to come over so we could go out for a romantic dinner. I did it for him, not me. I'm just as happy eating a pizza.

Tony: Yeah, but Maureen sabotaged the entire evening. All she talked about was how much money I should leave her in my will and how much for the kids' trust fund. I told her I did not want to discuss these things on our night out.

Therapist: But you did engage!

Tony: Yeah, she got me so mad, and when she pushes me to my limit, I just give in, get pussywhipped. I know when we were here last time we agreed that we would not discuss these things on our special night out.

Therapist: But you did!

Therapist (internally): As I listen to the word "loser," I get the sense that Tony is identifying with a negative part of himself. I also hear how Maureen magnificently coerces Tony to enact that role, how she unconsciously makes Tony out to be a loser. She provokes him to such a breaking point that he has no recourse but to submit. After he does that, he loses control, then lashes out and lets her have it! What Tony doesn't realize is that when he gets "pussywhipped," he does begin to feel inadequate. Maureen's ego impairment is so defective she is not able to see her participation. All she sees is an abusive stepfather. She confuses Tony's frustration with her as abuse and sadism, when in fact it is merely frustration. Okay, get ready. This is a good time to confront.

Therapist: I know you are hurting and are in a great deal of pain. When you are hurting it is hard to see your role. You only see Tony as cruel and abusive but you don't have a clue as to how you provoke him. Tony, you try and hold on to your word, but you fall weak before your wife and give way to the attack.

Tony: Well, what am I supposed to do?

Therapist: Have you ever heard of boundaries?

Maureen: Boundaries? Yes, you did mention boundaries. I still don't know what you're talking about.

Tony: Look, she pushes me to my limit.

Therapist (internally): I feel like shaking you. Tony, why don't you leave the room? Why do you put up with this? Be a man and stand up for yourself. Take a cab home. Do anything to avoid colluding with her provocations. Don't you see how you become the loser and the abuser, a role she coerces you into? You are weak and passive with Maureen, as you were with your father. You think yelling and screaming is being a man, but you are just being manipulated. Come on, stand up for yourself. You can do it!

Tony: Guess I got pussywhipped into it.

Therapist (internally): Good for you, Tony! You are beginning to see how you played into the loser game.

Maureen: I have no one else to discuss these things with. Tony is hardly home, so the only time I can bring up the stuff about the kids and the trust is when we go out for a romantic dinner once a week.

Therapist: We made a commitment that these issues would not be discussed during intimate times together. You say Tony sabotages the marriage. Don't you see how you not only sabotage the marriage, but also the treatment? You sabotaged what we agreed upon.

Maureen: Why are you taking sides? Why are you on Tony's side? Why don't you ever see my point of view?

Therapist (internally): Maybe you're right! Maybe I am taking sides! What do I do now? Okay, show empathy for how she feels betrayed and then zoom in like a laser! Joan, whatever you do, don't get sucked in. If you do you will become the loser, because this is what Tony does.

Therapist: I apologize if you feel I am not showing any empathy or understanding toward you. I imagine it must make you feel betrayed to think that your own therapist would not understand the frustration and pain you are in. But, with all due respect, there is no way I am taking sides. I don't take sides. The only side I take is the side of the relationship—the marriage.

Tony: It was nice to see you not giving in to Maureen. I feel as I do because I have no choice.

Therapist: In other words, I did not allow myself to get intimidated or feel guilty that I was doing something bad when I knew I was trying my best to be helpful to the relationship.

Therapist (internally): This was a wonderful moment. The dance between shame and guilt became crystal clear. I was supposed to feel guilty for taking sides and to worry that if I confronted Maureen I would make her wrong and she would feel shamed.

Tony: That was really cool. But still you are not in my situation at home when things are so tight and pressured. It is easy to succumb and just give in to Maureen's demands.

Therapist: No, it is not easier. It is harder, because if you give in then you become the very thing that Maureen coerces you to become—a loser. I understand how frustrated you become.

Tony: What do you mean?

Therapist (internally): Don't you see, by this masochistic surrender you remain weak and emotionally impotent. My head is spinning from this madness. Okay! Here goes! Joan, get moving! Go! But what if she leaves, storms out of the office (stirring up my own abandonment V-spot issues)? Warning: Joan, you are in ego failure. If you worry about being abandoned or her storming out, you will be identifying with Tony's fears.

Therapist: All you see is a mean, sadistic husband like your stepfather, who abused, beat, and violently mistreated you. You confuse your husband's frustration with abuse. He is frustrated, not sadistic! The part you don't see is how you unconsciously provoke him, set him up to be mean to you *(I know I'm going to get it now)*.

Maureen: What are you talking about? Are you saying I am the cause of his meanness? My analyst told me today I should leave him, get a divorce and find someone who will be nice to me.

Therapist: Now you are making me into a mean daddy, acting as though I am abusing you and being mean (couple transference). It is hard to see this is coming from a place of caring and desire to save your marriage. I am so tired of you distorting. Can't you see your husband wants you, is turned on by you, finds you sexy and attractive? Can't you appreciate that, let alone appreciate that I am trying to help you?

Maureen: I can see that a little.

Therapist: Good! I'll take what I can get. That is a start, and I do care, so please try and take the work we do as something productive.

Tony: We will be away next week.

Maureen: You know what that means?

Therapist: Have a great time. See you next week.

Maureen: You go first.

Tony: No, you go!

Primitive Defenses and Psychodynamics

Not only is there a dance between the couple, there is also a dance between their psychodynamics.

Within the dynamics of the couple, there are also back-and-forth movements between guilt/shame, envy/jealousy, domination–control/submission, dependency/omnipotence, and attachment/detachment, not to mention the dance between the V-spots. These occur both between the partners and between the couple and the therapist. The cast of characters who exhibit these types of primitive defenses presents a kind of turnabout scene, making it hard to know who is the abuser and who is the abused. To complicate things, the person who accuses the other is often the one who is doing the very thing he is accusing the other of. Let us examine these psychodynamic concepts a bit further.

Shame versus Guilt

Shame is one of the most common defenses that appears again and again in couple therapy. The shame in couples is being "needy," and couples mask and cover up what is usually felt to be their normal and healthy dependency needs. Shame is like a virus that invades and infects the psyche. It has to do with hiding, is more pronounced than guilt, and occurs in the paranoid-schizoid position. Shame is a matter between the person, the group, or society. Guilt, on the other hand, is between the person and the superego.

Guilt represents a higher form of development than shame and has an internal punitive voice that operates at the level of the superego. It occurs in the depressive position, followed by the desire to make reparation, to take responsibility for past acts, transgressions, or wrongdoings. Shame is associated with isolation and being abandoned by the group, tribe, or society. Guilt is a reaction against an act of doing and the remorse for that act (Lansky 1987). Shame is the preoccupation with what others think, while guilt is primarily a matter between a person and his conscience.

Although it is beyond the scope of this volume to expand on different kinds of guilt, it is noteworthy to mention that guilt can also relate to a sadistic superego, one that has run amok. Ethnic cleansing is an example of this type of guilt: the need to cleanse in order to get rid of the "dirty Jews" or the "dirty Kosovars."

Envy versus Jealousy

Envy, a part-object relationship, is destructive in nature and is considered to be the most primitive and fundamental emotion. It is not based on love, and its intent is to destroy that which is envied. Jealousy, on the other hand, is a whole-object relationship, whereby one desires the object, but does not seek to destroy it. It has a healthy component in that one desires to be part of the oedipal unit, the pack, or the group. We might say Maureen, as described previously, is possessed with envy, an internal force that drives her to destroy the object that feeds her.

Domination/Control versus Submission

Domination is a form of projective identification in which the object is forced either consciously or unconsciously to yield to the will of the other person. The person who is controlled or dominated often moves into a form of masochistic surrender whereby one gives up his/her own needs to satisfy and glorify the other. This is a part-object relationship in which the object does not seek to destroy the other but to subjugate part of the self that goes into submission and a state of victimization or the role of enabler. This is illustrated by the following vignette.

The Greek Wedding

Mr. and Mrs. P. and have been married for 30 years. They arrived in my office for conjoint therapy consultation. The father, Aram, is horrified that their daughter, Ani, wants to marry someone out of their culture and Greek Orthodox religion. Mr. and Mrs. P. come from a very well-to-do, tightly knit Greek family who believe that marrying someone outside of Greek Orthodoxy is strictly out of the question. The first session was like "shock and awe." The father kept blasting his wife, Surpoohie, for allowing their daughter to have a boyfriend who was not Greek, let alone a "low-class American" and a "curse" to the family. "He doesn't even make a living, was married before, has two kids and, she is only thirty-two. Besides, he seems to be cheap." In a loud voice, the father suddenly blurts out, "Everyone is talking about this at our church. I am so humiliated! Ani has shamed us! No one will tell her to her face that he is just a user. I simply will not allow this! If her grandfather, my father, were alive he would put his foot down and this would not happen."

Surpoohie expresses great resentment toward her husband's demands, control, and aggressiveness, and attempt to take control of Ani's life. "He tells all our friends that unless our daughter breaks up with her boyfriend he will not attend any of our events (church, parties, weddings). We're going to a big wedding and my husband threatens that 'if he [the boyfriend] is going to be there then I will not go.' That is why we are here today." After much confrontation, even to the point of telling the husband that he has no right to take over Ani's life, that she is no longer a little girl, Surpoohie simply has to concede.

Finally, the father takes on a different face and, much to our surprise, confesses that if he goes to the party, he will explode and humiliate everyone. "So it is best if I don't go!" At this point the therapist immediately goes into an empathic mode. "Ah, now this is the healthy side of you, the part of you that feels vulnerable and fearful that you will not be able to contain your emotions, that everything will just spill out." Toward the end of the session, Aram segues into a state of mourning hitherto never addressed. Not having mourned the death of his father, Aram unconsciously "becomes" his own father, identifying with a strict, harsh, punitive, demanding internal father. "So instead of letting us know how sad you feel about your father's death, you then have 'become' the replacement for him, his role, and his functions. To allow Ani to have her own life would be a 'curse' and betrayal to your deceased father (Ani's respected grandfather)."

At this juncture the entire mode shifts from mania and aggression to that of sadness, mourning, and loss. The therapeutic challenge in this case is how to confront the aggression and at the same time be empathic to the real issues and feelings of pain and humiliation this couple was experiencing (see chapter 7 on cross-cultural couples).

Omnipotence versus Dependency

The discussion of omnipotence and dependency is crucial because children whose formative years are deficient in maternal-caretaking capacities grow up never learning how to develop healthy dependency attachments. To ward off intolerable feelings of smallness and helplessness, the child grows up with a fantasy that it is bad to have needs, and will therefore project "needy" selves onto others. "It is you that is the needy one, the disgusting one, not me!" Omnipotence is the flip side of dependency. The omnipotent ones are those who never need anything or want anything because they have it all. "I don't need you, I don't need your advice, and I don't need this treatment."

Attachment versus Detachment

Attachment theory is based on the work of John Bowlby (1969), one of the first to recognize the importance of early attachment ties to maternal caretakers. He observes that when children are raised in abusive or deprived environments, severe disruptions with bonding occur. The loss of the object is accompanied by the infant's increasing signs of helplessness, hopelessness, and despair. When this occurs, the infant goes into detachment mode or pathological mourning. Apathy, lethargy, and listlessness become the replacement for affective experience (anger, rage, envy, betrayal, and abandonment). Detachment is not to be confused with denial and withdrawal. Bowlby stresses that when one withdraws, one still maintains a certain libidinal tie to the object; however, when one detaches, one goes into a state of despondency. Children who are left alone or are neglected over long periods of time enter into a phase of despair.

Projective Identification

Earlier it was mentioned that Melanie Klein's (1957) formulations of projective identification have proved invaluable in couple therapy. Her introjective/projective process helps therapists understand "the dance" of the couple and how certain behaviors and interactions go round and get transported back and forth. Projective identification is a one-way process wherein one tries to get rid of some unwanted part.

In conjoint treatment, for example, we see how certain dynamic mechanisms of the narcissist (grandiosity, entitlement, guilt, withdrawal) can arouse states of unworthiness and non-existence in the borderline (shame, blame, envy, abandonment, and persecutory anxieties).

Dual Projective Identification

Dual projective identification, a term that I devised, is more suitable for conjoint therapy than projective identification. It is a primitive mechanism that can explain what happens when one partner projects an intolerant part of the self into the other. It is a dynamic of great fascination to me because it shows movement back and forth, specifically how the "projector" can make the "projectee" feel the same way he or she feels. It is a method of getting rid of inner defects. Another fascinating aspect takes on a more delusional quality, whereby one makes false accusations against the other, and then accuses the other of the very same thing they are doing. For example, someone who is always late or always forgetful will accuse the other of always being the late or forgetful one. Through dual projective identification, one transmits dependency needs along with the accompanying affects to unconsciously express repressed urges, needs, and desires. (The case of Marley and Marv in chapter 6 offers a good example of dual projective identification.)

Table 5.1 indicates the kinds of dynamics both abusers and enablers project into one another. Because the dynamics are not clear entities, there may be some overlap.

Suggestions for the Couple

What follows are suggestions for the therapist to give to patients. These suggestions are broken down into segments for partners of narcissistic and bor-

Table 5.1. Psychodynamics

Narcissist/Borderline
- Guilt/shame
- Attack/blame/withdrawal
- Entitlement/victimization
- Omnipotence/dependency

Passive-Aggressive/Caretaker
- Shame/guilt
- Withdrawal/dependency
- Caretaker role/baby spouse role

Obsessive-Compulsive/Histrionic/Dependent
- Control/domination
- Guilt/shame (internal dirt)
- Obsession with order
- Emotional needs dirty/disgusting (internal dirt)

Schizoid/Histrionic/Dependent
- Clinginess/detachment
- Abandonment/dependency
- Sado-masochism
- Search/unavailable object

derline personalities, as well as passive-aggressive, obsessive-compulsive, and schizoid types. There are also general suggestions pertinent to all couples.

Suggestions for the Partner of the Narcissist

He has made you feel as though you are not entitled to anything because you think you are nothing and that he, the narcissist, is everything. That is a couple myth, a falsity. You have allowed yourself to identify with his negativity, his control, his domination. You need to go out with friends, get a support system, do things, buy things. Don't sit around and wait and wait. Join groups, make friends. Do whatever you have to do to make yourself feel worthy. This shift will make you feel more entitled and important. If you are told you are too needy, then go out immediately and get your needs met. Don't *become* neediness! This creates a dramatic shift in the dynamic within the relational love bond. It makes him begin to wonder where you are. But don't do it out of spite or retaliation. Do it for your own development. You will start to feel a new inner vitality.

Do not withhold from yourself. When you start acting like you are entitled, you will feel different and people will treat you differently. When he withdraws and gets out of line, don't sit around and mope; tell him that you will return and talk when he has calmed down. See friends, go to the theater—and have an alternate plan, just like you have plans in the event of an earthquake. For a change, he'll have to wait for you! Return happy and satisfied, like your own needs have been met. Begin developing your own new space of entitlement (the transitional space).

Suggestions for the Partner of the Borderline

Remember, at any given moment he may attack, insult, or betray you. You feel confused because only moments ago he promised you the world, was a wonderful lover, knew exactly how to please you, and was aware that you need a great deal of love, attention, and admiration. But as you are seduced into this luring scenario, you become the perfect target. With the borderline, you have to protect your V-spot against the feelings of shame and blame. On a more cautionary note, borderlines often confuse normal boundary or limit setting or even an innocent question for an attack as if they are bound by some kind of repressive regime. Women who need a great deal of love, attention, and admiration are perfect targets for these flare-ups.

Without provocation or warning, the borderline will suddenly turn on his spouse or mate. He will tell you your breasts are too small, will compare you to other women, sabotage your plans, not show up, embarrass you, etc. Do not play into this. Set boundaries and limits. Tell him exactly what you expect and what you will or will not tolerate. Do not threaten; be firm and speak with conviction. Mean what you say, do it, and stick to it even if it is something small. Because of the lack of boundaries, if you give an inch the other will take a mile (this is particularly pertinent in court mediation cases).

So, if he doesn't show up, tell him next time you will take your own car. You may feel that you are being punitive or abusive, but remember that you are actually being healthy and loving by creating boundaries. Try not to personalize, identify with, or collude with the craziness. This will create and exacerbate abandonment issues. Be strong and stick to the boundaries you have set. This will help you keep things straight and stop your V-spot from being wounded again.

Suggestions for the Partner of the Passive-Aggressive

Stop enabling him. If he continues to forget to go to the market, then there will be no food. If he forgets his checkbook, then no bills will be paid. Have alternate backups that can protect you. Do only the things for which you can follow through. Do it and mean it. Relieving him of responsibility will continue to stir up your V-spot and make you angry. Remember, even though you are a high-functioning woman, you are not his caretaker! Being the caretaker may work for you in the workplace, but not in your relationship. You are an equal partner. For example: The wife asks what the husband wants for dinner. He replies, "Anything, I don't care." She says, "How about fried worms!" No response; he falls asleep on the couch. Then cook for yourself or for you and the kids.

Suggestions for the Partner of the Obsessive-Compulsive
If he withholds by not allowing you to decorate the house, then go shopping or hire a decorator. Do whatever you can to take care of yourself and protect your V-spot. If he gets angry, enraged, or even abusive, then you will have to deal with that. Remember that you are not a child, you are an adult woman and you do have resources. Keep in mind that no one is allowed to abuse you, mistreat you, or injure you physically or emotionally.

Suggestions for the Partner of the Schizoid
If he is schizoid, he will withdraw at every opportunity. Do not allow this to occur. Keep him engaged and involved in every imaginative way you can. At parties, be sure to place him next to someone with whom he has shared interest (science, computers). This will be less threatening for him, and he will not embarrass you. Remember to do everything you can to protect your V-spot. If he withdraws from you while having sex, continually remind him that you are not engulfing him, that you are not his suffocating mother, that he is free to leave at any time. Remind him that he needs to express himself and not cut you off by detaching.

General Suggestions for All Couples

- Don't attack, retaliate, or get into the battle.
- Wait for a quiet time to engage in discussion, and be sure to follow through.
- Don't leave the room mad. If the person gets too "heated," reassure him that you will return in a short time when he/she calms down (do it and mean it).
- Stay differentiated. Don't get hooked into the deception or the manipulation.
- Trust that you have been manipulated and deceived; don't question it.
- Don't wait for the "right time." It is never the right time!
- If your partner withholds time or money or won't let you, for example, spend time or money on things you enjoy, don't attack. Show him you understand, but don't give up your own needs.
- If he's a borderline and flies into a rage, do not move. Remain absolutely still. Do not say a word. Agree to own up to the area in which

he might be correct, and repeat again and again that even if what he says is true he has no right to attack or verbally abuse you.

- If he gets angry, screams, yells, or complains that you are interfering with his work, his friends, or his family, remind him again and again that you come first, that you and the relationship are most important.

Discussion

This chapter has focused primarily on the psychodynamics of the couple—how various kinds of abusers and enablers form relational love bonds that are destructive and painful (traumatic bonding). A fantasy analysis, as well as analysis of a political couple, showed partners engaged in a collusive bond or *folie à deux* to enhance and dramatize the dance and the forever-evolving movements of their psychodynamics. The concept of *folie à deux* provides a global example of how an entire culture can be affected when early traumatic injury occurs—a cultural V-spot like the Milosevics'. Most people do not live with dictators, but they may feel just as imprisoned and tortured as if they did.

The next chapter deals with one of the most important aspects in identifying the V-spot, and can be quite valuable in helping the therapist efficiently zone in on the exact area of vulnerability experienced by those in couple therapy. This involves getting in contact with what Klein (1957) refers to as one's internal object, often the "bad breast" object that one internalizes. Chapter 6 expands on these terms to help explain why people stay bonded to their bad internal objects, or what I refer to as their internal and external abusers.

CHAPTER SIX

~

The Internal Abuser

If they be two, they are two so
As stiff twin compasses are two;
Thy soul, the fix'd foot, makes no show
To move, but doth, if th' other do.

—From John Donne's "A Valediction Forbidding Mourning"

This chapter focuses mainly on the internal abuser and the corresponding V-spots. Most patients who are enablers of emotional abusers will be quite surprised to discover that not only can there be an external abuser (someone who betrays and violates them), but there can also be an internal abuser (a harsh, critical, punitive, or persecutory object) who keeps them from having a full and intimate relationship. This is a very sensitive therapeutic point, because if we are too quick to interpret the internal abuser, the enabler may misinterpret or misconstrue this to mean that they are responsible for the abuse (which of course they are not). "My husband cheated on me! Are you saying that I am the cause of it?"

The process of helping patients identify and become acquainted with their internal abuser is not to shame them or make them feel guilty, but to empower them by relieving their feelings of persecution and paranoid anxiety. By healing and coming to terms with the internal abuser, one achieves a sense of control. As stated earlier, it is their "powerhouse." While we cannot always control the external abuser who will say and do all kinds of destructive things, we *can* control our internal abuser. "Oh, I'll never get a job!

Who'd want to hire me?" Seeing past the external abuser to the internal one is a very delicate process. This insight is only possible when the patient becomes fully aware that the external abuser's primary function is to ignite the inner abuser's V-spot. Then the healing process can proceed. This kind of therapeutic experience offers patients an opportunity to experience the real relationship, as opposed to the fantasized one.

Let us focus on internal/external objects and where their V-spots intersect. How does one partner project a negative feeling into the other? And how does the other then identify or over-identify with that which is being projected? To emphasize this point, the following section makes strong distinctions between a defense and a feeling.

What Is an Object?

Psychoanalytic literature discusses all kinds of objects—part objects, whole objects, split-off objects, internalized objects, projected objects. An object does not refer to a physical presence, such as a lamp, but to a specific function served within an interpersonal relationship. It is a living and breathing entity, with a life and a drive of its own. While Freud coined the term "object," it was Melanie Klein who assigned it new meaning (1975). Freud's object was solely biological and drive/instinct oriented, while Klein's objects were focused on the psychodynamics of moving back and forth between internal and external occurrences through the introjective and projective processes (1957).

The following example illustrates the projective identification process: A patient called to ask me if I was interested in buying a crystal chandelier from her. Two hours later she called and said she needed an appointment. One could interpret the offering as an invitation to make contact. But because of the patient's perceived omnipotence, she could not allow herself to be needy; therefore, she made me out to be the needy one, the one who needed her chandelier. She did not recognize that her needs were "objects of value."

Through the infant's early introjections, Klein (1975) assigned further importance to internal objects, noting their aggressive destiny and how they evoke unidentifiable sensations of persecution, retaliation, and danger. Subsequent concepts arising from her elaborations on infantile primitive defenses such as splitting, projection, projective identification, envy, and persecutory anxiety opened the door to an entire roster of object relations. Although stimulated by Freud's superego, Klein gravitated to a more primitive superego while still embracing its fantasy quality (1957). Freud's superego has a voice of the father, is more evolved, harsh, punitive, and guilt inducing. Klein's superego, although inspired by Freud, originated as more primitive, shameful, and persecutory in nature. From there ascended an entire internal-object world composed of part objects and later a more mature superego.

The neo-Kleinians (Fairbairn 1944; Winnicott 1965; Kernberg 1992) felt that the splitting of the object into the "good and bad breast" was somewhat limited. Fairbairn's (1940, 1946) notion of bonding to bad internal objects has had a major influence on couple therapy (Lachkar 1982, 2005). He, more than anyone else, helps explain why people stay forever faithful to one's "bad" internal objects. As mentioned earlier, Fairbairn (1940) provides a platform for us to consider why couples stay in painful, conflictual, and destructive relationships. Fairbairn expanded Klein's view to more than the good/bad breast to include the idea that the ego does not split merely into two parts but into a multitude of subdivisions (rejecting, tantalizing, tormenting, depriving, withholding, unavailable objects).

> She's like an albatross around my neck, yet I wouldn't wish her on my worst enemy.

Inspired by Fairbairn's work, I have extrapolated the concept of "internal/external" objects to illuminate the propensity of narcissistic/borderline partners, along with other primitive love bonds, to remain relentlessly attached to their "bad" internal objects. In treatment, it is our job to gradually wean the patient away from the bad external object and to the internal one. This is precisely where the V-spots join—an easy concept to express, but a hard one to find.

Fairbairn's description of splitting objects into various internal objects has relevance to V-spot theory. To elaborate, it is not enough to say that one has internalized or introjected a bad object. It is more important to pinpoint how one is bonding to that "spot" as it becomes an all-consuming force. This brings us to the discussion of pain (Mother of Pain). In many of my earlier contributions, I describe a certain segment of patients who bond with pain or the "Mother of Pain," a term borrowed from Sheldon Bach (1994, 14). "The pain of suffering defends against the greater pain of loss" (17). As no one can make up for early loss, the therapist can help patients learn to tolerate, mourn, and contain the pain of loss or cope with early trauma. Many of these patients unfortunately only get a semblance of aliveness when they are bonded to the pain. Therefore, it is necessary to gradually move the patients away from their bad and painful introjects, no matter how "comforting" or "familiar" these introjects may be.

Pain is often inextricably linked to the love object. This can most often be seen in the case of borderline patients, who have a predisposition to use pain as a means of bonding with their objects. The kinds of parasitic attachments they form are predestined to exacerbate an already existing condition of victimization and unworthiness. This creates ambivalence and chaos because, in spite of the desire to grow and develop, they bond with painful partners. This becomes even more confusing because the love object who can be cruel and sadistic can be loving and kind.

Because the pain is linked to the love object, it also becomes highly charged and sexualized—known as "traumatic bonding" (Dutton 1981). As bad as the pain is, it is familiar, and it is better than facing the abyss, the black hole, the void. This helps us understand why couples stay forever bonded to the painful object. The relationship is the transitional object to the internal world. It is, therefore, "the meaningless" that epitomizes states of terror rather than deprivation itself. Patients may feel enraged but at least they feel a "sense of aliveness instead of deadness" (Grotstein 1987).

Pain stirs up an amalgam of unresolved developmental issues as each partner seeks out the other to play out their internal drama or archaic injuries (V-spots). "At least I feel alive, I know I exist!" In more global terms and for a more graphic example, compare these partners to suicide bombers. "I'd rather die a suicide bomber to prove we as a people exist!" (Lachkar 2002). "Now I know I am alive! I have purpose and meaning to life; I shall give honor and status to my family."

To summarize, some partners bond with pain and choose to stay in painful, often conflictual, relationships for some of the following reasons:

- People who have had traumatic experiences are programmed to bond with a painful internal object that is familiar.
- It is better to bond in pain than to have to face the void, the black hole, the emptiness.
- Pain stirs up an amalgam of unresolved infantile issues.
- Pain becomes highly eroticized/sexualized.
- Pain is familiar (familiar internal bad object).
- Pain is confusing. The lover who can be cruel and sadistic can also be loving and kind.
- Pain is linked to internal part of the self that one wants to destroy/be rid of.

Part Object

According to Klein, part-object functioning occurs in the early stage of the paranoid-schizoid position (1957). It is the first contact that occurs between the mother and the baby in the feeding experience. The breast is believed to be the baby's first possession and is there for the sole purpose of serving the baby's needs on demand. A part object is a part of a person—such as a mouth, a hand, a breast, or an anus—that serves a specific function designed to be available for the sole purpose of gratification. During this stage, the other is not recognized as a "whole object." How one relates to an external object is fundamental to object-relations theory. This has immense value in couple therapy because often partners confuse healthy dependency needs with mania. "Of course you are upset when your husband leaves you and goes away on business trips, but it is your reaction that is of concern."

Examples:

- I need you desperately.
- I can't live without you.
- I don't need you at all.
- I feel lost without you.
- I can do it all myself.
- If you leave me I will kill myself.
- The only reason I stay is because you provide for me financially.

External Object

An external object is an actual person, place, or thing cathected to or invested with emotional energy that has the capacity to blame, shame, hurt, or project a negative feeling into the other. In this book, we have discussed various kinds of oppressors or abusers, such as the narcissist, the borderline, the schizoid, etc. Their characterological states, traits, and characteristics have been outlined to describe how they arouse the V-spots of the enablers that choose to stay with them.

Whole Object

The start of the depressive position is marked by the awareness that the other person has rights, feelings, needs, hopes, strengths, weaknesses, and insecurities of their own. The healthy baby grows to view the mother as a separate person with feelings and desires of her own. There is a relinquishment of paranoid anxiety, splitting, and projective identification with the emergence of a more integrated ego and mature superego.

Self Object

A self object is almost identical to an internal object located within the psyche and seeking an interpersonal object to relate to. Self object is a term Kohut devised to describe the developing child's need for the admiration and glee in the mother's eye as she gazes upon her child (1977). It is the ambitious role of the caretaker to offer such self-object needs as mirroring, empathic attunement, and reflection of the child's "normal" grandiose self.

Internal Object

The internal object requires more rigorous investigation and is far more intricate than a self object. Internal objects do not readily attach themselves to external stimuli that provide pleasure; rather, they first must be introjected into the psyche as something that arouses them and can subsequently be identified with. The term does not always have a clear definition because it is a complex concept. The internal object is the primitive way of bonding with the split-off part of the patient's inner world. It might even explain why people choose oppositional partners, for it compels them to get in contact with some destructive or negative aspects of themselves. This may explain why even empathic responses are misconstrued as negative and manipulative (especially for those with borderline pathology); the empathy might mirror the pain but will not identify with it.

For example, Mr. Joseph feels betrayed because all his employees left to work at another company. Meanwhile, he complains that he feels betrayed because he was so good to his employees, gave them everything, and was a real "nice guy." He said, "I became their best friend; when they wanted extra days off I gave it to them. When they needed money in advance, I gave it to them." A therapist would tell Mr. Joseph, "Yes, you gave them everything except your boundaries. You betrayed yourself by not being able to play the role of a boss (internal betrayer)."

Mediation

> Happy families are all alike; every unhappy family is unhappy in its own way.
>
> —Leo Tolstoy, *Anna Karenina*

No book of this scope would be complete without making reference to one of the most emotionally charged experience couples go through—divorce and custody battles. This may seem like a diversion, but many in clinical practice are confronted with the horrors that occur in court custody and divorce battles. In recent years, an increasing number of mediators, lawyers, and court officials have consulted extensively with psychoanalysts and other mental health professionals in order to deal with "impossible couples" in court settings. Nowhere do we see more emotions fly than in divorce court—V-spots everywhere! Court mediators, lawyers, judges, and other court officials are continually baffled as to why people continue to battle. Even when a resolution is offered, it is rebuffed. The couple involved makes constant demands for documentation, dredges up false accusations of child abuse/molestation, forges documents, purposely builds up huge legal bills, violates restraining orders, and yells/fights/lays blame in front of children. Another common abuse is the misuse of children as little mediators. These children grow up feeling guilty over their parents' divorce. They feel that they are somehow responsible: "If only I had been a better child this never would have happened." One man spent hundreds of thousands of dollars trying to prove that he was entitled to custody of his child, while his borderline wife manipulated the court into believing she was the helpless victim and he the abusive father. He finally won, but in doing so he had to confront his own internal psychological abuser (the projected "family" of the court as a re-enactment of his own abusive family). "Why is everyone turning against me?"

Mediation is a process whereby a trained and skilled third party assists in conflict resolution in order to negotiate a marital and custody settlement agreement. The role of the mediator is to improve communication, understanding, and consideration for all parties involved. Mediation attempts to minimize or avoid involvement with the legal or judicial system while at the same time maximizing the alternatives. It primarily addresses the needs of the couple and family by tearing down barriers that disrupt the process. Overall, mediation is a more economic and practical way to reach a settlement agreement.

In a paper I wrote some years ago, "Courts Beware of the Borderline" (1986), for the *Conciliation Court Review*, many judges and lawyers in the field of family law concurred that there were certain individuals who would sacrifice themselves because they were more concerned with vengeance and retaliation. I found that these people were truly getting back at the mommy/daddy/spouse who betrayed or abandoned them rather than trying to reach a conflict resolution. This is important because the divorce rate in recent decades has skyrocketed. Even after divorce or separation, these couples seem to maintain a bond, albeit a destructive one. Are they crazy, perverse, or just sadomasochistic? They cannot separate because they cannot feel alive unless they are fused in a dysfunctional, destructive attachment.

More and more mediators stuck in the quagmire of beleaguered relations are recognizing the need to become aware of the different kinds of personality disorders and search for more effective tools. It is helpful for them to know, for example, how the narcissist will feel entitled or overly entitled to everything (the house, all the money/furniture) as compared to the borderline, who does not feel entitled but instead will spend the rest of his or her life fighting, rebelling, retaliating, and doing anything to get even or get back at the spouse who abandoned or betrayed them. "I want more and more!" shouts the narcissist. "I don't care about winning. I just want to get back at the bad mommy/wife who betrayed and abandoned me!" shouts the borderline. The passive-aggressive will do it *mañana*, whereas the obsessive-compulsive will review everything again and again in great detail, never coming to a decision until everything is perfect. This brings us to the impossible couple.

The Impossible Couple

The impossible couple consists of any two personality types whose goals, desires, and aims are not directed toward maintaining an intimate relationship, but rather unconsciously seeking to destroy. What dominates is not the love or the intimacy, but such primitive defenses as control, domination, envy, jealousy, as well as splitting, projection, and projective identification (very similar to a pathological type of relationship). These are two people who live within their own inner world or the world of the other, making up their own stories, which they believe are the truth. Within these beleaguered relationships are two developmentally arrested people who coerce each other into playing out certain roles as they stir up archaic injuries and get lost in identifying or over-identifying with each other's projections. These are couples that, even after divorce or separation, maintain a destructive bond (often a sadomasochistic relationship). They must maintain the attachment to feel alive.

It can be confusing to talk about impossible couples because there are many types of impossible couples. These couples in conflict include abusive couples, dysfunctional couples, cross-cultural couples, interracial couples, blended couples, gay/hetero couples—but their fundamental dynamics share many common denominators that have been discussed in describing various personality disorders. These people cannot allow themselves the kind of dependency that intimacy requires. Feeling needy, dependent, and vulnerable stirs up early memories of archaic injuries, which are easily ignited during times of stress and trauma. "Why should I allow myself to be vulnerable? It will only lead to hurt and rejection!" Healthy, normal dependency needs are easily confused with feelings of impotence and imperfection. The court system and mediation process are designed to bash into their defense mechanisms, forcing them to relinquish control and break through the distortions, delusions, resistances, and defenses to help reach a workable resolution. The following case exemplifies how realizing that the seemingly unhealthy part of the self can truly be the healthy part and can help save what seems to be an impossible relationship.

Case of Stephan and Monica

Monica and Stephan have been in an on-and-off relationship for eight years. Monica has seen several therapists; each advised her to leave because the relationship was abusive and destructive. Most therapists saw no hope in continuing it. Monica moved out of Stephan's house, but one year later found him at her door begging her to return. Monica called quite distressed and confused, wondering why a professional or "high-functioning" woman like herself would subject herself to a man who was sadistic and cruel.

Monica: Well, we're back together, and I think we are even wasting our time being here.

Stephan: Right! We got back together, and nothing has changed. We are back to our old stuff.

Therapist: Yet, you are here!

Monica: Yes we are, and I guess I was hoping there would be some changes. But whatever I say, whatever I do, Stephan is always right, and I am always wrong.

Therapist listens.

Monica: Then when I try and show him I'm right, he blows up and gets raving mad. At this point, I can't even talk to him.

Stephan: But most of the time you *are* wrong. You talk nonsense. Just because she is a therapist, she thinks she knows it all.

Therapist: Well, no one can know it all.

Stephan: I do! Most of the time I *am* right. Ask her. She wanted to buy a stock, and I told her not to do it. She did and guess what happened? Right. It bombed.

Monica: He is not even working. He was a high school teacher but quit because he could not deal with the kids. He has so much anger.

Stephan: Hey, wait a minute. She is wrong again. I quit because the principal kept interfering with my class and wanted me to teach the way he wanted. Again, see how she distorts everything?

Monica: Okay, have it your way. See, this is what I always do, have to concede to him or else I never hear the end of it. Before we broke up, he smashed a glass, ran out, and slammed the door so hard I thought it would break.

Stephan: But she never listens to me!

Therapist: So, we have here Mr. and Mrs. Right. Mr. Right is always right, and Mrs. Right is always wrong.

Stephan: No, you don't know what you are talking about. It is not like that at all. It has nothing to do with being right or wrong; it has to do with her paying attention to me and listening to me.

Therapist: But when she does pay attention to you, Monica claims you attack her and get angry.

Stephan: You don't know the rest of the story. She then threatens to leave because she can't face that I know more than her.

Therapist: But, you also claim to know more than me.

Stephan: When did I do that?

Therapist: When I did the Mr. and Mrs. Right thing. *(The therapist, getting very angry and frustrated, feels like asking him to leave the office and never return. Instead, she decides to zone in on his V-spot.)*

Monica: He acts like he doesn't care when I leave him, but I know he does.

Stephan: She always threatens. But you know what? I don't care anymore.

Therapist: I think you do care. It is just hard for you to be vulnerable and admit the feelings of loss and abandonment.

Stephan: Why should I go through more losses? I've been through enough.

Therapist: Like?

Stephan remains silent.

Monica: His mother slit her throat when he was six years old, and his father then married a woman Stephan despised.

Therapist: Stephan, I'm sorry to hear that. That is very tragic for a young child. This helps me understand why it is so difficult for you to allow yourself to feel vulnerable and how big and powerful you must feel when you know it all.

Stephan: Who wants to feel small and weak?

Therapist: You do!

Stephan: What? Are you crazy?

Therapist: Well, if you can allow yourself to feel small and weak, then you can acquire the dependency needs an intimate relationship requires.

Monica: What should I do when he has his outbursts of rage?

Therapist: The worst thing to do is threaten to leave. Just tell Stephan to cool off, and when he is ready to have a conversation with you, you will engage with him.

Monica: But even when I do talk to him, it still ends up with him yelling and screaming.

Therapist: Well, when you return and Stephan calms down, tell him you would like to have a dialogue with him. However, if he wants to have a dialogue with himself or give a monologue, you can only sit in the audience and applaud because it is not a conversation.

Stephan: This whole thing is a bunch of nonsense.

Therapist: Now, Stephan, you are doing the same thing with me as you do with Monica, having a conversation with yourself. It is hard for you to believe that the "knowing you" is not the healthy part of you, but the "little you."

The you that can be vulnerable is the healthy you. Monica, you think the submissive/giving in you is the healthy part, but it's not. It just makes you into a victim and even more of a target for other people's aggression. If you both continue on with the "dance" that you do, there never will be a chance of any resolution.

Stephan: So?

Therapist: If you can allow yourself to take in something from me, then you will have a chance to heal from old wounds and be able to have a nurturing relationship that can feed you.

Monica: Thank you, doctor. I think you helped us get to the core. Guess I was too quick to apologize, to think I was wrong. Because of my early deprivation, I tend to be submissive and do anything to get his approval.

Therapist: Ah, now we are having a conversation. You have both been very helpful in giving me a sense of what is going on in your relationship, and I shall look forward to seeing you both next week. And yes, I will be here!

Even with this "impossible couple," we can still see how in the dance of the V-spots, Stephan turns his sadistic self against his masochistic submissive partner, and how Monica, in order to get Stephan's approval, will do anything to quell his rage. "I'll even say you're right when you're wrong!" The therapist was able to contain her intense countertransference reaction of anger and rage toward Stephan as soon as she was able to get in contact with Stephan's V-spot: the fear of dependency. After hearing his tragic history of loss and realizing his defenses against loss, the therapist was able to help Stephan to know that it was his vulnerable self that was the healthy part of him, while his know-it-all self was the destructive part.

The Betraying Object

A patient who lives and breathes betrayal is another example of bonding with an internal object. Wherever she goes, betrayal is lurking in the shadows. According to V-spot theory, it is not only that you *feel* betrayed, but you have *become* the betrayal. This is the internal betrayer that fools you into thinking all the betrayal is external, but the real betrayer is the internal one.

Anita is a 40-year-old actor, the daughter of a famous Hollywood star. She presents a history of both emotional and physical abuse—constant put-downs of her talents and her desire to become a performer. Wherever she goes, whatever she does, she is confronted with betrayal—whether it be a man she meets who seems to fall head over heels for her but never calls her back; or an agent who is blown away by her talent but never calls her; or a beloved friend who gets married and moves away, cutting off contact; or her therapist, who may say something positive about her abusive father. "How dare you say anything positive about my father? Don't you realize what he did to me? Now you are betraying me!"

One day Anita commented about the flowers in my office. I told her that she would like to bloom like a flower but had felt much oppressed in her growing years. The treatment encouraged Anita to take major risks, to go to auditions, and to seek out an agent. She was extremely beautiful, talented, bright, and very gifted. However, with each encounter she was put down and rejected, and was unable to recognize that the entertainment industry is like a home-bred cult of narcissists hungry for attention, fame, and success. Anita could not see how she set herself up for failure. If the audition called for a brunette, she would go as a blonde. If the part required a short, petite type, she would show up anyway, although she was a tall, voluptuous type. "How come they never choose me?" Hollywood became a mother who failed to recognize her child's talents and specialness.

Case of Marley and Marv

This case is an example of dual projective identification, of two people who stir up each other's V-spots by bringing unresolved, unconscious issues into their relationship.

Marley: We have been together for eight months. Marv shows no initiative to do anything or go anywhere.

Therapist: Not go anywhere!

Marley: Not only that, he never has given me a card, a gift, or even a flower, not even any mention of a future together. Yet he acts like he's mad about me!

Therapist: Oh!

Marley: Yes, of course we go to dinner. I drive to his house every weekend to Santa Barbara from Marina del Rey. He is very well to do, and I am currently not working. He never offers to pay for my gas, nor does he ever make an effort to come to my place. He says he wants to hang loose.

Therapist: What happens when you bring these things up to him?

Marley: I actually have stopped discussing any of these issues because when I do he accuses me of pressuring him.

Therapist: What's wrong with pressure? Sounds like he needs some pressuring.

Marley: He says he had a very suffocating mother who always pressured him. He has had two wives, and his last girlfriend did the same thing. He says he wants to do it differently with me. He tells me to be patient, and if I am patient he will give me the world.

Therapist: And in the meantime?

Marley: In the meantime I am to wait and not make demands on him.

Therapist: So it's all about him, isn't it?

Marley: Yep!

Therapist: How does this make you feel?

Marley: I feel as though I am going to explode/suffocate. It is as though someone has given me an enema, and I can't let it out.

Therapist: So you're telling me you are picking up his anal retentive stuff, and everything he feels, he projects onto you. Now you, Marley, are the one that has to withhold and feel suffocated (projective identification) as he puts his feelings into you.

Marley: Exactly. But what do I do?

Therapist: First of all, Marley, you need to recognize that you are identifying with his negative projections and taking them in. So what if you pressure him? So what if he doesn't like it? That is not your problem. That is his stuff. What does his therapist say about this?

Marley: His therapist says he should trust his feelings.

Therapist: His feelings! Marley, those are not feelings; those are his defenses. It is a shame how so many people confuse feelings with defenses.

Marley: That makes sense. But I am scared to do what you are suggesting. My feelings tell me not to invade his space.

Therapist: Marley, now you are saying the same things. Your fear is not a feeling. It is a defense, just as his fear of engulfment and entrapment are not true feelings.

Marley: Are you saying I should get beyond my fear and not worry about hurting him or pressuring him?

Therapist: That is exactly what I am saying. I'm not saying you should attack him or get unduly aggressive, but I do think you need to deal with your needs more realistically, or your internal contents will explode. Go for it. Don't be afraid. What's the worse thing that can happen?

Marley: He'll leave me.

Therapist: Those are your abandonment issues.

Marley: Okay, let me think about this pretty heavy stuff.

Therapist: And a heavy heart. See you next time, Marley. Have a good week!

Marley: Bye!

Case of Beth and Sam: The Nag and the Asshole

The following is an example of dual projective identification illustrating how one partner projects into the other a negative feeling, and how each identifies or overidentifies each others negative projections—or each others corresponding V-spots.

Beth: He ignores me and pays no attention to my needs. He shames, ridicules me, and makes me feel like a nothing. When I ask him about our holiday plans, he says something sarcastic like, "Okay, why don't we just have a picnic in our backyard?"

Sam: See what a nag she is! Big deal, why should I support Hilton Hotel or Sheraton Hotels. They are all a bunch of rip offs, and the comforts of home are by bar much better.

Beth (internally): *He is just a cheap bastard and an asshole.*

Therapist: Simple—because it is customary to plan vacations, time away from home, and if you care about Beth you will try and please her because you love her.

Sam: But why doesn't she do the same for me? After all, I have needs too.

Therapist: But just last week you were telling us how happy you are just doing nothing like watching sports on TV and basically had no needs.

Sam: But, I do have needs! I need time to myself. I need space. I need to not be badgered. I need time to be alone.

Beth: This is what he always does. What is he, a space cadet?

Therapist (acknowledging the wife's pain): Of course those things are important. We all need time alone, but, Bob, within the context of this relationship, those are not needs.

Therapist (internally): He doesn't know the difference between a defense mechanism and a need. He is withdrawing, I am loosing him. How do I get this across?

Sam: If these are not needs, then what are they?

Therapist: Those are your defenses. I don't mean to invade into your space and bother you with all this, but what you do is a defense not a need. It is the defense of isolation and withdrawal.

Sam: But she still nags, or whatever you call it.

Therapist: What you calling nagging, we might call the desire for closeness, intimacy and communication. She at least wants a connection with you and time together.

Beth: That's exactly right. This is where I get confused. When he starts telling me about space, I start to feel a terrible sense of shame for having all these needs while he doesn't seem to need anything! I feel as though I'm just someone who gets in his way (Beth identifying with Sam's negative projections).

Therapist (internally): Beth doesn't realize that this is her V-spot—how she feels shame because there is an internal part of her that identifies with his negativity. Maybe she does feel she is too needy. How do I get this across?

Therapist: But your needs are important, and you do need to start paying more attention to them. Beth, it is not your needs that get in the way; it is your way of identifying with the negative responses from your husband, then you start to believe you really are a nuisance, instead of having the legitimate needs any woman has in an intimate relationship.

Sam: This is such a waste of time. Why don't we get down to the real issues about our marriage.

Therapist: Like what? (Beth looks on curiously).

Sam (unabashedly): The fact that I can't get it up?

Therapist: Now, Sam, I see you are making a real connection here, but you seem quite anxious.

Sam: You bet. It makes me feel like a fool to even have to bring this up, like an "asshole."

Therapist: It makes you feel like an asshole to connect with your needs so instead you "withhold" from yourself, Beth, or from me. To ask for your needs also makes you feel vulnerable and dependent, but actually this is the very healthy side of you, and I'm ready to help.

Beth: So why can't he get it up?

Therapist: Sounds to me we are really talking about Sam's emotional impotence—getting his feelings "up" here.

Sam: Now you're talking (pensively). I never thought of that before—the idea that my physical impotence can be connected to emotional impotence.

Therapist: This may sound very strange to you, but facing this dependent part of you is actually facing the healthy and potent part.

Linda: This happens all the time. He always has to act so macho, as if he is the one who knows everything, has everything, and never needs anything from me.

Bob: Well, I must say I have been to many therapists before, but never has anyone connected my inability to "get it up" with emotional impotence.

Therapist: Before we stop, I would like to reiterate how important your needs are, so let's start here. Please feel free to say anything, ask anything, and I will do my best to respond.

Bob: Uh, I did. By the way, I want to ask you if you will hold my check.

Therapist: Ah, sounds like you're getting healthy already.

Bob: Well, I never thought it would end up like this.

Therapist: Good. I look forward to seeing you both next week.

In this case, we see how the narcissistic "sucker" projects his "bad boy" self into Beth, making her out to be the needy one who nags and nags. For him, needs are dangerous and persecutory, tantamount to being a "sucker." The therapist does not allow herself to get duped into believing that his girlfriend's needs are outrageous and out of line when they appear to be perfectly normal. Because of the early trauma in her own life, she internalized the "bad girl" syndrome every time she was accused of being a nag, therefore confusing healthy needs with paranoid anxiety. She threatens him and represents a part of himself that must face his own emotional impotency.

Discussion

Patients who exhibit primitive defenses tend to use/misuse/abuse the therapist as a transference object. They have a magnificent way of zeroing in on the therapist's V-spot, and they know precisely how to get the most mileage from it.

Borderline patients, for instance, invariably are described as exhibiting intense aggression, magical thinking, paranoid ideation, and severe mood swings. They have a striking ability to convince the therapist that they are truly the helpless victims by using pain as the transitional object to form a parasitic bonding relationship. In the case of Beth and Sam, we see how Sam not only withholds from Beth, feels shame in expressing his needs to the therapist, but also withholds from his "erections" (metaphorically speaking of course). In couple therapy I continue to wonder and to be baffled by what it is that perpetuates conflict, that keeps people in painful, destructive relationships (bonded to the "Mother of Pain"), whereby conflict resolution becomes virtually impossible. Couples involved in these regressive, primitive bonds share a collective couple fantasy. They think that by repeating the trauma of abuse, they somehow will be healed, for example, Sam withholds and Linda nags. Part of the healing process is to help these individuals move beyond the repetition to a new space (very much as yoga teaches practitioners to stretch their bodies into a new space), rather than repeating the same destructive behavior again and again. The enabler can heal from emotional abuse by zoning into her V-spot and then locate her internal abuser, the part of the self that has incorporated the bad internal object long before ever meeting the external one. This entails making the vulnerable partner aware not only of the abuse but of how identifying with it affects and distorts almost every aspect of that person's life.

This chapter has focused primarily on the internal abuser and the corresponding V-spot. Confronting this internal abuser is a highly sensitive and delicate matter; introducing the enabler to her partner's internal object precipitously can constitute a shame/blame reaction. "Are you telling me I am responsible for the abuse?" The therapist has to use his/her own sensibility to know when the timing is right. When this does occur, a new therapeutic space opens and the healing process begins. Chapter 7 adheres closely to my earlier works on cross-cultural couples (1998, 2004). However, a new dimension has been added to explore the possibility of a collective V-spot. It examines how this group ideology relates to various cultural backgrounds.

Chapter 7 expands my earlier works on cross-cultural couples (1997, 2004), adding a new dimension to explore the possibility of a collective "cultural" V-spot as it examines group phenomenon in relation to various cultural backgrounds. It questions, where do the boundaries of culture and pathology meet? This chapter discusses the treatment of cross-cultural couples and how to distinguish how much of their V-spot activitation is cultural and how much is pathological. It also outlines a treatment procedure in accordance to the individual and cultural V-spots in couples, as well as the arousal of the therapist V-spots vis-à-vis countertransference.

CHAPTER SEVEN

~

Group Psychology and Cross-Cultural Considerations

> What the Japanese consider sexy is different from the Western ideal. The whole idea is to have mystery . . . it's all about hidden treasures.
>
> —Colleen Atwood, Academy Award–winning kimono designer for the movie *Memoirs of a Geisha*

Today our consultation rooms are beginning to look like a mini United Nations (Lachkar 1997, 2004, 2008). An increasing number of clinicians are becoming aware of the diversity of their patients (Lachkar 2004). We live in an ever-changing world in which individuals and couples from various cultural backgrounds share their various and rich backgrounds (multicultural couples, cross-cultural couples, interracial couples, interethnic couples, same-sex couples, blended marriages/families, stepfamily marriages, etc.). A person who intermarries is not only marrying another person but tying the knot with an entire culture—with religious, political, and ideological heritages (Lachkar 1997, 2004, 2008). Therapists face new challenges in the global environment in which we live. There is a growing understanding that clinical practices based on the assumption that all couples are white, heterosexual, and married may not be adequate when working with interracial and cross-cultural couples.

I first became aware of cross-cultural and interracial differences when I worked as a teacher at a school where the majority of children were African American. I noticed that they would laugh and play, but as soon as someone criticized or made some demeaning remark about someone else's mother, a typical defensive response was, "Hey, don't you talk about my momma!" This was quite strange, particularly to someone like myself coming from a Jewish immigrant background in which most of our entertainment was derived by making humorous remarks about our Jewish mothers. I soon learned to respect and recognize that these sentiments had historical and social roots and implications.

Is there such a thing as a cultural vulnerability or a cultural V-spot? Do cultures share painful archaic injuries through wars, loss, or a lifetime of governmental abuse or indifference that keeps them forever embroiled in endless feuds? To penetrate these seemingly impermeable borders, we must take into account how such dynamics as shame, guilt, envy, jealousy, dependency, and issues around separation-individuation are qualitatively experienced and differentiated. While writing a recent article, "The Psychopathology of Terrorism" (2008), these differences became more glaringly apparent to me. In this article, I question if terrorists have a mental illness or if their acts of violence are cultural. If they have a mental illness, do we have the right to diagnose a group of people? To do so we must take into account three broad categories: (1) child-rearing practices, ideology, religion, and mythology, (2) governments who disregard the human rights of their people, and (3) psychodynamics such as shame, guilt, envy, jealousy, control/domination, and oedipal issues, including rivals.

One cannot effectively treat emotional vulnerabilities without understanding these qualitative distinctions. Emotional abuse extends beyond geographical borders to encompass the differences in psychodynamics of these vulnerabilities. For example, if you have a Korean patient, it is not enough to analyze their anger or rage without considering the Korean concept of *han* (interminable rage). *Han* is a concept with deep historical significance stemming from the Japanese invasion and occupation of Korea, during which the women had to fend for themselves while the majority of the men were killed and slaughtered. Nor is it enough to understand the concept of self without considering the group self. In Asian and Middle Eastern societies, an individual self is virtually non-existent; it is the group self that plays the dominant role. In these countries, it is not enough to understand shame without considering the notion of "saving face." The same holds true for the concept of true and false self (Winnicott 1965). In Japanese society this is known as the private and the public self (*honne* and *tatamae*). How does an American-trained therapist deal with this? The entire spectrum of self-development takes on a different shape, meaning, and value when viewed from a worldwide perspective. "I'm here to help you develop a true sense of self" does not hold water in Asian and Middle Eastern societies.

In many of my earlier works (Lachkar 1992, 1998, 2004), I discussed "shared couple myths and shared couple fantasies," whereby two partners form a *folie à deux* (or "the dance"). To expand these concepts further, we need to turn to group psychology and psychohistory for background on what happens when two people bring together two opposing worlds. One culture's narcissist or borderline may be another culture's embodiment of mental health. Let us say, then, that narcissistic and borderline vulnerabilities can be understood within the context of their historical and cultural heritage. Later, these points will be examined from a psychological/psychoanalytic viewpoint, incorporating both the intersubjective and objective perspective.

Defining Culture

Culture can be defined as a system of values and beliefs that people share and that offers a system of implicit and explicit designs for living. Implicit in culture are many collective group fantasies that are socially transmitted, particularly by the way people behave, think, and perceive reality, thus offering a blueprint on how to live. It is the organizing principle whereby values and traditions become transmitted through the culture's ideologies, religion, political beliefs, social system, child-rearing practices, and art. It is a process of enculturation and socialization in which one learns a systematic pattern of behavior fundamental to the individual's emotional survival. Culture definitively shapes the individual's ideologies, belief system, and values. In an ever-changing world, our clinical practice takes on a new shape, especially when we take into consideration different family values, child-rearing practices, and religious and political beliefs.

Cross Culture versus Transculture

Robert Endleman (1989) describes very clearly the difference between cross-culture and transculture. Cross-culture is a means of looking at the culture from within. It holds to the notion that we are culturally and psychologically different. Since we are governed by different principles, we do not share the same instinctual drives of sex, aggression, and oedipal conflicts. He implies that in many societies, aggression is enacted masochistically, whereby the child has to suffer to prove his self-worth. Transculture means looking at culture from without. It attests that we are culturally different but psychologically the same and share the basic principles of child development fundamental for all human beings. In other words, Endleman argues that every culture strives to master and overcome oedipal rivals, that oedipal conflicts are universal, and that stages of separation and individuation are inherent in all human beings. Societies or religious groups that cannot find healthy ways to deal with aggression or dependency needs hide under the rubric of religion to assuage their shame or guilt—a "toilet receptacle" to mask their torrid rage. The healthy way to deal with mental pain (loss, betrayal, or abandonment) is through reparation and mourning of the loss, not revenge and retaliation. Women become easy targets for the pent-up rage and aggression of men who have not sufficiently mourned and confronted loss.

These concepts have relevance not only for understanding what people bring to their relationships, but also for the workplace. It is not unusual to become frustrated by a Japanese colleague, employee, or staff member who says "yes" when they mean "no." To be more specific, Japanese people tend to respond more to a negative question than the answer (Berton 2001). How about someone who says she will do it today but really means tomorrow? Or how someone in a Muslim country promises something, then suddenly changes his mind saying, "It was the will of Allah"?

Berton (1995, 2001) has written extensively on Japanese negotiating behavior, indicating that the Japanese have 16 ways to avoid saying "no." Japanese communication is usually quite loose in logical connections. One can go on talking for hours, even gracefully, without coming to the point. That is why it is sometimes extremely difficult for Westerners and the Japanese to communicate, especially in business matters (Doi, quoted in Berton 1995). In order to avoid conflict and offense and maintain a sense of harmony (*wa*), the Japanese are reluctant to say "no," which is felt to be too direct, abrupt, and ultimately impolite. This is why much of Japanese communication is based on non-verbal expression (*haragei*), so as to not offend or hurt.

Where Do Pathology and Culture Interface?

Common questions when treating cross-cultural couples are: From what perspective do we view culture? How do we find pathology? Where do pathology and culture lie? Where do the boundaries between aggression, cruelty, and cultural tradition interface? What are the forces mutual to individual psychopathology and political relationships (Lachkar 1993, 2002, 2004, 2008)? Psychohistorians cannot ignore the psychodynamic aspects of political and psychological vulnerabilities within the matrix of culture and societal traditions.

The question frequently asked is: Do we have the right as Western analysts to apply these concepts to people of varying ethnic backgrounds? My contention is that we do. Kris Yi (1995) argues that Western psychotherapy deals ineffectively with other cultures, particularly Asian cultures, because of the indiscriminate use of psychoanalytic principles that claim universal application. She does not exclude psychoanalysis as a main organizing principle and proposes that psychoanalysis has been ineffective because of the lack of attunement, which leads to an impasse and discontinuity. The following is an example of this kind of discontinuity.

> I am from Israel, and my wife is a Protestant American. When we first got married she agreed to convert to Judaism, but after we had our kids she began to get very uncomfortable attending religious services, feeling disgusted by the guttural sounds of the Hebrew prayers. We saw a therapist, and she just didn't get it! Whenever I said "Shalom" to her, she would respond, "How are you today?" On Rosh Hashanah, I would greet her and say "Shana Tova," and she would respond, "Hope you have a nice weekend." I didn't expect much; just a few words of my tradition.

Similarly, it is imperative that a Jewish therapist say "Merry Christmas" to those patients who celebrate the Christian tradition. Let us now turn to group psychology and psychohistory as we segue into the discussion of the varying psychodynamics and their applicability to cross-cultural couples and their corresponding V-spots.

Group Psychology

Only recently has the study of group psychology gained popularity. Since psychoanalysis was intended for the individual, many psychoanalysts have looked askance at applying analytic concepts and principles to group behaviors. Individual pathology becomes even more glaringly apparent within a group than when the individual is isolated from the herd. Freud (1914) was the first to recognize animal instincts within the group (Lachkar 1993, 276–87) when he looked for the forces that bind people together. Freud recognized the existence of a collective mind, a concept that I have extended to the "couple mind." Just as couples do, groups guard against painful effects by using aggression, primitive defenses, and collective fantasies.

Many theorists believe that group psychology can offer insights into the behavior of individuals who exhibit properties similar to those involved in group dynamics. In the treatment of individuals and cross-cultural couples, we ask ourselves: Can we analyze and diagnose a couple or group mind? One must survey various disciplines—including anthropology, psychohistory, and sociology—to provide the necessary background information.

Understanding group myths and shared group fantasies can be valuable in treating couples from diverse backgrounds. Lloyd deMause (2002a) maintains that the roots of group fantasies are inextricably linked to child-rearing practices. He offers a chilling account of life in Islamic fundamentalist societies filled with violence, cruelty, and sexual exploitation of children. DeMause (2002b) links harsh child-rearing practices among German mothers, for example, as a cause of wars and genocide, including the Holocaust (204). These are familiar themes in countries that do not stress the importance of healthy child development.

Kernberg's discussion of the use and misuse of aggression provides valuable guidelines for our understanding of the regressive nature of relationships. His premise is that if aggression goes in the wrong direction, primitive defenses such as envy take over, and thus infect and dominate the relationship. Just think what happens when the same thing occurs in a group. Those who form highly charged, eroticized, sadomasochistic relational ties operate within their own network—stripped and brainwashed of all capacity for individual thought. According to Wilfred Bion (1961), group thinking is not motivated by rational thought but rather by dogma, pedagogy, and group leaders who have the charisma and persuasion to influence the group "mind." He describes two kinds of groups, which I find applicable to group formation. The first is the "Work Group," composed of members who are goal oriented/directed and do not allow primitive defenses to divert them from the task at hand, which is their primary concern. The second group is the "Basic Assumption Group." By contrast, the members of this group, the regressed group, are dominated by primitive defenses and get diverted from the task at hand. The group opposes new ideas and has a cult-like mentality. Members are not to question, challenge, or disrupt the group's harmony and sense of purpose or togetherness. There is a tendency for members of the "Basic Assumption Group" to form parasitic attachments to leaders, to idealize and go along with the false sense of security and safety they offer.

Psychohistory

Psychohistory is currently becoming an important area of research. According to Peter Loewenberg (1995), psychoanalysis is to the individual what psychohistory is to a culture's mythology. Psychohistory offers a broader perspective from which to view cross-cultural differences. An increasing number of mental health professionals are beginning to recognize that they cannot ignore the psychodynamic aspects of character and culture.

At one time, social scientists would have been criticized for analyzing and diagnosing groups, cultures, or nations, standing accused of grand-scale stereotyping and wild speculation. In recent years, however, social scientists, analysts, anthropologists, and psychohistorians have gone beyond the individual in applying their skills and knowledge. For decades, critics questioned whether psychologists had any business considering moral and political issues. Many continue to feel there is insufficient justification for analyzing groups in individual terms, considering it difficult enough making distinctions among individuals, let alone tackling group diagnoses. Thus, psychotherapists have long shied away from psychohistory, claiming that it would lead to dramatic, wildly speculative interpretations. I liken it to the practice of yoga—one must extend into "the beyond" in order to discover new dimensions and space.

I first ventured into psychohistory by delving into the Middle East, examining the historical, mythological, psychological, and religious past of the area. I felt compelled to understand what binds these groups in ongoing, circular, painful, destructive battles that make conflict resolution virtually impossible. Paradoxically, through my interest in the Middle East, I began to see the Arab-Israeli conflict as similar to the interactions of the narcissistic/borderline couple (Lachkar 1983, 1985, 1992, 2004, 2008). This paved the way for my in-depth work on marital therapy. The elements that perpetuate political/religious conflicts are the same elements that keep marital partners enmeshed in these primitive bonds.

We, of course, cannot stereotype or make sweeping generalizations about all Arabs and Jews or any other ethnic/religious group. However, just as an analyst has the right to analyze a patient's dreams, we have the right to analyze a country's mythology, religion, leaders, ideologies, child-rearing practices, shared myths, and collective group fantasies. It has been said that the people who identify with certain leaders who perpetuate a group's mythology are the ones who perpetuate conflict. Thus, it is critical to understand the mythology, folklore, and collective ideologies that give rise to the psyche of a group. This is the essence of psychohistory. Could we say, for example, that Sarah abandoning Hagar and Ishmael in the desert after Sarah gave birth to Isaac was the original archaic injury? Would the V-spot then be a woman's act of abandonment, which took away a son's birthright? Is this the original injury, a biblical V-spot the Arabs have never reconciled or made peace with? Have the Arabs never mourned the loss?

I refer to two recurring myths in the Bible and the Koran that had significance in fueling the Arab-Israeli conflict. The first myth is the belief that Jews are God's "chosen people," which led to a collective "Israeli-Jewish" narcissistic disorder (dominated by such defenses as guilt, grandiosity, and excessive entitlement fantasies). This leads to the belief that Arabs are a "fatherless," orphaned society, which explains a collective "Arab-Muslim" borderline diagnosis (dominated by shame/blame, with corresponding abandonment anxieties). Stemming from these mythic origins are age-old sentiments, passions, and feelings that continually resurface, giving rise to many shared, collective group fantasies.

The Arab-Israeli conflict, with its confluence of psychoanalysis and psychohistory, has striking similarities to the marital discord I have observed in my clinical practice. Just as couples "think" they are battling over sex, money, or custody (external events), they are really disputing self-identity and oedipal conflicts (boundaries, dependency needs, bonding, attachment, betrayal, abandonment anxiety, and entitlement). Similarly, tensions in the Middle East are not really over land or occupied territories, but stem from shame, saving face, betrayal, dependency, entitlement, domination/control, oedipal rivals, boundaries, bonding, delusion, attachment needs, and self-identity development. We all have a universal need to master our pre-oedipal rivals (relational or political) and to preserve self-identity or the collective group identity. The preservation of the self or the collective group self becomes more pervasive than life itself (Lachkar 1998, 2004, 2007, 2008).

What does this have to do with the V-spot? An example of an aroused cultural V-spot can be seen in a Jewish Gaza settler's inability to mourn the loss upon leaving his home. The sentiments get short-circuited, and the everlasting pain festers. When Gaza settlers were forced from their homes (*Los Angeles Times* 2005), Yuval and his family were some of the last settlers to leave. While waiting for a miracle instead of packing, they began to cook, play guitar, and engage in sing-a-longs. The psychohistorian might interpret leaving Gaza as not only representing the loss of a home but, for Yuval, like so many others, as representing the burning of the First and Second temples, something from which Jews have never recovered. Thus, this is an example of a collective V-spot, the earliest archaic injury a group of people mutually share and never forget. This double cultural V-spot injury was not a far cry from post-traumatic stress disorder: first, to have your temple burned down by non-Jews and later to be betrayed by your own people.

Psychodynamics from a Cross-Cultural Perspective

Exploring the following psychodynamics—aggression, shame, guilt, the true and false self, and dependency—can give us insight into what motivates and drives humans, as individuals or members of groups, to behave the way they do.

Aggression

Aggression is an ongoing process by which a person, group, organization, nation, or government psychologically—consciously or unconsciously—imposes and attempts to destroy the will of human beings. It is an attempt to control or dominate by forcing people into compliance, either physically or emotionally, against their will, beliefs, and perceptions. According to Freud, as cited by his biographer Peter Gay (1988), "Aggression can become a source of a pleasure that human beings are reluctant to give up once they have enjoyed it." Aggression feeds upon itself and can become addictive, so that one does not feel comfortable without it. The libidinal ties that bind members of a group in affection and cooperation are strengthened if the group has outsiders it can hate—the projected enemy or scapegoat (549). Scapegoating is a common phenomenon to avoid the "enemy" (real or fantasized).

Shame

Many Asian and Middle Eastern cultures have been described as "shame societies," as opposed to Christian societies such as Germany, which are perceived as "guilt societies" with a need for reparation. Put simply, shame comes from without, whereas guilt comes from within. A major theme in Japanese society is the emphasis on *shame* and *saving face* (as opposed to guilt). Professor Peter Berton (1995), an international relations and foreign affairs scholar and psychoanalyst whose main area of expertise is East Asia and Russia, testifies that the most common threat that a Japanese mother will use to discourage certain behaviors is to say, "People will laugh and make fun of you!" (*Warawareru Wo Yo*).

In most Christian societies in the West, people are dominated more by guilt than shame. In Japan and other Asian and Middle Eastern societies, shame is a major sanction; people are chagrined. In the West, guilt is relieved by confession and atonement, but chagrin cannot be relieved in this manner. A man who has sinned can get relief by either confessing to a priest or to a secular therapist. This partially may explain the relative lack of popularity of psychoanalysis and other psychotherapies in Japan.

Shame is a matter between the person and the group. It is concerned with what others think, whereas guilt is a matter between a person and their conscience (superego). Shame is the need to hide one's true inner feelings, which are repressed. The Japanese, like many other Asians, are heavily invested in "saving face." Obedience to others is of utmost importance. One must strive not to compete, show feelings, induce competition, or be unique. The parent will ridicule or humiliate a child to keep him in check. In a shame society, culpable acts remain unspoken.

Guilt

One major difference between guilt and shame is the ability to mourn, face one's losses, and come to terms with guilt. According to Klein, guilt occurs in the depressive position, when one faces grief, along with a desire to make reparation for all wrongdoings. It is interesting to note how citizens of countries such as Germany allow themselves to mourn, face their destructive acts, and make reparation. In contrast, the Japanese, not having come to terms with guilt, do everything they can to save face and cover up. Does Japan hide its war crimes because of shame?

Germany is a good example of a country that has "developmentally evolved" to a state of wishing to make atonement. This contrasts with the Japanese, who have never come to terms with their war crimes (Lachkar and Berton 1997). Peter Loewenberg (1987) discusses how Germans tried to prove their superiority by projecting their own depreciated and unwanted dirty/anal parts of themselves onto the Jews, and then relishing the anguish and humiliation they were imposing by "debasing the Jews, treating them as contaminants." They postulated a new degradation, and in fantasy placed themselves in the position of the Jew to experience how it felt. According to Loewenberg, transforming Jews became a fecal triumphant orgy. In my analysis, this was a reflection of harsh child-rearing practices by obsessive-compulsive mothers who forced their children to be perfect. The resulting consequence was an ultimate sadistic superego—that is, superegos running amuck.

True and False Self

The terms true and false self were originally described by D. W. Winnicott (1965). He described the false self as a defense against the true self. As the self that belies the true self, the false self is a major focal point in psychotherapy. A Western analyst will devote much treatment time to helping patients achieve not only a sense of self or self-identity, but also a true self (Winnicott 1965). In Japanese societies, for example, the false self is the shield that protects the self from shame. The eminent Japanese psychoanalyst Takeo Doi followed his *amae* research in a book-length study of *tatemae* (false self) and *honne* (true self), which draws a distinction between appearance and reality, or form and content. He defines *tatemae* as the public self, where one behaves and speaks as society expects (conformity). This could cause a great deal of confusion in treatment with a Western analyst because a Japanese person would be least likely to freely associate in a "public office."

Dependency

The Japanese view the concept of *amae* as the desire to merge with others. Doi (1973; Johnson 1994) called *amae* a key concept for understanding Japanese personality structure. *Amae* is "to depend and presume upon another's benevolence." Doi acknowledges that this longing for dependency can be fulfilled in infancy, but it cannot be easily satisfied as one grows up. However, the need for *amae* continues. It is argued that the search for *amae* beyond infancy is unique to Japan.

The concept of *amae* is very complex and has been the subject of debate among Japanese and American analysts. Some scholars have intimated that the need for *amae* beyond infancy is a sign of pathology in Japanese society (Iga 1984). *Amae* is a form of dependency relating to the mother's intense internalization and identification with her child's needs, especially her male child. It embodies the feelings that all normal infants have toward the mother's dependence, the desire to be passively loved, and the unwillingness to be separated from the warm mother-child circle and cast into a world of objective "reality." It manifests itself as the desire to merge or fuse with others; however, this love creates extreme forms of ambivalence and hostility. Under the guise of "closeness," the mother will co-sleep, co-bathe, and in some instances engage in incest by masturbating baby boys to relieve their erections (Adams and Hill 1997). This longing for fusion is normal in infancy, but in Japan the need for *amae* continues and manifests itself in a variety of social conventions and characteristics.

What dependency represents for a Westerner is in sharp contrast to what dependency represents in Japanese, Middle Eastern, or Asian societies. A Western psychoanalyst will endeavor to help the patient ask directly for what the patient needs and will expect the patient to express himself as openly as possible; whereas a Japanese patient will invariably remain silent, waiting for the analyst to offer what he or she needs (*amae*). As a corollary to the mother/infant relationship, whereby the mother indulges the child in a lifelong dependency on her, the expectation is that the mother will be exquisitely attuned to the child's non-verbal communication. In Middle Eastern societies, dependency is maintained throughout the Muslim world via Arab unification, where all Arabs share the same beliefs, traditions, ideologies, and collective group fantasies, and nothing should come between them. Israel may be viewed as the oedipal object or interloper disrupting this state of symbiotic harmony and bliss (Lachkar 1998, 2004).

The Western notion is that the infant is born dependent and then goes through stages of separation individuation and eventually develops autonomous ego functioning. In Asian societies, the process of individuation is not encouraged. Instead, interdependence is developed. In Japan, there is a lack of differentiation between self and other that would be regarded with horror by Western psychiatrists; self-identity is organized around the dependence of the group. The psychological center of gravity is embedded in the "other" and what the "other" is feeling, thinking, or doing.

The following is an example of *amae*: A Japanese scholar came to visit the United States for the first time. He was invited to the home of a colleague as a guest. His colleague's wife asked him if he was hungry and if he would like something to eat. He responded by telling her he was not hungry, humbly bowed, and thanked her graciously for her kind offer. Shortly after, he began to feel a festering rage and realized that she (the hostess) did not offer *amae*. "If she cared about me, she would just know I was hungry and would have offered me food. In Japan, guests are always offered food even if they claim they are not hungry."

Amae's Impact on a Narcissistic/Borderline Japanese/American Couple

An American man married to a Japanese wife complained that he felt suffocated by his wife's relationship with their son. She infantilized the son, and even though he was more than two years old she continued to breastfeed him. "I can't stand it; she's arranged to take him everywhere—to work, to social events, to bed. All she does is hold him, breastfeed him, and never lets him cry. She attends to his every whim. This just isn't right! She doesn't allow her son to grow up."

Another kind of dependency relationship is maternal fusion, exemplified here by the relationship between an American Jewish husband and his Italian wife. A narcissistic American-Jewish husband, a corporate executive, complained that he is a busy man and that his Italian wife didn't allow him any space to work or to go on business trips. All the complaints she experienced in the relationship became reenacted with the therapist (in the "couple transference"). Things began to climax when I confronted her about her difficulty in leaving at the end of the session. She would take an endless amount of time to get out of her chair, gather her belongings, and ask a slew of questions. At the door she would begin another barrage of complaints about her husband and her abusive father. At home she would clutter my voice mail with messages, my e-mail with endless documents and pictures. When I confronted her about our "culture clash," she said: "I'm Italian and in Italy people are very close. Even therapists become part of the family. They visit in the home, go out socially, and are not so standoffish. You act like a cold fish, a complete stranger. I tell you everything about myself, and you tell me nothing. I need more from you, and you aren't willing to give it."

At the end of each session, I began to feel more and more invaded and intruded upon. When I confronted her about this, her response was: "I need it! I need it! In Italy, I could stay at my appointment and talk if I wished, and my analyst would never rush me out the door like you do. In fact, he would even offer me something to drink, something to eat, help me on with my coat. You have never even offered me a cup of coffee. We are Italians. We take our time. You Americans are all crazy; you rush, rush. You are so typical of people in the States where everyone is so cold, aloof. It's just not that way in my country."

I began to show her that beyond our "cultural differences" was an internal mother she experienced as cold and indifferent. I also reminded her of a father who always brushed her aside and who ousted her when her younger brothers were born. The hunger and yearnings to feel included drove her compulsive search to fuse with the maternal object. Briefly stated, ensuing issues reached far beyond "cultural correctness."

Individual Self versus Group Self

In many societies, particularly in Asian and Middle Eastern countries, the individual self is virtually nonexistent. Americans are considered to be an individualistic culture, with emphasis on self-development. Asian and Middle Eastern societies are considered to be a collectivistic culture, with emphasis on the group self. More pervasive is the cultural group self or the collective group self. According to Yi (1995), American culture places emphasis on the autonomous self, which stresses uniqueness and self-expression, whereas Asian societies lean toward an interdependence that stresses heavy reliance on the group and others. But when we talk about a cultural self, are we talking about an individual self? A group self? A self-actualized self? Or a collective group self? Miyamoto refers to this as selfless devotion to the group, for example, not taking allowable vacations or Japanese masochism.

I am reminded of a young Japanese graduate student who came in for treatment in my early years of clinical practice. He walked in with his head down and did not make any eye contact. After sitting silently for many minutes and obviously feeling very anxious, he said he was gay and felt very fearful that his family was soon to discover his preference for men. I proceeded to tell him how he had to do what was right for him and not live his life for his family and friends, and how wonderful it was that he could come for treatment and begin to develop his own sense of self. He looked at me quizzically, as if I were from Mars. "What is a sense of self?"

Who is the "we," and who is the "you"? Most Western psychotherapists assume that there are two individuals interacting together during therapy, or as Roland clearly states, an "I-self," with more or less firm ego boundaries between them (Roland 1996, 72). He states that the Japanese therapist assumes a different kind of self based on a "we-self," which is fundamental to the Japanese mode of hierarchical relationships (72). "How can I be a 'we' with you? We are not equal." Roland explains that this is quite different from American egalitarianism. Turning again to the *amae* relationship, "When we are a 'we,' I don't have to tell you how I feel. You will just know."

If we compare the cultural differences between Japan and the United States in the allowance for individuality or conformity, we would find that a Japanese person would be careful not to show negative emotions and would have a tendency to pretend not to see the emotions or expressions in others. In contrast, people in the United States, a country that encourages individuality, would encourage both the expression and perception of negative emotions. Again, in Japan the emphasis is on conformity, so emotions would be considered a threat to the group's harmony (*wa*).

One could argue that Western psychoanalytic theorists also promulgate lifelong dependency relationships. In keeping with this idea, Roland reminds us of Winnicott's famous statement, "There is no such thing as a baby" (1996, 80). Also, we could accuse Klein, with her emphasis on maternal attachment as a lifelong bond, and Kohut's concept of a lifelong search for mirroring and self objects, as fostering lifelong dependency bonds. The difference, as Roland so eloquently explains (1996), is that even within this milieu, the Western individual still desires and aspires to achieve "at-one-ment" through uniqueness, creativity, and individuality.

Case of the Armenian Sisters

Two Armenian sisters came for consultation. The older sister was enraged that the younger sister would dare to fall in love with a non-Armenian man. "I will not allow it. If my father were still alive, he would never permit this to happen." I immediately confronted her aggression, saying that under the guise of "culture" she was enacting some kind of early injury or traumatic experience. She said she was angry. I told her that even if she was angry, she still was overstepping her boundaries. (For a few moments my V-spot was grossly stirred. My older sister used to boss me around. I almost wanted to give way to her because that was the pattern with my sister, who was relentless until I did what she wanted. I quickly got hold of myself, remembering that I was not a little kid acting obediently to an older sibling.) "What gives you the right to order your sister around? You are not her parent; you are her sister." She told me it was cultural. I then responded quickly, "Ahh . . . now I understand why you do this. So instead of mourning the loss of your father, you have become him and have taken over his function. This is your way of remaining loyal to him, but you do not see how you are not your father and do not have his rights."

Hierarchy and Obligatory Bonds

In Middle Eastern and Asian societies, parents and elders are prioritized; deference and devotion to parents is a strong, long-standing attachment. Therapists must have some knowledge of obligatory relational bonds. The following is an example of a Persian husband and his American wife's dilemma surrounding these bonds:

> I need to spend special time with mother, my father, my brothers, my uncles, and my cousins. Besides, she doesn't fit in. She doesn't speak Farsi, and we talk about many private things that are our personal business. In my country, parents come first, and if my mother wants to be with "her" family and me, well, that has priority.

The following is another example of how this attitude can ignite powerful feelings of rejection in a partner who was exposed to a dramatic cultural shock:

> I was born in California; my husband is Sephardic Israeli. We went to Israel to visit my husband's parents. When we arrived, I found out that it was my husband's parents' anniversary. It also happened to be my birthday. When I confronted my husband and asked why he made such a fuss over his parents and ignored me, he said that parents come first.

The image of mother as self sacrificing and all giving becomes a strongly internalized object. In Asian societies it is based on Confucianism, in which dependent and interdependent interactions are clearly delineated: parent to child, husband to wife, older brother to younger brother, employer to employee. In China and Japan, the father-son relationship is considered to be the most important dyad. The rank of commander and subordinates is quite clear: boss-employee, elder-younger, teacher-student, master-servant, husband-wife. These relations require benevolence, authority, responsibility, and wisdom from the authority figures. The subordinates must comply with obedience and subservience.

In Japan, the primary responsibility is not to the family but to the boss, although another important relationship is the mother-child *amae* bond. Outside of the home (*soto*), women occupy subordinate positions with few individual rights and little power. Inside the home (*uchi*), women as mothers hold stable and powerful positions (unlike Korean wives, who are totally dependent on their husbands) (Lachkar 2004, 2008). In Kleinian terms, this could be interpreted as part-object functioning (paranoid-schizoid position), where mother is the giver, the provider, and the nurturer, the all-encompassing breast, not viewed as someone with needs in her own right or as a whole object.

In Korea the obligatory bonds are quite clear, starting with king to subject, parent to child, husband to wife, older sibling to younger sibling. The Korean father is highly revered and idealized. He becomes the all-encompassing king, the benevolent lord and master. He is viewed as an all-powerful, all-giving being whose main task is to care and provide for the family. When this fantasy is disrupted, it can provoke severe fragmentation and rage, or what is known in Korea as *han*. During World War II, after the Japanese invasion, the image of the benevolent father was shattered. He "betrayed" them and let them down. Korean women had to endure the tragic losses of their husbands and fathers, and had to fend for themselves by becoming aggressive and very revengeful.

Han comes out more in the United States than in Korea. When in the United States, Koreans are without the support or a "holding environment." In Korea, there is the support of the tribe, the group. When Koreans leave, they betray the group. Furthermore, marrying a foreigner is tantamount to marrying "a pig." One might ask why the Koreans' subservient attitude does not carry over into the United States. In Korea, the family and village serve as a container or holding environment for the group's rage and feelings. The woman is supported in her compliance. Without the support of the "container," the woman is thrown into a frenzy, a state of intense fragmentation. The biggest problem Koreans face when they come to this country is feelings of profound loneliness, confusion, and powerlessness. Adaptation is especially stressful for women as newly assigned roles such as "working mother" disrupt the child-mother symbiosis. Women not only suffered tragic losses before and after the Korean War, but they now struggle with new identities as women and mothers.

Treatment of Women

Men who violate women's rights under the flag of culture claim women as their property, and they feel a sense of entitlement and ownership. Men from other cultures can act out their most heinous aggression under the guise of tradition and religion. "In my country it is our duty to see to it that our wives obey."

Case of the American Woman and the Italian Husband

Our courtship was magical. I met my Italian lover, my Romeo, my handsome prince from Tuscany. He was every woman's dream: handsome, debonair, a man who loved fine foods, wine, music, opera. I was smitten from the beginning. We got married and had two wonderful children, when suddenly I started to get suspicious of his financial ventures. I could not help myself. I started to go through all of his accounts, sales receipts, and even his e-mail. I was horrified to discover that he was involved in some kind of a financial scam. He caught me probing through his records and started to beat me. I wanted to scream but didn't want the kids to find out. He made me feel that his brutality was justified because in Italy women are taught to obey their husband, not question or interrogate them. "A good wife cooks, takes care of the kids, and that's it."

Today, women are being beaten, raped, stoned to death, traded as chattel, clitorectomized, and degraded in many other ways—often sanctioned by abusive governmental leaders and dictators. We would be remiss if we neglected some reference to the cultural views of gender and the role of women. Men who abuse women under the banner of "cultural differences" claim such behavior is an intrinsic element of their culture or society. Today, women's and human rights groups are demanding action.

Recently, an increasing number of Western men and women have converted to Islam. According to prison psychiatrist Theodore Dalrymple, who has worked with Muslim prisoners in Britain, "a large part of the attraction of Islam to increasingly and essentially secularized men" is the opportunity Islam allows for the "abominable abuse of women" (Chesler and Kobrin 2005).

Nothing better depicts the differences between Islamic and Western views on the treatment of women than a comment in the *Los Angeles Times* (2005) about how Muslims interpret Western films. In viewing *Titanic*, what perturbed the Muslim viewers more than the nude scene was, as the Iranians argued, that Rose, the protagonist, had no right to leave her abusive fiancé, "not even for Leonardo DiCaprio."

The following case provides another example of an all-too-frequent occurrence. Women who fall in love, marry, and have children with Middle Eastern men (who come from governments that repress and violate women's rights) always have in the back of their minds the concern that even though this person lives in this country, he cannot easily adapt to our ways. Although the husband in the following example was loving and charming, there was always the fear he could run off with the children to Saudi Arabia, never to return with them.

Case of the Middle Eastern Husband and the American Wife (Lachkar 1998, 2004)

Therapist: Hello, Salaam! Who would like to start?

Abdul: I really don't want to be here because I don't believe in therapy. In my country, this is unheard of. If we have a problem, we pray to Allah for forgiveness, and our will and destiny are in his hands.

Mary: This is what my children and I have to put up with all the time. I don't believe in prayer, magical thinking, wishes, and dreams. He turns to the Koran as if it is gospel truth. I am a practical person, well-educated and well-informed, and can't believe I'm with someone who does all this "hocus pocus" stuff. I believe in talking things over and working things out. Every time there is a problem, Abdul talks about Allah. He can't even keep a promise. When he doesn't follow through he says, "Well, it was the will of Allah. Inshallah!" Baloney! Can't he realize he is in America now? This is not the Middle East. When there were just the two of us, I could ignore it, but now this is very difficult for our children.

Therapist: Yes, it does sound as though there are some real cultural differences that are causing stress and very hurtful feelings.

Mary: We went to Saudi Arabia last year and took the children to visit Abdul's parents. My daughters and I vowed we would not wear veils (*chadors*), but when we arrived wearing our American garb, we found ourselves being stared down. Not only were we viewed as foreign and strange, their eyes were burning through our clothes, as if we were prostitutes. I was scared. I knew I should obey. I always felt the threat that if I didn't, he could keep the children there and I would have no recourse.

Abdul: (laughing) Yes, and you should have seen how quick they put on their *chadors* and *hijabs*. Have you ever visited my country? There, the women don't even have a say. They aren't even allowed an opinion. My wife doesn't know how lucky she is that I am not like that.

Mary: He may not be like that, but he doesn't realize how difficult it has become to talk freely. Maybe we can do that here.

There have been many instances in these cross-cultural relationships in which men leave the country and never return with the children:

> The nightmare fell upon me. We returned to the States, and without my knowing, he took our baby son and went to Lebanon. I spent a year screaming, "My baby, my baby! I need my baby back," but to no avail. After a long legal process, there was nothing I could do (Lachkar 2004, 142).

This illustration has particular clinical relevance because, in an age of feminism and human rights, a female therapist may be horrified to hear of these abuses. Conversely, men who come from male-dominated societies may have tremendous resistance to opening up to a female therapist. "I know you don't want to be here, but you also may not want to be here because I, like your wife, am a female."

The Artistic V-Spot and Creativity

Another form of societal aggression is halting one's creativity, forcing the government's values upon the individual. Kohut (1977) recognized the importance of creative freedom for the artist as an important extension of the self for "those who show total devotion to their art form" (121). Many oppressive regimes suppress these expressions and deprive people of their rights as individuals (religious freedom of expression, women's rights, etc.). They also deprive the artist of artistic and creative freedom and expression. Most societies today encourage music, dance, and art, but those that encourage conformity as opposed to individual expression are doing an injustice. Many students from Asian countries, for example, have been shocked to hear American art teachers say, "Let your mind go and draw or paint whatever comes to mind." Culturally mandated artistic suppression has resulted in what could be called "an artistic V-spot" for many people in countries that demand conformity. My article "Narcissism in Dance" (2001) further discusses the idea of aesthetic survival and what happens to societies and individuals when artists are mistreated or deprived of their artistic endeavors and creativity.

In many of my previous works, I discuss the need for artistic expression as a very basic human phenomenon. It is noteworthy to mention that in terms of stirring up old hurts and archaic injuries, totalitarian dictatorships can curtail freedom and expression as well as a depriving parent can.

The most glaring example of artistic repression was during the last dynasty to rule in China—the Qing/Ch'ing dynasty. This corrupt dynasty oppressed its people by shutting down all their artistic outlets. Literature was ever under attack. They outlawed any writing against the government and allowed the government to decide at random what was acceptable and what was not. The horror of these artistic deprivations was depicted in the 1999 movie *The Red Violin*, directed by François Girard. It relates the history of a famous violin's journey, moving from the hands of a common seventeenth-century fiddlemaker in Cremona, Italy, to a young orphan with a prodigious musical talent in eighteenth-century Vienna, to a famous British lord performing during the reign of King George III, to a lover of Western music, and ending up with the struggles during the Chinese Cultural Revolution, where all musical instruments were banned and all artistic expression severely censored. In this film, the violin comes into the possession of Xiang Pei (Sylvia Chang) in Shanghai, but she is forced to hide it or face punishment from an establishment that deems all Western instruments to be a corrupting influence.

Discussion

The dilemma faced and feared by many therapists treating cross-cultural couples is that they may not be sufficiently knowledgeable. However, the therapist need only be familiar with a few phrases in the language and some basic customs and traditions to effectively analyze the role culture plays in strained relations between cross-cultural partners so that the healing process can begin. This chapter is not meant to intimidate therapists who are not familiar with treating couples from varying ethnic backgrounds. Quite the contrary, the intent is to broaden awareness of the global underpinnings of cross-cultural roots and the corresponding treatment of emotional abuse in couples. It is reassuring to know one does not have to be a linguist, an anthropologist, and a great specialist to effectively treat cross-cultural couples. It is amazing how someone from another country—when greeted with a *buenos días*, *salaam*, or *bonjour*—gets a warm rush, a feeling of connectedness, and thus an opening to the therapeutic bonding experience.

Therapists can no longer ignore the cultural, ethical, and religious aspects of psychotherapy, although it can befuddle therapists to have to integrate these new approaches into their clinical practices. In treating couples from various cultures, we sometimes deal with societies that identify with destructive leaders, have been brainwashed, and have enculturated painful bonds of sacrifice and victimization. We might deal with countries that have stripped and hijacked their citizens of their normal human rights. Some patients may come from societies that do not stress separation from the maternal object but instead maintain a lasting bond in a maternal fusion.

Countries like Iraq, Saudi Arabia, and North Korea will need to invest years into infant studies, child development, and psychological research relating to the development of human growth (as the French, German, British, and Americans have) to free citizens from oppressive patterns.

The next chapter discusses treatment procedures and techniques including expanding a new perspective on three phases of treatment as outlined in my earlier works (1992, 2004).

CHAPTER EIGHT

Treatment Procedures and Techniques

In my previous work (1992, 1998, 2004), I outlined three distinct developmental phases that couples move through, similar to the two positions outlined by Melanie Klein (1957)—the paranoid-schizoid and the depressive position. I equate these three phases with three periods in European history: (1) the Age of Darkness, (2) the Age of Enlightenment, and (3) the Age of Reason. Movements between these positions tend to vacillate back and forth, occurring throughout life as various states of fragmentation to that of wholeness. As Grotstein (1981) reminds us, development moves on dual tracks (87). Movement and growth are essential in all forms of treatment; however, growth and change are not always lineal.

The attainment of this progression may be baffling, because often couples confuse mania with mental health. With the depressive position come feelings of sadness, guilt, and remorse. Patients with low self-esteem cannot tolerate or contain these emotions and think they are getting worse instead of better. Phase Three focuses on this point. "I think I am getting worse. I feel so depressed, so guilty about the affair I had and how it messed up my marriage and my family!" To this a therapist might respond, "You think you are getting worse? Actually, you are getting better! Your idea is that mania and excitement are growth. What you are feeling and experiencing now is progress." Overall, the therapeutic challenge is to gradually wean the partners away from "the relationship" and toward self-development (Lachkar 2004).

This chapter details the following: (1) three phases of treatment; (2) a six-step treatment procedure; (3) treatment points and techniques; (4) qualities of the therapist; (5) therapeutic functions—including transference, countertransference, and couple transference; (6) how to listen for a theme and suggestions for the couple; and, finally, (7) treatment points and techniques for cross-cultural couples.

Three Phases of Treatment

What follows are three distinct phases that couples move through. Although these are not clear and distinct phases—because individuals and couples don't move on single track—these phases are provided as guidelines to assist the therapist in monitoring and diagnosing (see figures 8.1, 8.2, and 8.3).

Phase One: The Phase of Darkness

- The state of fusion, collusion, and delusion; little differentiation between self and other (paranoid-schizoid position)
- Primitive defenses dominate the relationship (envy, jealousy, blame/shame, control, oedipal rivalry).
- Each partner feels the other is responsible for the other's archaic pain/injury (V-spot).
- No awareness of an identification with an internal object (everything externalized)
- Partners project and identify with each other's negative projections and are unaware of their internal "bad" objects ("I don't deprive myself; he is the one who deprives me!").
- Each partner feels they have to walk on eggshells to not inflame the other's "V-spot."

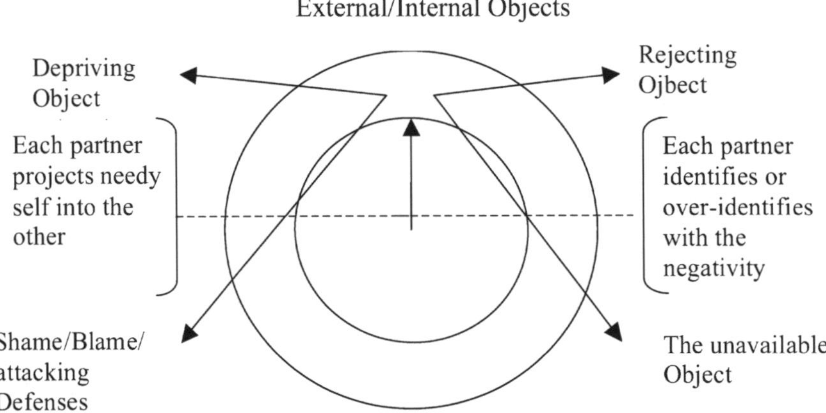

Figure 8.1. Each partner lives emotionally inside the other.

In this stage the therapist takes a very active role in setting the stage and the boundaries, mainly of safety and containment. It becomes clear to both partners that, no matter how injured or pained they are, aggression such as shouting, yelling, and interrupting must be curtailed. Often in the beginning stage, the therapist is unsuccessful because there is so much anguish and pain. At least the therapist can outline a clear structure of the expectations. In addition, if both partners are seeing individual therapists, many therapists will arrange a time period in which to work. For example: "Let us work for six weeks, discuss the treatment goals, decide what we would like to accomplish, and then we can always reevaluate."

It is noteworthy to mention that it is quite common for spouses in individual treatment to see therapists with different theoretical perspectives. Often the couple therapist and the individual therapist are asked to consult. As beneficial as this may sound, it can also create more confusion and chaos. For instance, one partner may be seeing a self psychologist while the other is seeing a behavioral or an object-relational therapist. This can sometimes create treatment barriers, with consulting leading to more confusion. The differences in orientation is sometimes woven into the couple transference: "It is okay for us to have divergent views. We all have the same goal in mind: to help you with your relationship and ensuing conflicts." I am reminded what Breuer told Nietzsche in Yalom's book, *When Nietzsche Wept* (1992). He remarked that consulting with too may authorities or getting too many opinions and consultations is like "reading a play before it is performed" (51). It is my contention that the real answers unfold in the transference or as in the case of the couple, the "couple transference."

The first stage marks the initial phase of treatment: the couple living in the phase of "darkness." I liken it to the Middle Ages (the Dark Ages), where one lives "inside" the psychic space of the other. In this phase, there is very little room for introspection, awareness, and self-reflection; people are dominated by myths, dogma, and beliefs that have been prescripted and preprogrammed. When any of these beliefs are questioned, one responds with rage in trying to defend the sense of self. It is a state of oneness, fusion/collusion with the other, with no differentiation between self and other (paranoid-schizoid position). It is a shame-blame phase, each one blaming the other for all the shortcomings in the relationship (who is right, who is wrong, finding fault, getting even, and retaliation). There is much stonewalling, and each partner shows little awareness of the inner forces that invade the psyche—often described as the void or the black hole—along with a preponderance of primitive defenses such as splitting, projection, and projective identification. There is often a prevalence of magical thinking: "He should just know

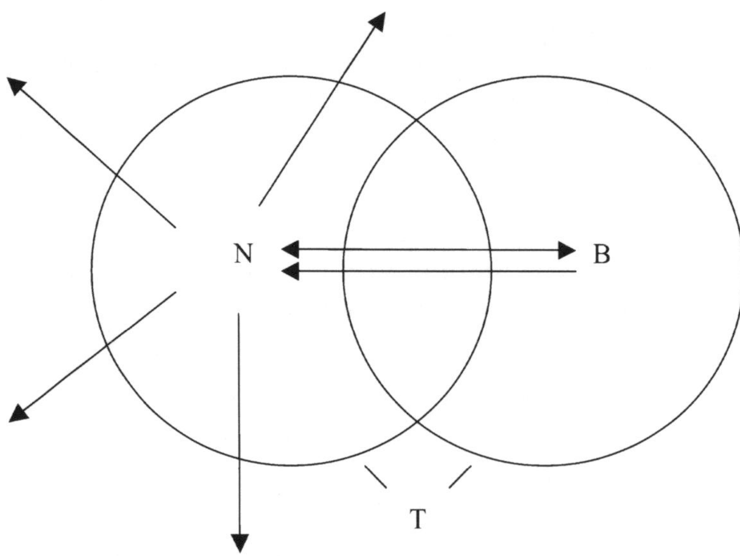

Figure 8.2. Boundaries of twoness (ability to move into a new transitional space). (N = The Narcissist, B = The Borderline, T = The Therapist.)

what I need/want without my having to tell him." In this phase there is little room for insight and introspection.

Phase Two: The Phase of Enlightenment

- A gradual shifting away from blaming/shaming/attacking defenses (moving toward the depressive position)
- More awareness of the internal abuser and disidentification with each other's negative projections
- Bonding with the therapist as someone helpful; beginning of healthy dependency needs

The Enlightenment period was a philosophical movement in eighteenth-century England, France, and the United States that emphasized use of reason. This enlightenment phase for couples is not quite the phase of reason, but it marks the emergence of rational thought, wherein one is recognized for having his or her own mind and judgment. In this phase of "two-ness"—two separate emotional states—each partner can tolerate the separateness and uniqueness of the other. There is more tolerance for ambiguity, budding insights into unconscious motivations (internal objects), and other compelling forces. It is the beginning of bonding with the therapist and a "weaning" away from living emotionally "inside" the object to move toward mutual interdependence. As

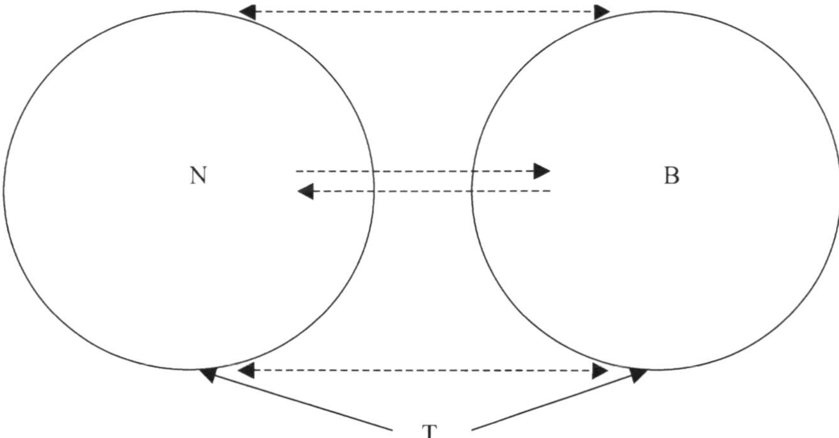

Figure 8.3. Boundaries to two separate but bonded, dependent yet interdependent, individuals.

the therapist emerges as a new self object, there is an opening of a new therapeutic space (transitional space). It is a hopeful stage with a burst of new energy and feelings of excitement. A profound shift occurs, a movement away from blaming/attacking and "doing" to that of feeling/thinking and "being." The therapist gradually helps the partners recognize and identify emotional vulnerability concomitant with distorted thinking.

Phase Three: The Phase of Reason

- Less splitting and projection
- More awareness of internal objects
- Love, intimacy, and dependency replace dependency needs.
- State of remorse where one comes to terms with guilt
- Each partner takes more responsibility for his or her own "V-spot" and does not make the other feel responsible.
- Each partner begins to form his or her own unique relationship with the therapist: "T."

This phase marks the beginning of two emotional states that work dependently and interdependently concomitantly. It is a stage at which a person relinquishes manic defenses and persecutory anxieties, leading to higher ego functioning; therefore, the "phase of reason." Healthy dependency needs emerge as both partners begin to sense that the therapist can be helpful. There is more tolerance for ambiguity, budding insights into unconscious motivations (internal objects), and other compelling forces. It is the beginning of bonding with the therapist and a "weaning" away from living emotionally "inside" the object toward mutual interdependence.

As the therapist emerges as a new self object, there is an opening of a new therapeutic space (transitional space). As it is a hopeful stage with a burst of new energy and feelings of containment, with it comes confusion about what is mental health. As mentioned earlier, many patients with severe personality disorders cannot fathom the idea that sadness and guilt are within the normal mental state of mind. Here the therapist has the opportunity to display her major trump card, a predominant shift away from blaming/attacking as opposed to the delusional and distorted thinking associated with the vulnerability that occurs in the paranoid-schizoid position.

According to Albert Mason (1981), mania is often equated with exciting objects such as the affair, the medical degree, or the hot date. But acquiring these "manic" cures depends on control of an external object to produce a fantasy of self-endowment. In reality, it only produces persecutory anxiety. Mason implies that as one becomes more dependent upon the object, as opposed to possessing the object, the more tolerance there is for pain and vulnerability. This is where real aspirations are embraced.

Six-Step Treatment Procedure

This six-step treatment procedure was originally designed for narcissistic/borderline relationships, but it has clinical relevance and applicability to a wide range of couples. The first step is for the therapist to see the couple together in order to form a safe bond before transitioning into individual therapy. On a cautionary note, it is best not to move the couple into individual therapy until the couple is ready. Too early a separation can induce a "rapprochement crisis."

Example: A new couple was seen conjointly and soon after individually. The wife appreciated that I saw her, and we agreed to see her husband. She had a dream that she went into a woman's house but ended up getting raped by a man, who urinated and ejaculated all over her. Both had their clothes on. Her associations were with a parent who would do things behind her back and a mother who forced her to eat contaminated chicken. I pointed out how unconsciously she felt the treatment was contaminated, that my seeing her husband alone made her feel betrayed, as though I were doing things behind her back.

The second step is to be aware of the qualitative differences and how each partner experiences anxiety differently. Couple interaction can diminish individuality. It is important to avoid such statements as "You *both* are suffering from abandonment anxiety," or "You both get angry when you feel your partner is withholding." Statements like these touch and inflame the V-spot. Instead, utilize specific, targeted statements. To the borderline say, "You attack when you feel betrayed or abandoned" while saying to the narcissist, "You withdraw and isolate yourself when personally injured."

Third, the therapeutic alliance must be joined with a member who is predominantly narcissistic. Because of rampant narcissistic injury, the tendency to flight/flee, isolate, and withdraw can pose a serious threat to treatment. As long as the narcissistic is provided with empathic responses and therapeutic bonding is occurring, the borderline will not feel abandoned and will be able to tolerate the process (sometimes a knowing look, a wink, or a nod can help).

Example: A narcissist husband was mortified to find out about the many affairs his borderline wife was having. I tried to be empathic toward her (the borderline) by attempting to "understand" how she may need many "daddies" to make up for the loss of her father. Her husband leaves, never to return, interpreting my "empathic" stance as confirmation/validation of her behavior. I soon learned how important it is to bond first with the narcissist (his damaged vulnerable self).

The fourth step addresses the importance of technique and qualities of the therapist. For instance, use few words, and when you interpret, speak with meaning and conviction. It is especially important to use good eye contact (see section later in chapter, "Qualities of a Therapist").

The fifth step is being aware that the more primitive the couple, the more structure, simplicity, and clarity they need. Some therapists are very firm about securing the therapeutic frame from the onset, while others allow the frame to gradually evolve. It may take time to develop clear treatment boundaries. This is fine and is not considered as negligence on part of the therapist as long as the ultimate goal is to create boundaries. As the resistance unfolds, we weave into "couple transference," saying, "Just as it is important for you both to feel safe in your relationship, it is also important to feel safe here." The main goal is to gradually wean the partners away from the relationship and into the process of self-development. Try to provide a secure frame while not expecting immediate results.

The sixth and final step is understanding that when individual treatment occurs at the same time as conjoint treatment with the same therapist, the therapist has the right to use discretion about what to share. Issues of confidentiality are still under the umbrella and guidelines of conjoint treatment.

Treatment Points and Techniques

To expand on the six-step treatment procedure, let us now move into more specific treatment points and techniques, such as the following:

- Don't be afraid to confront the aggression. Speak directly to the aggressor with technical neutrality by making clear, definitive statements.
- Be empathic toward the pain and the patient's vulnerabilities, but avoid getting drawn into the couple's battle.
- Set goals and continually reevaluate and remind patients of these treatment goals (why they came in the first place!).
- Avoid asking too many questions and obtaining lengthy histories. Don't waste time. Start right in. The history and background information will automatically unfold within the context of the therapeutic experience and the transference.
- Avoid self-disclosure, touching or consoling the patient, or making concessions.
- Listen and be attentive. Maintain good eye contact throughout the conversation. Speak with meaning and conviction. Talk directly to the issues.
- Use short, clear sentences. Keep responses direct. Mirror and reflect sentiments with simple responses and few questions.
- Keep in mind a "normal couple" or "ideal couple." This image will sharpen your focus and safeguard you from getting lost within the couple's psychological "dance."
- Explain how one may project a negative feeling into the other, but try to understand why the other identifies with what is being projected (focus on the dual projective identification).
- Listen for the theme. Be aware of repetitive themes. The subject and feelings may change, but the theme is pervasive (betrayal, abandonment, rejection fantasies).
- Help the couple recognize "normal" and healthy dependency needs.
- Summarize and clarify the issues and dynamics at the end of each session or at the end of the treatment sessions. Be sure to remind the couple of the treatment goals.

Example:

> We have met for eight weeks. Today is our final session. The focus has been on commitment, helping you solidify your relationship. Although we have not

achieved the actual goal of commitment, we do have a sense of what the resistances or fears are.

For you, Sidney, the fear is that you cannot trust that Nicole will maintain her love and caring for you. Even now when you see Nicole express the slightest emotion or need, you do not see Nicole for who she is, but an infantile unavailable histrionic mother.

For you, Nicole, the fear is that you will not have enough feelings of entitlement to set limits and boundaries with Sidney, that this relationship will drag on and on for another six years. (See the case of Sidney and Nicole later in this chapter.)

Qualities of a Therapist

Psychoanalytic technique and theory alone are meaningless unless artistically, emotionally, and creatively executed. Psychological movements, like dance steps, involve interpretation that must be poignantly expressed with purpose and a direct focus. Every movement and gesture must be understood internally, processed, and related to a feeling state or to a mode of experience before it is executed into the external experience. In dance, an arm gesture must conjure up a thought, an image, or a feeling (it can't just be an arm sticking out in space) in order to give the movement meaning; otherwise, the gesture becomes robotic/statue-like, empty and meaningless. So must the therapist speak with meaning, passion, and conviction if the offered interpretations are to carry any weight. It is not sufficient for a musician to merely play the notes. Eye contact, tone of voice, gestures, phrasing, and timing all parallel the therapeutic process.

I cannot help but equate the qualities of a therapist with those of a fine artist, be it violinist, pianist, dancer, or other virtuoso. I am particularly inspired by Isaac Stern, the violin virtuoso, who claims that there are three qualities a musician must embody. The first is confidence, the second is empathic attunement, and the third is "enough arrogance to carry it off." Can we say the same applies to a therapist, needing enough conviction to break through the patient's resistances and defenses? The outcome of successful marital therapy is greatly enhanced if the therapist can speak with meaning and conviction and recognize that couple conflict is often a projection of one's internal chaotic world (Lachkar 2004).

I can remember a very specific moment in a dance class many years ago when Carmelita Maracci was teaching a master ballet class. That particular day, members of the American Ballet Theatre came to take class. No sooner did class begin, in the midst of the adagio of a Bach Sarabande, then in stomped my overweight immigrant Polish-German Jewish mother. We all stopped and looked up (of course with much embarrassment on my part). Just then Carmelita looked at my mother, glanced at the pianist, then turned to the class and said, "Now look at Joan's mother when she comes into a room. She makes a statement! The rest of you all look like prancing little nymphs!" It was at that moment that I knew what carrying out an interpretation meant; one must not just mouth the words but speak with meaning and conviction.

Therapeutic Functions

This section focuses on therapeutic functions, including transference and countertransference issues, and a concept I devised that is applicable for conjoint treatment, "the couple transference."

What follows is a list of therapeutic functions. I am reminded of a woman who came for supervision feeling guilty that she was getting paid for not doing "anything" except listening. Listening, I say, is a therapeutic function, embodying the following:

- Empathy/understanding
- Using the patient's words/metaphors
- Introspection
- Therapist as mirroring object
- Therapist as self object
- Therapist as container (hard object)
- Therapist as transitional object, the bonding/weaning mommy
- Therapist as holding and environmental mommy
- Therapist as "being" versus "doing" mommy (remembering the patient's experiences and affects)
- Therapist as interpreter/thinker
- Therapist as transferential object

Transference and Countertransference

Transference occurs in response to the patient's issues, with the therapist internalizing them as if they are his or her own. In some instances the therapist may feel so angry with the patient that he or she may react in an opposite manner—for example, become unduly kind and understanding and fuse with the patient's pathogenesis. In other instances, the analyst may overreact and become a strict, harsh, punitive parent. "What! You're late again! How come you keep forgetting your check book?"

Transference and countertransference issues take on a different shape when we take into consideration ego functioning as it intersects with the V-spots of analyst and patient. One supervisee told me he was enraged every time his patients were late because they reminded him of his ex-wife who took three hours to get dressed and was late to every function they attended. This brings us to the analyst's V-spot and countertransference. We need another approach to viewing transference and countertransference reactions because instead of two people, there are now three. Within the matrix of conjoint therapy, I have devised the term "couple transference" to encompass transference and countertransference issues (Lachkar 1998, 2004).

The Couple Transference

Couple transference does for the couple what transference does for the individual. Couple transference interpretations are derived from the analyst's experience and insights in order to produce a transformation within the dyadic relationship. Couple transference refers to the mutual projections, delusions, and distortions—or shared couple fantasies—that become displaced onto the therapist. The notion of "couple/therapist transference" opens up an entirely new therapeutic vista or transitional space in which to work. It is within this space that "real" issues come to life. For example, both partners may project shame or guilt onto the therapist for having needs, turning him or her into a money-hungry therapist.

Who Comes First?

A frequent conflict that occurs in conjoint therapy is the dilemma: Who comes first? The children, the spouse, the job, the dog, the sailboat? Who or what among these has priority? In the previous chapter, we discussed obligatory bonds, for which the demarcation lines are very clear—for example, God, father, elder brother, younger brother, mother, children, wife, etc. In Western society, these boundaries are indistinguishable from each other. In couple therapy, we must take the preliminary assumption that the relationship has first and foremost priority. Children, airplanes, hobbies, or pets ultimately cannot replace lifelong partners.

The following example illustrates another typical conflict scenario that occurs when one partner keeps the other on hold while he makes up his mind about whether to commit.

Case of Nicole and Sidney: The Couple in Waiting

Nicole and Sidney have been together for six years. Sidney was married and has a five-year-old son. Sidney insists he loves Nicole more than any other woman in the world but fears that because she is emotionally volatile, the relationship will become a replay of his histrionic mother and ex-wife. He therefore keeps his partner of six years endlessly waiting while he decides whether or not to make a commitment. Meanwhile, Nicole feels her biological clock is running out while Sidney sits back and does nothing until he is ready.

Therapist: Hi, Nicole and Sidney:

Nicole: (crying) My biological clock is running out of time, and Sidney already has a child. I'm forty-one years old, and my gynecologist tells me my hormonal level is already lowering.

Sidney: She's always rushing me, and I'm just not ready.

Therapist: Well, I guess if you were ready to live with Nicole for six years, you would be ready for commitment.

Sidney: I can't be pressured and pushed.

Nicole: (hysterically crying, but later calms down) See what I mean? Look, I have been patient with you. I love you and will do anything for you, but if you are not ready then let's take a break.

Sidney: Well, I love you, too. I don't want a break. I'm here in therapy. Doesn't that show you that I'm working on it? (Turns to therapist). Look, it is only recently that Nicole has been calm and given me a feeling of confidence.

Therapist: But you have been living with her all these years, even when you felt insecure.

Sidney: That is because I love her.

Therapist (thinking internally): I start getting very impatient, recognizing his narcissism and entitlement thinking, that he has the right to keep someone on hold while he takes his time to get ready. This stirs up my V-spot, but I pull myself out of it and with the utmost technical neutrality I mirror Sidney.

Therapist: Yes, it is very scary to see Nicole lose it like your mother, whereby you had to become the parent for her. In fact, you never even had a childhood because you had to care for her, and there was no father around to take over. Now you feel you are in the same position and scared that all the emotional responsibility will fall on your shoulders.

Sidney: That's exactly how I feel, and I don't want to be pushed. I am not ready to give her a ring or make a commitment.

Therapist (internally): Okay, Joan, you have mirrored him, now go for it. Remember in ballet class how you take three steps back and then suddenly you go? You attack the step. Should I now try it?

Therapist: Yet, you feel ready to keep her on hold, not considering her situation, as if this is all about you.

Sidney: I resent that. Now you are taking her side.

Therapist: I think I am taking the side of the relationship, because your idea is to wait and wait, thinking that the longer you wait the more secure you will feel, when in fact it is the opposite. It is the commitment that brings security and holds the love bond together.

Sidney: I can understand that.

Therapist: I know you're upset with me for pressuring you.

Nicole: (smiling) Joan, that was brave!

Therapist: Well, someone here has to stand up to something, and if I don't then I will become the weak, passive, inadequate mother and that would not make either of you feel safe here.

This case presents a real therapeutic challenge because it involves the question of what and who comes first: Sidney's waiting to be ready, or Nicole's desire to tie the knot, have children, and face the reality of her biological clock? If the basic assumption is that the commitment takes priority and that "waiting" is a defensive operation, this gives the therapist a direction to follow.

Another question is, who is in therapy: the individual or the relationship? My approach begins with the relationship as the patient, gradually weaning the patient away from "the relationship" to the self-development that usually occurs in phase three (see Treatment Phases discussion earlier in this chapter). According to Arnold Rothstein (1998), a stern disciplinarian of psychoanalysis who entered couple therapy by treating a couple for a colleague as a favor, success occurs when partners are transformed into analytic patients. He views couple therapy as a defensive operation covering up internal conflicts. Without relinquishing his classical training, Rothstein remains faithful to the psychoanalytic model.

I may not agree completely with Rothstein's stern position, but I cannot help but hear his voice guide me as I consistently ask myself, "What is being covered up?" or "What is the couple defended against?" or "What is being projected? Denied? Avoided?" To this I now add, "How do we locate the V-spots as they translocate into the quagmire of the couple conflict?" More specifically, "When they are inflamed, how do the V-spots impact ego functioning and the capacity for healthy object relations?" In the midst of her presentation, one therapist commented, in a frustrated voice, "I am so sick of this woman complaining and complaining about her relationship. I feel like telling her to get a life!" This therapist was not too far off. She was recognizing that sometimes the relationship can be a defense or replacement of many underlying issues and conflicts denied or avoided.

One very narcissistic husband, caught by his wife having an affair with his research assistant, couldn't understand why his wife felt so hurt. "He just doesn't get it! He thinks because I was busy with a new baby and two small kids, that he was entitled to just go out and screw someone." As we can see from this example, although the emphasis was on the pain the affair stirred, underlying factors were fear of victimization and insecurity on her part and lack of empathy on his. "What is wrong with him that he can't understand I am hurting?" "Can't she ever stop grilling me, months and months of endless interrogations: 'Was she pretty?' 'Was she sexier than me?' 'How old was she?' 'Where did you meet her?' 'Did you buy her gifts?' 'How come you bought her gifts and not me?'"

How to Listen for a Theme:
Listen to the Words (External/Internal Objects)

- Robber (External Robber-Internal Robber)
- Judge (External Judge-Internal Judge)
- Policeman (External Policeman-Internal Policeman)
- Rapist (External Rapist-Internal Rapist)
- Bankrupter (External Bankrupter-Internal Bankrupter)
- Traffic (External Traffic-Internal Traffic)
- Betrayer (External Betrayer-Internal Betrayer)
- Loser (External Loser-Internal Loser)

"Yes, there can be an external betrayer: your husband, whom you caught having an affair. But there can also be an internal betrayer part of yourself that betrays you." These internal-external objects are inextricably linked to V-spots, and getting in contact with them is where the power is. We cannot always control how others betray or violate us, but we can control our internal betrayer. For example, a woman is horrified to discover her husband has been having an affair. She screams, she yells, she attacks, but to no avail; he continues to have affairs. She does not want to divorce her husband. In order to regain her own power, she gets in contact with a part of herself she has neglected—wanting to go back to work as an architect. Yet, every time she picks up the phone to call a contact, she hears this voice saying, "Who would hire you? You're a nothing. Even though you think you are good at what you're doing, look at all the competition you have out there!"

"Yes, there can be an external judge, your husband, who controls and watches over your every move. But there also can be a very harsh internal critical judge who inhibits your every move and desire (the harsh superego)."

"Yes, there can be an external robber, someone who takes time, attention away from you. But there can also be an internal robber part of yourself that robs yourself of pleasure.

"Yes, there can be an external rapist husband, one who rapes your mind, takes over your thinking. But there can also be an internal rapist, one who disavows your thoughts, devalues your own ideas, goals, and wishes."

Suggestions for the Couple Once a Theme Is Established

- Don't attack, retaliate, or get into the battle.
- Wait for a quiet time to engage in discussion, and be sure to follow through.
- Don't leave the room mad. If the person gets too "heated," reassure him/her that you will return in a short time when he/she calms down (do it and mean it).
- Stay differentiated; don't get hooked into the deception or the manipulation.
- Trust that you have been manipulated and deceived; don't question it.
- Don't wait for the "right time"; it is never the right time!
- If your partner withholds time, money, and won't let you, for example, decorate the house, go out immediately and hire a decorator, and spend money (the "real relationship" will unfold).
- If your partner is a narcissist, be sure to address his strength, attributes, and what you appreciate about him; gradually let him know what he does that is hurtful to you. Don't attack. Show him you understand, but don't give up your own needs.
- If he's a borderline and flies into a rage, do not move; remain absolutely still. Do not say a word. Agree to own up to the part he might be right about, and repeat again and again that even if what he says is true, he has no right to attack or verbally abuse you.
- If he gets angry, screams, yells, complains that you are interfering with his work, his friends, his family, remind him again and again that you come first, that you and the relationship are most important.

Treatment Points and Techniques for Cross-Cultural Couples

The entire spectrum of psychoanalytic theory takes on a different shape when treating cross-cultural couples. Drawing from many different theoretical approaches—including concepts from classical psychoanalysis, self psychology, object relations, group psychology, and psychohistory—I have found self psychology most suitable for the treatment of couples of varying ethnic backgrounds because of its mirroring and empathic techniques. The treatment approach outlined here is constructed to help therapists understand the interplay of the various psychodynamics described in chapter 7, with its idiosyncratic nature and all its cultural contours.

At one time, psychologists and social scientists attracted a great deal of criticism by analyzing or diagnosing groups, cultures, or nations, and were accused of grand-scale stereotyping. In recent years, however, more mental health professionals and psychohistorians are making use of therapists' analytic tools and knowledge to investigate the dynamics of other cultures. For example, Peter Berton, a world-renowned international scholar in international relations and psychoanalysis, has written and published extensively on Japan, including his book *Japan on the Psychologist's Couch* (2001). While we, of course, cannot stereotype or make sweeping generalizations about ethnic or religious groups, it is critical to understand the mythology, folklore, and collective ideologies that gave rise to the psyche of the group—the essence of psychohistory. In recent years, social scientists, analysts, anthropologists, and psychohistorians have gone beyond individual analysis in applying their skills and knowledge when putting societies "on the couch." In a joint article (Lachkar and Berton 1997, 2004, 2008), we discussed the differences between Japanese and German attitudes toward World War II war crimes, noting that Japan can be characterized as a shame society and Germany as a guilt society; these cultural attitudes affect how individuals act.

In treating couples whose values are at complete odds with one another, I have employed a technique I call the "cultural contrast hook," whereby the patient claims his behavior is cultural and the therapist, in turn, makes a case to show that even the person's culture does not support the pathology. For example, Kimora was withholding money from Patricia and felt he had to be in total control. He tried to manipulate the therapist into thinking that in Japan, the man is the head of the household and that women are subservient to them. The therapist in a most sensitive way waited for an opportunity to explore the withholding and controlling nature of Kimora's behavior. She clarified that even though what he says is true about women being subservient in Japan, she had done enough research to warrant the following response to Kimora: "Yes, you are right about women being subservient to men in your country, but even in your country it is the woman who is the sole keeper of finances in the home." The therapist found distortion and misrepresentation even within Kimora's own culture.

Another technique is to provide many illustrative examples that convey a cultural contrast. Let us examine an extreme example. A man in Saudi Arabia says it is okay to beat his wife because that is "what they do in my country when a woman misbehaves." When this Middle Eastern man complains that his wife disobeys him and only listens when he beats her, the therapist has an opportunity to apply the cultural contrast hook, "Yes, I do understand how this is your tradition. Imagine if your wife came from a tribe in central Africa where most of the people were cannibalistic and their tradition was to eat the body parts of their fellow human beings? How would you feel if your wife took a bite of you and said it was customary? You are a family man. Imagine now if you lived in China and you were restricted to only having one child."

It is not uncommon for a man from a male-dominated aggressor society (a "macho" society) to seek out a woman who is submissive and subservient. The following case is an illustration of how the therapist must not only be "culturally sensitive" to people from different cultures, but also must be able to separate culture from aggression. One Russian scientist came to this country and started dating American women. Not only did he find them "too demanding," needy, and spoiled, he got the sense that they would not serve his emotional and sexual needs. He met an immigrant Chinese exchange student 20 years his junior. Shortly thereafter she moved in with him. Not only was she required to be at his beck and call to meet all his sexual demands, prepare the meals, bring his morning coffee, and clean the house, she was verbally abused (name calling, put-downs, racial slurs, and innuendos). In exchange, he hooked her by offering her money and a credit card, and he helped her get a driver's license. Whenever she would complain that she was not happy and was being mistreated, he "shamed" her for not being grateful for all he had done for her.

Besides the cultural contrast hook, there are many other techniques and methods to keep in mind when working with cross-cultural couples. The following is a condensed list of applicable suggestions:

- Learn the fundamental dynamics of the culture; mirror and reflect.
- Be aware that self psychology provides the most effective method to mirror and understand the subjective experience.
- Know something about the foods, holidays, and traditions of the patient.
- Learn a few words of the respective language—at least "hello" and "good-bye." If the patient is Asian, serve tea and bow slightly. If Korean, say how you love kimchi.
- Be empathic to the cultural differences, not to the aggression.
- Be aware of the differences between the individual and group self.
- Be aware of special treatment needs. Try to bond through some common ground (music, food, dance, etc.; for example, "I love Arabic music" or "I would love to learn how to make hummus."

- Be aware of body language—e.g., with Asians, keep your distance; with Persians and Italians, stay close.
- Find pathology within the individual.
- Find pathology within the government.
- Find pathology within the culture.
- Find pathology within the couple transference.
- Remind the couple why they are in treatment.
- Mirror the conflict, don't try to fix it.
- Empathize with the vulnerabilities, not the aggression.
- Use the "cultural contrast hook."
- Use humor and play, and provide many illustrative examples. "What would happen if I showed up in your country de-veiled or pregnant out of wedlock?
- Keep in mind that many people from other cultures are consumed by persecutory anxieties. It is important to speak in a calm and caring manner.

The Therapist's V-Spot and Cross-Cultural Couples

We cannot overlook the therapist's V-spot when it comes to cross-cultural couples. Men who abuse women under the guise of tradition or culture arouse anger in many therapists raised within a democratic society with Western values and traditions. Following are some examples of common countertransferences that occur in working with cross-cultural couples:

- Therapist is not being sufficiently culturally sensitive.
- Therapist has an inadequate understanding of the patient's culture.
- Therapist goes overboard trying to adjust to the patient's culture.
- Therapist goes overboard trying to please.
- Therapist is frightened of the person's culture and aggression.
- Therapist fears rejection.
- Therapist identifies with the projections of shame/guilt.
- Therapist may be denying that there are cultural differences.
- Therapist to be aware of his or her own cultural V-spot.

For example, an Israeli microbiologist that I have been treating for the past three years tells me I'm not a "good friend," that I never go to lunch, out for coffee, or just stop at her club. She says that she does so much for me, is so caring, and I do not reciprocate her kindness and generosity. Knowing that I am a psychohistorian, she always apprises me of events going on the Middle East. She was the first to call to tell me about the attack on the World Trade Center on 9/11. "When you went to Israel, I was the one who warned you not to go into the Palestinian Authority's area, and you didn't listen."

My V-spot got a double dose: first, my own countertransference issue about not being "good enough," a reminder of a mother who always told me to be a "good girl" (meaning complacent); second, the cultural aspects (see chapter 7). In Israel people are very close, or shall I say "fused." Because of the political climate, living in constant fear forces people to maintain very strong attachments. Friends, family, siblings, and yes, therapists as well, stay very closely tied. It is not unusual for a therapist to visit the homes of patients and join in at social events. Getting in contact with my V-spot made it possible for me to treat this patient with more clarity and not give way to the seduction and guilt being induced in me (coercing me into the role of the "bad little girl," ultimately a split part of the patient's unanalyzed pathology projected into me).

Discussion

This chapter has focused on treatment—mainly addressing the dilemma of distinguishing how much of a problem is cultural and how much is pathological, especially when two people—along with their corresponding cultures—enter into a marital bond. I have discussed the three phases of treatment that couples move through—states of mental darkness into states of awareness, introspection, and, finally, separateness. I included treatment points and techniques for treating a cross-cultural couple, introducing the techniques of the "cross-cultural hook" and emphasizing that both object relations and self psychology appear to be the most effective treatment modalities for cross-cultural couples because self psychology offers the mirroring and empathic responses to help enter the nearly impermeable walls of defense, while object relations contains and deals with the aggressive and destructive aspects of the relationship. Where do narcissistic and borderline pathology meet? How do we discover a "self" within the borderline who comes from a shame society that accepts shame as a way to conform, as a normal aspect of life? Therapists need to probe deeply enough to find pathology within the individual and the vertex of conflict within his/her own culture (Lachkar 2004).

This brings us to the final chapter, in which I will widen my perspective from the individual to the global to encompass treatment challenges that the ever-changing world and our environment bring to our clinical practices. Our excursion has taken us from the domestic level to the global—cross-cultural couples exposing their ever-ready, explosive V-spots. Our focus has been on abuse, primarily emotional abuse, and the vulnerabilities that abusive relationships reveal.

From the individual, to the couple, to the global, to the political, to the artistic—each facet of the concept of the V-spot has been explored. Although the idea may sound simple at first, I hope by now the reader has gotten a sense of not only its complexity but also its psychological and clinical relevance. Homing in on the exact area of vulnerability opens new therapeutic avenues within the context of various personality types, cultures, traditions, and ideologies.

CHAPTER NINE

Final Thoughts

Couple therapy is a deep, emotional experience with intense communication and feelings occurring between the couple and the therapist. The task is to alleviate the early anxieties and modify the harshness of internalized objects and inner persecutors. This is done by analyzing and interpreting couple transference, which offers a new lens with which to view the conflict and an opportunity to move away from the relationship to working though more individual issues.

In *The Narcissistic/Borderline Couple*, I define a specific type of a beleaguered love bond between two developmentally arrested people who coerce each other into certain roles as each brings into their current reality archaic experiences embedded in their V-spots. Together they play out a drama characterized by painful, never-ending patterns of destructive behavior and form a parasitic bond that thwarts growth and development. What it is about these love bonds that attract? It is not really important how they find each other; more important is the glue that keeps them together. They "do the dance," as if they have some extraordinary built-in sonar system (Lachkar 2004).

The narcissistic personality is inclined to attract a borderline personality as an "object choice." Each stirs up some unconscious or conscious unresolved developmental issue in the other: the narcissist "needs" a borderline, and the borderline "needs" a narcissist. Ironically, two narcissists or two borderlines do not make it, but when paired, these oppositional types appear to maintain a bond. With a narcissistic/borderline couple, the blending of V-spots becomes very apparent: the narcissist feels attacked and guilty while the borderline feels betrayed and abandoned. At the same time, these patients readily evoke reactions in the therapist's V-spot.

As an intern frantically trying to find specific treatment procedures for couple therapy, I discovered that not much had been written on technique and procedures, much less from an object-relations perspective. Thus, I devised my own theories, techniques, and treatment procedures. Since writing *The Narcissistic/Borderline Couple*, I have been amazed at the number of authors who have expanded beyond narcissistic/borderline relations, risking the challenge of assigning diagnostic categories.

Although the idea of abuse was implied, it was not until writing *The Many Faces of Abuse* (Lachkar, 1998a) that I, too, ventured beyond narcissistic and borderline relations to encompass a variety of dyadic configurations, exploring how the grandiose self can infect and invade other types of relational love bonds. For example, what happens when a histrionic hooks up with an obsessive-compulsive, or an obsessive-compulsive with a passive-aggressive, or a schizoid with a dependent? This gets very confusing because not only are there narcissistic borderlines, narcissistic obsessive-compulsives, and narcissistic passive-aggressives, there are also many faces and phases of narcissism.

Therapists have moved from the individual to the global, encompassing treatment challenges that our ever-changing world and environment bring to our clinical practices. Our excursion has taken us from the domestic level to cross-cultural couples and their explosive V-spots. Our focus has been on abuse—primarily emotional abuse—and the vulnerabilities that get stirred within five different kinds of abusive relationships. Although she may not be buried under coals as Burmese brides sometimes are, or have her throat slit for committing adultery or becoming pregnant out of wedlock as some cultures practice, the American woman who is emotionally abused may feel just as pained as if she were being physically abused.

Treating cross-cultural couples is one of the therapist's most difficult challenges because we cannot effectively work with cross-cultural couples without understanding their respective cultures. We cannot understand various cultures unless we understand how the history, religion, child-rearing practices, and treatment of woman shape them. We cannot describe culture without the risk of stereotyping groups of people who fall into certain diagnostic categories. The clash between East and West brings a variety of psychodynamics that we attempt to reconcile.

The individual's V-spot is based on early archaic injuries and the memories that spark traumatic experience. The cultural V-spot is a collective group experience of shared mutual archaic injuries emanating from the group's mythological and historical past. We cannot speak of abuse or V-spots (individual or collective) unless we address the culture's history, government-sponsored abuse, violations of human rights, the treatment of women, and child-rearing practices that foster abuse. We struggle as well with the term "abuse." What seems like abuse or forced submission to people in the West is often considered normal in other cultures.

We must be careful not to assume that all human behavior and relationships are pathological. Pathology cannot be the excuse for causing pain in another human being. Conjoint therapy is not the road to the Promised Land; it is merely an introduction and precursor to individual treatment. Whether the two people that make up a couple come from the West or the East, both are subject to erosion of personal responsibility and, with all our piety and wit, we as clinicians are able to offer nothing that can replace accountability. Analogously, the human condition is such that conflicts do exist and are not always pathological. Furthermore, therapists must be careful to not become the replacement for family, society, and support. As one couple said, "We love our conflicts and would not give them up for the world." Often therapists are quick to tell an enabler to just leave an abusive relationship without any regard to the understanding of the undeveloped issues the conflict stirs—for example, the dance between guilt/shame, envy/jealousy, and domination/submission.

Many theorists believe that group psychology can offer insights into the behavior of individuals who exhibit characteristics similar to those involved in group dynamics. Perhaps this is especially true in couple therapy. Within narcissistic and borderline relationships, the shared couple myth needs to be understood in terms of the couple as a unit, as well as in terms of each person's delusions, distortions, and projections. Can we diagnose a "couple mind" in terms of the partners' collective defenses? Is it possible to understand that one partner will inflict pain on the other to dehumanize and destroy the will of that person? Understanding group myths and the shared emotional fantasies of couples can help objectify the highly charged passions that are so difficult for many couples to face. Successful couple therapy requires us to deal with both individual and couple transferences.

This journey has taken our dynamics all over the world in the attempt to find universal application and relevance to our Western style of psychotherapy; it has also been a journey inside—into the V-spots of ourselves and the people we treat. We have seen that when treating couples from diverse societies, we need to learn something about their language and culture. We also need to learn the special language of the various pathological disorders that we treat. For this reason, I have developed the language of "empathology" (Lachkar, 2008b) to match the various personalities that we meet and treat. Just as we need to learn how to speak to Asian, Hispanic, or Muslim patients, we also must adapt ourselves to empathically attune ourselves to speak with various personality disorders. I find that understanding these diversified groups—within the context of their corresponding V-spots—brings further clarity and value to the work we do behind the closed curtains in our own consultation rooms.

Where the V-spot was, ego shall be!

~

Glossary

Borderline Personality: This term designates a defect in the maternal attachment bond as an over-concern with the "other." Many mental health professionals have affixed the term "as-if personalities" to borderlines, who tend to subjugate or compromise themselves. They question their sense of existence, suffer from acute abandonment anxiety, persecutory anxiety, and tend to merge with others in very painful ways in order to get a sense of bonding. Under close scrutiny and under stress, they distort, misperceive, have poor impulse control, and turn suddenly against self and others to attack, blame, find fault, and get even.

Containment: This is a term employed by Wilfred Bion to describe the interaction between the mother and the infant. Bion believed all psychological barriers universally dissolve when the mind acts as receiver of other people's projections and evacuative material, which the mother does in the state of reverie by using her own alpha function. Containment is the capacity for transformation of the data of emotional experience into meaningful feelings and thoughts. The mother's capacity to withstand the child's anger, frustrations, and intolerable feelings becomes the container for these effects. This can occur if the mother can sustain intolerable behaviors long enough to decode or detoxify painful feelings into a more digestible form.

Cultural V-Spot: The cultural V-spot is a collectively shared archaic experience from the mythological or historical past that evokes painful thoughts and memories for the group, e.g., for Jews, the burning of the Temple, loss of holy land, the expulsion of Ishmael to the desert with his abandoned mother, Hagar.

Depressive Position: This is a term devised by Melanie Klein to describe a state of mourning and sadness. It is the state in which integration and reparation take place. Not everything is seen in terms of black and white. There is more tolerance of guilt, remorse, self-doubt, frustration, pain, and confusion. One is more responsible for one's action. There is the realization not of what things should be, but the way they are, that there is "no breast." As verbal expression increases, one may feel sadness, but one also feels a newly regained sense of aliveness.

Ego: The ego is part of an intrapsychic system responsible for functioning. It is the mediator between the id and superego. The function of the ego is to observe the external world, preserving a true picture by eliminating old memory traces left by early impressions and perceptions.

Envy: Klein made a distinction between envy and jealousy. Envy is a part-object function and is not based on love. She considers envy to be the most primitive and fundamental emotion. It exhausts external objects and is destructive in nature. Envy is possessive, controlling, and does not allow outsiders in.

***Folie à deux*:** In general terms, *folie à deux* refers to Melanie Klein's notion of projective identification, whereby two people project their delusional fantasies back and forth, engaging in a foolish "dance." The partners are wrapped up in a shared delusional fantasy, and each engages and believes in the outrageous scheme of the other. Usually the term applies to both oppositional and collusive couples. In some cases there is triangulation, which is a three-part relationship in which two people form a covert or overt bond against another member.

Guilt: Guilt is a higher form of development than shame. Guilt has an internal punitive voice that operates at the level of the superego (an internalized, punitive, harsh parental figure). There are two kinds of guilt: valid guilt and invalid guilt.

Internal Objects: This is an intrapsychic process whereby unconscious fantasies that are felt to be persecutory, threatening, or dangerous are denounced, split off, and projected. Internal objects emanate from the part of the ego that has been introjected. Klein believed that an infant can internalize "good objects" or the "good breast." If the infant perceives the world as bad and dangerous, the infant internalizes the "bad breast."

Jealousy: Jealousy, a higher form of development than envy, is a whole-object relationship whereby one desires the object but does not seek to destroy it or the oedipal rival (father and siblings, those who take mother away). Jealousy, unlike envy, is a triangular relationship based on love, wherein one desires to be part of or included in the group, family, clan, or nation.

Manic Defenses: The experience of excitement (mania) offsets feelings of despair, loss, anxiety, and vulnerability. Manic defenses evolve as a defense against depressive anxiety, guilt, and loss. They are based on omnipotent denial of psychic reality and object relations characterized by a mass degree of triumph, control, and hostility. Some manic defenses work in the ego.

Mirroring: This is a term devised by Heinz Kohut that describes the "gleam" in a mother's eye, which mirrors the child's exhibitionistic display, and other forms of maternal participation. Mirroring is a specific response to the child's narcissistic-exhibitionist displays, confirming the child's self-esteem. Eventually these responses are channeled into more realistic aims.

Narcissistic/Borderline Relationship: These two personality types enter into a psychological "dance" and consciously or unconsciously stir up highly charged feelings that fulfill early unresolved conflicts in the other. Each partner needs the other to play out his or her own personal relational drama. Engaging in these beleaguered relationships are developmentally arrested people who bring archaic experiences embedded in old sentiments into their current relationships.

Narcissistic Personality: Omnipotence, grandiosity, and exhibitionist features dominate this type of personality. These individuals become strongly invested in others and thus experience them as self objects. In order to preserve this "special" relationship with their self objects (others), they tend to withdraw or isolate themselves by concentrating on perfection and power.

Object Relations: Object relations is a theory of unconscious internal objects in a dynamic interplay with current interpersonal experience. It is an approach to understanding internal intrapsychic and internal conflict, including the patients' projections, introjections, fantasies, distortions, delusions, and split-off aspects of the self. This psychodynamic theory is based on how one relates to and interacts with others in the external world. Klein developed the idea of pathological splitting of "good" and "bad" objects through the defensive process of projection and introjection in relation to primitive anxiety and the death instinct (based on biology). Object relations is one of the most powerful theories in examining unconscious fantasies/motivations, reflecting how a person can distort reality by projecting and identifying with bad objects.

Obsessive-Compulsive Personality Disorder: The obsessive-compulsive abuser has difficulty completing tasks, becomes preoccupied with small tedious duties, has strict rules, and is obsessed with details, lists, and organization; he will, for example, redo a schedule or a spreadsheet to the extent of overlooking major tasks. Obsessive-compulsives make unreasonable demands, including perfection, and have excessive devotion to work and productivity to the dismissal of leisure activities and family and social relations.

Paranoid-Schizoid Position: The paranoid-schizoid position is a fragmented position in which thoughts and feelings are split off and projected because the psyche cannot tolerate the feelings of pain, emptiness, loneliness, rejection, humiliation, or ambiguity. Klein viewed this position as the earliest phase of development—part-object functioning—and the beginning of the primitive superego (undeveloped). If the child views the mother as a "good breast," the child will maintain good, warm, and hopeful feelings about the environment. If, on the other hand, the infant experiences mother as a "bad breast," the child is more likely to experience the environment as bad, attacking, and persecutory. Klein, more than any of her followers, understood the mother/the breast as of primary importance.

Part Objects: The first relational unit is the feeding experience with the mother and the infant's relation to the breast. Klein believed the breast is the child's first possession, but because it is so desired, it also becomes the source of the infant's envy, greed, and hatred and is therefore susceptible to the infant's fantasized attacks. The infant internalizes the mother as good or bad, a "part object" (a "good breast" or "bad breast"). As the breast is felt to contain a great part of the infant's death instinct (persecutory anxiety), it simultaneously establishes libidinal forces, giving way to the baby's first ambivalence. One part of the mother is loved and idealized, while the other is destroyed by the infant's oral, anal, sadistic, or aggressive impulses. In clinical terms, Klein referred to this as pathological splitting. Here a parent is seen only as a *function* for what the parent can provide, e.g., in infancy, the breast; in later life money, material objects, etc. Men, for example, may only see women as part objects. "I love her because she has big breasts!"

Passive-Aggressive Personality: Passive-aggressive personalities are often dependent, products of sibling rivalry with avoidance aspects. The passive-aggressive typically procrastinates until the last minute, feigns inefficiency, and invariably finds a conundrum of excuses why things were not accomplished. They claim others make unrealistic demands on them, especially with respect to authority, and defend against commitments by ineptness, forgetfulness, devaluing the importance of the task, and devaluing the needs of others. The passive-aggressive's stories of mishaps are endless: "Gee, honey, the store was closed!" Decoded, the message is a form of projective identification, saying, "Now, I'm going to show you, 'wife/mommy,' how it feels to be locked out/unfed!"

Persecutory Anxiety: Persecutory anxiety is the part of the psyche that threatens and terrifies the patient. It relates to what Klein has referred to as the primitive superego, an undifferentiated state that continually warns the patient of eminent danger (mostly unfounded). Paranoid anxiety is a feature associated with the death instinct and is more persecutory in nature. That implies that the kind of anxiety from the primitive superego is more explosive and volatile than the kind experienced by the more developed superego.

Projective Identification: This is a process whereby one splits off an unwanted aspect of the self and puts it into the object, which identifies or over-identifies with that which is being projected. It is a psychic mechanism whereby the self experiences the unconscious defensive mechanism and translocates itself into the other. Under the influence of projective identification, one becomes vulnerable to the coercion, manipulation, or control of the person doing the projecting.

Psychohistory: Psychohistory does for the group what psychoanalysis does for the individual. Psychohistory offers a broader perspective from which to view cross-cultural differences. Using psychoanalytic tools and concepts, psychohistory allows a better understanding of famous individuals, nations, governments, and political events—very much as a therapist analyzes the couple as a symbolic representation of a political group or nation.

Reparation: The desire for the ego to restore an injured love object by coming to terms with one's own guilt and ambivalence. The process of reparation begins in the depressive position and starts when one develops the capacity to mourn and to tolerate and contain the feelings of loss and guilt.

Schizoid Personality: The central features of the schizoid are their defenses of attachment, aloofness, and indifference to others. The schizoid, although difficult to treat, is usually motivated, unlike the passive-aggressive. However, because of his detachment and aloofness, the schizoid personality lacks the capacity to achieve social and sexual gratification. A close relationship invites the danger of being overwhelmed or suffocated, for the schizoid may envision a relinquishing of his independence. The schizoid differs from the obsessive-compulsive personality in that the obsessive-compulsive feels great discomfort with emotions, whereas the schizoid is lacking in the capacity but at least recognizes the need. Schizoids differ from narcissists in that they are self sufficient and self contained. They do not experience or suffer the same feelings of loss borderlines and narcissists do. "Who, me? I don't care, I have my work, my computer, etc.!"

Self Objects: This is a term devised by Heinz Kohut. A forerunner of self psychology, the term refers to an interpersonal process whereby the analyst provides basic functions for the patient. These functions make up for failures in the past by caretakers who were lacking in mirroring and empathic attunement, and who had faulty responses with their children. Kohut reminds us that psychological disturbances are caused by failures from idealized objects, and patients may need self objects who provide good mirroring responses for the rest of their lives.

Self Psychology: Heinz Kohut revolutionized analytic thinking when he introduced this new psychology of the self that stresses the patient's subjective experience and considers the patient's "reality." The patient's reality, unlike object relations, is not considered as a distortion or as a projection, but rather as the patient's truth. It is the patient's experience that is considered of utmost importance. Self psychology, with its emphasis on the empathic mode, implies that the narcissistic personality is more susceptible to classical interpretations. Recognition of splitting and projection is virtually nonexistent among self psychologists.

Shame: Shame is a matter between the person and his group or society (in contrast to guilt, which is primarily a matter between a person and his conscience). Shame is the defense against the humiliation of having needs that are felt to be dangerous and persecutory. Shame is associated with anticipatory anxiety and annihilation fantasies. "If I tell my boyfriend what I really need, he will abandon me!"

Single and Dual Projective Identification (as it pertains to conjoint treatment): In single projective identification, one takes in the other person's projections by identifying with that which is being projected. Dual projective identification is a term I originated whereby both partners take in the projections of the other and identify or over-identify with that which is being projected (the splitting of the ego). Thus, one may project guilt while the other projects shame. "You should be ashamed of yourself for being so needy! When you're so needy, I feel guilty!"

Splitting: Splitting is when a person can't keep two contradictory thoughts or feelings in mind at the same time and therefore keeps the conflicting feelings apart, focusing on just one of them.

Superego: The literature refers to different kinds of superegos. Freud's superego concerns itself with moral judgment (what people think). It depicts an introjected whole figure, a parental voice or image that operates from a point of view of morality, telling children how to follow the rules, and what happens if they don't. It is often the "dos, don'ts, oughts, and shoulds," and represents the child's compliance and conformity with strong parental figures. Freud's superego is the internalized image that continues to live inside the child's life, controlling or punishing. Klein's superego centers on the shame and humiliation of having needs, thoughts, and feelings that are felt to be more persecutory and hostile in nature, and the superego invades the psyche as an unmentalized experience.

V-Spot: The V-spot is a term I devised to describe the most sensitive area of emotional vulnerability that gets aroused when one's partner hits an emotional raw spot in the object. Although oppositional—the G-spot gives pleasure and the V-spot gives pain—they are both are areas of profound stimulation. It is the emotional counterpart to the physical "G-spot." The V-spot is the heart of our most fragile area of emotional sensitivity, known in the literature as the archaic injury, a product of early trauma that one holds on to and unwittingly arouses in the other. When the V-spot is aroused, with it comes the loss of sense and sensibility; everything shakes and shifts like an earthquake (memory, perception, judgment, and reality).

Whole Objects: The beginning of the depressive position is marked by the infant's awareness of his mother as a "whole object." As the infant matures and as verbal expression increases, he achieves more cognitive ability and acquires the capacity to love her as a separate person with separate needs, feelings, and desires. In the depressive position, guilt and jealousy become the replacement for shame and envy. Ambivalence and guilt are experienced and tolerated in relation to whole objects. One no longer seeks to destroy the objects or the oedipal rival (father and siblings, those who take the mother away), but can begin to live amicably with them side by side.

Withdrawal/Detachment: Detachment should not be confused with withdrawal. Withdrawal is a healthier state because it maintains a certain libidinal attachment to the object. When one detaches, one splits off and goes into a state of despondency. Children who are left alone, ignored, or neglected for long periods of time enter into a phase of despair, according to Bowlby. The child's active protest for the missing or absent mother gradually diminishes when the child no longer makes demands. When this occurs, the infant goes into withdrawal, detachment mode, or pathological mourning. Apathy, lethargy, and listlessness become the replacement for feelings (anger, rage, betrayal, abandonment). Typically these kinds of children grow up with almost autistic qualities. These defenses often impact the personality in that they limit the capacity to think and communicate. "He just doesn't seem to get it, just can't connect the dots."

References

Adams, A., and L. Hill. 1997. The phallic female in Japanese group-fantasy. *Journal of Psychohistory* 25 (1): 33–66.

Alexander, Franz, and Thomas M. French, et al. 1946. *Psychoanalytic therapy: principles and application*. New York: Ronald Press, chapters 2, 4, and 17.

Bach, S. 1994. *The language of perversion and the language of love*. Northvale, N.J.: Jason Aronson.

Ball, A. L. 2004. Women who become undone: Review of *The many faces of abuse*, *Oprah Magazine*, September, 300–305, 327.

Benjamin, J. 1988. *The bonds of love*. New York: Pantheon.

Berton, P. 1995. Understanding Japanese negotiating behavior. *ISOP Intercom* 18.2: 1–8.

Berton, P. 2001. *Japan on the psychologist's couch*. Los Angeles: University of Southern California: Emerti Center.

Bion, W. R. 1959. Attacks on linking. *International Journal of Psychoanalysis* 40, 308.

Bion, W. R. 1961. *Experiences in groups and other papers*. London: Tavistock.

Bion, W. R. 1967. *Second thoughts: Selected papers on psycho-analysis*. New York: Jason Aronson.

Bion, W. R. 1977. *Seven servants: four works by Wildred R. Bion*. New York: Jason Aronson.

Bird, M. 1959. Marriage patterns: The "lovesick" wife and the "cold sick" husband. *Psychiatry* 22: 245–9.

Blackman, J. 2004. *101 defenses: How the mind shields itself*. New York. Brunner Routledge.

Blanck, G., and R. Blanck. 1974. *Ego psychology theory and practice*. New York: Columbia University Press.

Bowlby, J. 1969. *Attachment and loss*. 3 vols. New York: Basic Books.

Brandchaft, B., and R. Stolorow. 1984. The borderline concept: Pathological character or iatrogenic myth? In *Empathy II*, ed. J. Lichtenberg, et al. Hillsdale, N.J.: Analytic Press, 333–57.

Carlson, J., and L. Sperry, eds. 1998. *The disordered couple*. New York: Brunner/Mazel.

Chesler, P., and N. Kobrin. 2005. The white Moor as willing executioner. *Tech Central Station*. Online at: http://76.12.0.56/index.php?option=com_content&task=view&id=180&Itemid=36.

Cocks, G. 1994. *The curve of life correspondence of Heinz Kohut 1923–1981*. Chicago and London: The University of Chicago Press.

deMause, L. 2002a. The childhood origins of terrorism. *The Journal of Psychohistory* 29: 340–49.

deMause, L. 2002b. *The emotional life of nations*. New York. Karnac Books.

deMause, L. 2006. The childhood origins of the Holocaust. *The Journal of Psychohistory* 33: 204.

Deutsch, H. 1942. Some forms of emotional disturbances and their relationship to schizophrenia. *Contemporary Psychoanalysis* 11, 301–21.

Dicks, H. V. 1967. *Marital tensions: Clinical studies toward a psychological theory of interaction*. New York: Basic Books.

Doder, D. 1999. *Portrait of a tyrant*. New York: Simon & Schuster.

Doi, T. 1973. *The anatomy of dependence*. Tokyo: Kodansha.

Dutton, D. and S. L. Painter. 1981. Traumatic bonding: the development of emotional attachments in battered women and other relationships of intermittent abuse. *Victimology: An International Journal* 6, 139–55.

Ellingwood, Ken. 2005. For Gaza settlers, "the miracle" never came. *Los Angeles Times*, Sept. 21, p. A12.

Endleman, R. 1989. *Love and sex in twelve cultures*. New York: Psychic Press.

Fairbairn, W. R. D. 1940. Schizoid factors in the personality. In *Psychoanalytic studies of the personality*, 3–27. London: Routledge & Kegan Paul.

Fairbairn, W. R. D. 1944–1952. Object relationships and dynamic structures. In *Psychoanalytic studies of the personality*. Boston: Routledge Paul, 137–51.

Fairbairn, W. R. D. 1946–1952. A revised psychopathology of the psychosis and psychoneurosis. In *Psychoanalytic studies of the personality*. Boston: Routledge Paul. 28–58.

Fisher, H. 1992. *The anatomy of love*. New York: Norton.

Foster, R., M. Moskowitz, and R. Javier. 1996. *Reaching across boundaries of culture and class*. Northvale, N.J.: Jason Aronson.

Freud, S. 1922. *Beyond the pleasure principle*. Boni and Liveright Publishers.

Freud, S. 1923. *The ego and id*. New York: Norton.

Freud, S. 1924. The loss of reality in neurosis and psychosis. In J. Strachey (ed. and trans.), *The standard edition of the complete works of Sigmund Freud*, Vol. 19, pp. 140–153. London: Hogarth Press.

Freud, S. 1936. *The ego and the mechanisms of defense*. New York: International Universities Press, 30–32.

Freud, S. 1955. Notes upon a case of obsessional neurosis. In *The standard edition of the complete works of Sigmund Freud*, ed. J. Strachey, vol. 10, 153–318. London: Hogarth Press. (Original work published in 1909.)

Freud, S. 1957. On narcissism: An introduction. In *The standard edition of the complete works of Sigmund Freud*, ed. J. Strachey, vol. 14, 69–102. London: Hogarth Press. (Original work published in 1914.)

Freud, S. 1979. Group psychology and the analysis of the ego. In *The standard edition of the complete works of Sigmund Freud*, ed. J. Strachey, vol. 18, 65–143. London: Hogarth Press. (Original work published in 1921.)

Gay, P. 1988. *Freud: A life for our times*. New York: Norton.

Grinberg, L., D. Sor, and E. T. de Bianchedi. 1977. *Introduction to the works of Bion: Groups, knowledge, psychosis, thoughts, transformations, psychoanalytic practice*. New York: Jason Aronson.

Grotstein, J. 1981. *Splitting and projective identification*. New York: Jason Aronson.

Grotstein, J. 1986. Schizophrenia personality disorder: ". . . And if I should die before I wake." In *Towards a complete model of schizophrenic disorders*, ed. D. B. Feinsilver, 29–71. Hillsdale, N.J.: Analytic Press.

Grotstein, J. 1987. Meaning, meaningless, and the "black hole." In "Self and international regulation as a new paradigm for psychoanalysis and neuroscience: An introduction." Unpublished manuscript.

Grotstein, J. 1993. Boundary difficulties in borderline patients. In *Master clinicians: On treating the regressed patient*, ed. L. Bryce Boyer and Peter Giovacchini, 107–42. Northvale, N.J., and London: Jason Aronson.

Hartmann, H. 1939. *Ego psychology and the problem of adaptation*. New York: International Universities Press (1958).

Hartmann, H. 1958. *Ego psychology and the problem of adaptation*. New York: International Universities Press.

Iga, M. 1986. *The thorn in the chrysanthemum*. Berkeley: University of California Press.

Johnson, R. 1994. *Dependency and Japanese socialization: psychoanalytic and anthropological investigation into Amae*. New York: New York University Press.

Kernberg, O. 1980. *Internal world and external reality*. New York: Jason Aronson.

Kernberg, O. April 1990. Between conventionality and aggression: the boundaries of passion. Presented at the Cutting Edge Conference, University of California, San Diego, CA.

Kernberg, O. 1991. Sadomasochism, sexual excitement, and perversion. *Journal of the American Psychoanalytic Association* 39: 333–62.

Kernberg, O. 1992. *Aggression in personality disorders and perversions*. New Haven: Yale University Press.

Kernberg, O. 1995. *Love relations: Normality and pathology*. New Haven and London: Yale University Press.

Klein, M. 1957. *Envy and gratitude*. New York: Basic Books.

Klein, M. 1975. Love, guilt and reparation. In *The writings of Melanie Klein, Vol. I—Love, guilt and reparation and other works 1921–1945*, ed. R. E. Money-Kryle, 306–43. New York: The Free Press. (Original work published in 1937.)

Kohut, H. 1971. *The analysis of the self*. New York: International Universities Press.

Kohut, H. 1977. *The restoration of the self*. New York: International Universities Press.

Kobrin, N. (2006). "The Sheikh's New Clothes: Islamic Suicide Terrorism and What It's Really All About." New York: Loosleaf Law.

Lachkar, J. 1983. The Arab-Israeli conflict: A psychoanalytic study. Doctoral dissertation. Los Angeles: International College.

Lachkar, J. 1984. Narcissistic/borderline couples: A psychoanalytic perspective to family therapy. *International Journal of Family Psychiatry* 5.2: 169–89.

Lachkar, J. 1985. Narcissistic/borderline couples: Theoretical implications for treatment. *Dynamic Psychotherapy* 3.2: 109–27.

Lachkar, J. 1986. Narcissistic/borderline couples: Implications for mediation. *Conciliation Courts Review* 24.1: 31–43.

Lachkar, J. 1991. Primitive defenses in the Persian Gulf. Unpublished paper presented at the International Psychohistorical Association, John Jay College, New York.

Lachkar, J. 1992. *The narcissistic/borderline couple: A psychoanalytic perspective to marital conflict*. New York: Brunner/Mazel.

Lachkar, J. 1993a. Paradox of peace: Folie à deux in marital and political relationships. *Journal of Psychohistory* 20.3: 275–87.

Lachkar, J. 1993b. Political and marital conflict. *Journal of Psychohistory* 22.2: 199–211.

Lachkar, J. 1997. Narcissistic/borderline couples: A psychodynamic approach to conjoint treatment. In *The Disordered Couple*, ed. J. Carlson and L. Sperry, 259–82. New York: Brunner/Mazel.

Lachkar, J. 1998a. *The many faces of abuse: Treating the emotional abuse of high-functioning women*. Northvale, N.J.: Jason Aronson.

Lachkar, J. (1998b, July). Aggression and cruelty in cross-cultural couples. Paper presented at the Psychohistory Congress, Paris.

Lachkar, J. 2000. Slobodan and Mirjana Milosevic: The dysfunctional couple that destroyed the Balkans. (unpublished paper)

Lachkar, J. 2001. Narcissism in dance. *Choreography and Dance: An International Journal* 6: 23–30.

Lachkar, J. 2002. The psychological make-up of a suicide bomber. *Journal of Psychohistory* 29.4: 349–67.

Lachkar, J. 2004. *The narcissistic/borderline couple: New approaches to marital therapy*. 2nd ed. New York: Branner-Routledge.

Lachkar, J. 2007. The psychopathology of terrorism: A cultural "V-spot." *Journal of Psychohistory* 20 (2): 111–28

Lachkar, J. 2008. *How to talk to a narcissist*. New York: Routledge.

Lachkar, J., and P. Berton. 1997. Japanese and German reactions to their aggression in World War II: A psychoanalytic study. Unpublished paper presented at the first convention of the International Psychohistorical Association, Amsterdam.

Lachkar, J., and P. Berton. 2004. Japanese and German reactions to their aggression in World War II: A psychoanalytic study presented at the Sixth International Biennial (bicentennial) Conference of Sino-Japanese Relations, Beijing, September 18–19, 2004.

Lansky, M. 1987. Shame in the family relationships of borderline patients. In *The borderline patient: Emerging concepts in diagnosis, psychodynamics and treatment*, vol. 2., ed. J. Grotstein, M. Solomon, and J. Lang. Hillsdale, N.J.: Analytic Press.

Loewenberg, P. 1987. The Kristallnacht as a public degradation in ritual. In *Leo Baeck Institute Yearbook* vol. 32, 308–23. London: Secker & Warburg.

Loewenberg, P. 1995. *Fantasy and reality in history*. New York: Oxford University Press.

Loring, M. T. 1994. *Emotional abuse*. New York: Lexington Books.

Los Angeles Times. 2005. Primate party gone horribly awry, March 5, p. A1.

Los Angeles Times. 2005. LA Magazine, November 20, p. 11.

Mahler, M. S., F. Pine, and A. Bergman. 1975. *The psychological birth of the human infant*. New York: Basic Books.

Masaaki, I. 1981. *16 ways to avoid saying no*. Tokyo: The Nihon Keizai Shimbun.

Mason, A. 1981. The suffocating super-ego. Psychotic break and claustrophobia. In *Do I dare disturb the universe? A memorial to Wilfred R. Bion*, ed. J. Grotstein. Beverly Hills, Calif.: Caesura Press.

Mason, A. 1994. *Quick Otto and slow Leopold: The Freud-Fliess relationship*. Los Angeles: Psychoanalytic Center of California.

Matsunoto, D. 1996. *Creative psychology*. Pacific Grove, Calif.: Brooks/Cole Publishing Company.

McCormack, Charles. 2000. *Treating borderline states in marriage: dealing with oppositionalism, ruthless aggression, and severe resistance*. Northvale, NJ: Jason Aronson.

Miyamoto, M. 1994. *Straitjacket society: An insider's irreverent view of bureaucratic Japan*. Tokyo: Kodansha International.

Ogden, T. 1980. On the nature of schizophrenic conflict. *International Journal of Psycho-Analysis* 61: 513.

Ogden, T. H. 1986. *The matrix of the mind: Object relations and the psychoanalytic dialogue*. Northvale, N.J.: Jason Aronson.

Puhar, A. 1993. On childhood orgins of violence in Yugoslavia. *Journal of Psychohistory* 21 (2).

Puhar, A. 1994. Childhood nightmare and dreams of revenge. *Journal of Psychohistory* 22 (2): 131–70.

Roland, A. 1988. *In search of self in India and Japan: Toward a cross-cultural psychology*. Princeton: University Press.

Roland, A. 1996. How universal is the psychoanalytic self? In *Reaching across boundaries of culture and class: Widening the scope of psychotherapy*, ed. R. P. Foster, M. Moskowitz, and R. A. Javier. Northvale, N.J.: Jason Aronson.

Rothstein, A. 1998. *Psychoanalytic technique and the creation of analytic patients*. Madison, Conn.: International Universities Press.

Scarf, M. 1987. *Intimate partners*. New York: Random House.

Scharff, D., and J. S. Scharff. 1987. *Object relations in family therapy*. Northvale, N.J.: Jason Aronson.

Segal, H. 1964. *Introduction to the works of* Melanie *Klein*. New York: Basic Books.

Seinfeld, J. 1990. *The bad object: Handling the negative therapeutic reaction in psychotherapy*. Northvale, N.J.: Jason Aronson.

Sharpe, S. A. 1981. The symbiotic marriage: A diagnostic profile. *Bulletin of the Menninger Clinic* 45.2: 89–114.

Slavik, S. 1997. The passive-aggressive couple. In *The disordered couple*, ed. J. Carlson and L. Sperry, 299–312. New York: Brunner/Mazel.

Slipp, S. 1984. *Object relations: A dynamic bridge between individual and family treatment*. New York: Jason Aronson.

Tuch, R. 2000. *The single woman–married man syndrome*. Northvale, N.J.: Jason Aronson.

Vaknin, S., and L. Vaknin. 2007. *Malignant self love—Narcissism revisited*. Czech Republic: Narcissus Publications.

Willi, J. 1982. *Couples in collusion. The unconscious dimension in partner relationships*. Claremont, Calif.: Hunter House.

Winnicott, D. W. 1965. *The maturational process and the facilitating environment*. New York: International Universities Press.

Yalom, I. 1992. *When Nietzsche wept*. New York: Perennial Press.

Yi, K. 1995. Psychoanalytic psychotherapy with Asian clients: Transference and therapeutic considerations. *Journal of Psychotherapy* 32: 308–16.

Index

abuser types, *50*; borderline, 34–39, *38–39*, 167; narcissistic, 31–33, 53, 169; obsessive-compulsive, *38*, 45–46, 170; passive-aggressive, *38*, 41–42, 170–71; schizoid, *39*, 47–48, 171–72; "silent," 42; warning sign behaviors of, 62–63. *See also* emotional abuse; enablers; internal abusers
addictions, 23–25
Age of Darkness, 143, 145
Age of Enlightenment, 143, 146
Age of Reason, 143
aggression: attachment and, 76, 83–87, 128; confronting, 84–87, 150; cross-cultural consideration of, 131, 159; defining, 15, 131; psychodynamics of, 131
Aggression in Personality Disorders and Perversions (Kernberg), 77
alpha thinking, 76
amae (dependency), 133–35
The Anatomy of Love (Fisher), 24
anxiety, persecutory, 171
Arab-Israeli conflict, 6, 129–30
archaic injury, 3, 4, 9–10
Armenian societies, 136–37
artistic expression, 141–42, 151–52
Asian societies, 127, 131, 134. *See also* Japanese societies; Korean societies
"as if" personalities, 37, *38*, 167. *See also* borderline personalities
attachment: aggression and, 76, 83–87, 128; confronting, case study on, 84–86; detachment versus, 101–2; theory, 71, 68. *See also* love bonds
Atwood, Colleen, 123

Bach, Sheldon, 109
Beethoven, Ludwig van, 15
Benjamin, Jessica, 76
Berton, Peter, 131, 158
beta thinking, 76
betraying objects, 117–21
Bible, 129–30
Bion, Wilfred, 10, 19, 68; containment defined by, 167; group psychology defined by, 128; K and −K theory of,

75–76; projective identification theory of, 75
Bird, Martin, 46
Blackman, Jerome, 14, 15
blame. *See* shame/blame
bonds: hierarchical obligatory, 137–38, 153; "traumatic," 78, 110. *See also* love bonds; mother/child bonding
borderline personalities, 2; abusers with, 34–39, *38–39*, 167; *amae*'s impact on, 134–35; in business, 40; cultural, *39*; defining, 34–39, *38–39*, 167; enablers of, 39–40, *50*, 104; histrionic, *38*; love bonds of, 2, 33–34, 39–40, *50*, 78, *103*, 103–4, 163–64, 169; paranoid, *39*, 92; passive-aggressive, *38*; reality testing, 16; schizoid, *39*; therapist suggestions for partner of, 104; types of, *38–39*. *See also* narcissist/borderline relationships
Bowlby, John, 66, 68, 70, 101–2
breasts, good versus bad, 36, 71–72, 109, 111, 168, 170
business: borderline personalities in, 40; cross-cultural considerations in, 126; passive-aggressive personalities in, 25–26

caretaker personalities: love bonds of, 41–42, *50*, *103*; understanding, 16
Carlson, Jon, 65–66
case studies: *amae*, 134–35; betraying objects, 118–21; confronting attachment, 84–86; conjoint treatment, 153–55; detachment, 27–28; dual projective identification, 79–83, 118–21; emotional abuse, 54–55; *folie à deux*, 91–98; HFW, lower level, 58–62; impossible couple, 115–17; individual self versus group self, 136–37; internal abuser, 114–21; interracial relationship, 134–37, 139–41, 158–59; passive-aggressive, 25–26, 42–45; projective identification, 79–83; psychosis, 19–20, 27–28; psychotic versus neurotic ego function, 19–23; reality testing, 16–19; reverse superego, 25–26; schizoid, 49; treatment priority, 153–55; unavailable partner, 21–23; V-Spot of therapist, 3–4; waiting game, 16–19, 20–21, 154–55; Wolfman, 35; women, treatment of, 138–41
cathexis, 67
children. *See* mother/child bonding
Chinese Cultural Revolution, 141–42
Christianity, 131
Civilization and Its Discontents (Freud, S.), 51
classic psychoanalysis, 67–69, 70
communication: alpha and beta level, 76; Japanese approach to, 126; mediator's role of, 113
conjoint treatment: case studies, 153–55; cross-cultural, 157–61; individual versus, 145, 149; for primitive defense mechanisms, 102–6; six-step procedure for, 148–49; therapist suggestions for, 75, 102–6, 153–61, 157. *See also* couples; projective identification
containment, 167
control. *See* domination/control
countertransference, 3–4, 152–53, 160, 161
couples: cross-cultural, 157–61; impossible, 114–17; interracial, 134–37, 139–41, 158–59; mediation of, 112–14; self development phases of, 143; therapists, individual versus, 145, 149; transference, 149, 153
"Courts Beware of the Borderline" (Lachkar), 113
creativity: need for, 151–52; suppressing, 141–42

cross-cultural considerations: of aggressor societies, 131, 159; *amae* and, 133–35; in business, 126; for conjoint treatment, 157–61; of creativity, suppressing, 141–42; of *folie à deux*, 91–95; group psychology for, 123–42, 158; individual self versus group self in, 135–37; introduction to, 123–25; of obligatory bonds, 137–38, 153; pathology versus culture and, 126–27; for psychodynamics, 130–34, 165; psychohistory of, 128–30; religious, 126, 127, 129–30, 131, 132, 139; of self development, 124, 132, 133–34, 135–36; therapist suggestions for, 159–60; transculture versus, 125–26; of women, 138–41. *See also specific country's cross-cultural considerations*
cultural borderline personalities, *39*
"cultural contrast hook," 158–59
culture: defining, 125; pathology and, 126–27; V-Spots, 164–65, 167–68. *See also* cross-cultural considerations
custody battles, 112–14

Dalrymple, Theodore, 139
the "dance," 2, 71, 72, 99, 163, 168
dancers, 151–52
Dark Ages, 143, 145
darkness phase, of treatment, 143, *144*, 144–46
death instinct, 14, 35, 170, 171
defense. *See* manic defenses; primitive defense mechanisms
deMause, Lloyd, 128
dependency: *amae* as Japanese concept of, 133–35; cross-cultural psychodynamics of, 133–34; healthy, 147–48; interracial relationships, 134–37; life-long, 136; omnipotence versus, 101
dependent personalities, 48–49, *50*, *103*
depressive position, 143, 146, 168, 171, 173
detachment: attachment versus, 101–2; case study of, 27–28; withdrawal versus, 173
"detoxification," 12
Deutsch, Helene, 37
Dicks, Henry, 90
The Disordered Couple (Carlson and Sperry), 65–66
divorce, 112–14
Doi, Takeo, 132, 133
domination/control, submission versus, 100–1
Don Juan Syndrome, 37, 47, 53
Donne, John, 107
dopamine, 24
dual projective identification: betraying objects, 118–21; case study, 79–83, 118–21; defining, 172; primitive defenses, 102; psychodynamics, 102

ego: defining, 13–15, 168; dysfunctionality of, 19; id versus, 13, 14, 68, 69, 73, 168; psychotic versus neurotic, 19–23; subjective versus objective, 15–19; superego versus, 13, 14, 69, 108–9. *See also* theories
ego psychology, 14–15, 68, 69–70, 101
emotional abuse: case study of, 54–55; defining, 55–56; fears, common, 56; HFW's reaction to, 56–62; men's versus women's tendencies toward, 51; overview of, 51–55; warning signs of, 62–63
empathy/mirroring, 73–74, 83, 150, 169
enablers: of borderlines, 39–40, *50*, *104*; defining, 52; of narcissists, 33–34, *50*, *103–4*; of obsessive-compulsives, 46–47, *50*, *105*; of passive-aggressives, 41, 42–45, *50*, *104–5*; of schizoids, 48–49, *50*, *105*; victims versus, 52. *See also* love bonds

Endleman, Robert, 125–26
enlightenment phase, of treatment, 143, *146*, 146–47
envy, jealousy versus, 99–100, 168–69
external objects: darkness phase of treatment and, *144*; defining, 111; themes, 156

Fairbairn, W. R. D., 68, 109
false self, 37, *38*, 92, 124, 132
fantasy. *See folie à deux*
fears, common emotional abuse, 56
"feeding" experience, 36, 71–72, 109, 111, 168, 170. *See also* mother/child bonding
Fisher, Judy, 24
Fliess, Wilhelm, 90
folie à deux, 48, 106; case studies of, 91–98; cross-cultural, 91–95; defining, 90–91, 168
folklore, 128–30
Freud, Anna, 66
Freud, Sigmund, 19, 51, 79, 90, 108, 172–73; aggression defined by, 131; borderline defined by, 35; ego psychology theory of, 14–15; love bond concept of, 24, 67; narcissism concept of, 67–69; objects defined by, 108–9; sabotage explained by, 10; schizophrenia defined by, 26
Frost, Robert, 65

Gay, Peter, 15, 131
German societies, 128, 131, 132, 158
Grotstein, James, 36
group psychology: cross-cultural considerations of, 123–42, 158; defining, 127–28; hierarchy of, obligatory bond, 137–38, 153; individual self versus, 133, 135–37; psychohistory of, 128–30; thinking, 128. *See also* culture
G-Spot, 3, 9, 173
guilt: cross-cultural psychodynamics of, 132; defining, 168; shame versus, 99, 131–32, 168

han (interminable rage), 124, 138
Hartmann, Heinz, 68, 69–70
healing process, 10–11, 12–13
HFW (high-functioning women), 53; higher level, 56–57; lower level, 57–62
hierarchy, of obligatory bonds, 137–38, 153
high-functioning women. *See* HFW
"His Majesty the Narcissist" (Freud), 67–68
history. *See* psychohistory
histrionic personalities: borderline, *38*; love bonds of, 46–47, *50*, *103*
honne (private, or true, self), 124, 132

id, 13, 14, 68, 69, 73, 168
identification. *See* projective identification
impossible couples, 114–17
individual: self, group self versus, 133, 135–37; treatment, conjoint versus, 145, 149. *See also* self
infants. *See* mother/child bonding
instincts. *See* death instinct; mother/child bonding
internal abusers: betraying objects and, 117–21; case study of, 114–21; impossible couple as, 114–17; mediation of, 112–14; objects of, 108–12; overview, 107–8
internal objects: betraying, 117–21; darkness phase of treatment and, *144*; defining, 112, 168; impossible couple and, 114–17; meditation and, 112–14; pain and, 109–10; themes, 156; theories, 108–9

interracial relationships, 134–37, 139–41, 158–59. *See also* cross-cultural considerations
introjective/projective process, 71–72
Islam, 139
Israeli societies, 161. *See also* Arab-Israeli conflict
Italian societies, 134–35, 139

Japanese societies, 123; *amae* as dependency concept of, 133–35; communication approach to, 126; hierarchy and obligatory bonds in, 138; interracial relationships and, 158; self development concept of, 133, 135–36; shame versus guilt psychodynamics of, 131, 132; true versus false self of, 124, 132
Japan on the Psychologist's Couch (Berton), 158
jealousy, envy versus, 99–100, 168–69
Jewish societies, 127, 128, 129–30, 132, 134–35
judges: court, 113; as internal/external theme, 156
judgment, distortion of, 19–23

K and −K links, 75–76
Kernberg, Otto, 47, 68, 76–80, 132; aggression and attachment work of, 76, 128; ego defined by, 14; emotional tendencies of men versus women, 51; love bond types defined by, 76–79; reality testing defined by, 16
Klein, Melanie, 143, 170, 171, 173; borderline defined by, 35–36; depressive position defined by, 168; mother/child bonding theory of, 36, 71–72, 109, 111, 168, 170; object relations theory of, 68, 71–72, 110–11, 169; objects defined by, 108–9; projective identification theory of, 66, 68, 71–72
knowledge, 75–76. *See also* thinking
Kohut, Heinz, 4, 9, 66, 68, 141; mirroring defined by, 169; mother/child bonding theory of, 70–71; narcissism concept of, 68; self object defined by, 111–12, 172; self psychology theory of, 73–74, 172
Koran, 129–30
Korean societies, 124, 138

lawyers, 113
liars, 19, 58–59, 93
listening, 152, 156–57
Loewenberg, Peter, 128, 132
Loring, M. T., 53
love: falling in, 1, 23–24; pain confused with, 54–55
love bonds: borderline, 2, 33–34, 39–40, 50, 78, *103*, 103–4, 163–64, 169; caretaker, 41–42, *50*, *103*; dependent, 48–49, *50*, *103*; Freud's, Sigmund, concept of, 24, 67; histrionic, 46–47, *50*, *103*; mature, 78–79; narcissistic, 2, 33–34, 39–40, *50*, 78, *103*, 103–4, 163–64, 169; normal, 77, 147–48, 150; obsessive-compulsive, 42–45, 46–47, *50*, *103*; Otto's concept of, 76–79; passive-aggressive, 41–45, *50*, *103*; pathological, 77–78; perverse, 78; psychodynamics of, 99–105, *103*; schizoid, 48–49, *50*, *103*; "traumatic," 77, 110; types of, *50*, *77*, 76–79

Mahler, Margaret, 68
manic defenses, 148, 169
The Many Faces of Abuse: Treating the Emotional Abuse of High-Functioning Women (Lachkar), 2, 51, 62, 164
Maracci, Carmelita, 151–52

Marital Tensions (Dick), 90
marriage. *See* conjoint treatment; couples; *folie à deux*
masochism, 51, 54, 64, 76
Mason, Albert, 90, 148
mature love bonds, 78–79
McCormack, 48
mediation, 112–14
Middle Eastern societies: dependency psychodynamics of, 133; *folie à deux* case study of, 91–95; interracial couples and, 139–40, 158–59; psychohistory of, 6, 129–30; shame psychodynamics of, 131; true versus false self of, 124
Milosevic, Mirjana, 91–95
Milosevic, Slobodan, 91–95
mirroring, 73–74, 83, 150, 169
money issues, 81. *See also* business
Monroe, Marilyn, 33–34, 40
mother/child bonding: absence of, 173; containment as, 167; ego psychology and, 69–70, 101; separation-individuation process and, 70–71; single, 52–53; suffocating, 48, 49, 79–83; theories, 36, 68, 69–70, 71–72, 109, 111, 168, 170. *See also* self development
"Mother of Pain," 109
Much Ado about Nothing (Shakespeare), 89
Muslims, 129–30, 133, 139
mythology, 128–30

"Narcissism in Dance" (Lachkar), 141
narcissist/borderline relationships, 50; about, 2, 33–34, 39–40; love bond psychodynamics of, *103*, 103–4; as object choices, 163–64; as pathological love, 78
The Narcissistic/Borderline Couple (Lachkar), 2, 163, 164
narcissist personalities, 2, 164; abusers with, 31–33, 53, 169; *amae*'s impact on, 134–35; defining, 31–33, 53, 169; enablers of, 33–34, 50, 103–4; Freud's, Sigmund, concept of, 67–69; Kohut's concept of, 68; love bonds of, 2, 33–34, 39–40, 50, 78, *103*, 103–4, 163–64, 169; primary versus secondary, 68–69; reality testing, 15; schizoid versus, 47–48, 172; self psychology theory of, 72–73; therapist suggestions for partner of, 103–4; treatment of, 149
Narcissus, 67
"negative therapeutic reaction," 10
neurotic ego, psychotic versus, 19–23
normal love bonds, 77–78, 147–48, 150

objective ego, subjective versus, 15–19
object relations: defining, 169; narcissist/borderline, 163–64; self psychology versus, 73–74; theory, Klein's, 68, 71–72, 110–11, 169
objects: betraying, 117–21; defining, 108–10; external, 111, *144*, 156; internal abuser, 108–12; part, 110–11, 170; self, 111–12, 148, 172; splitting, 109, 169; transitional, 68; unavailable, 21–23; whole, 111, 173. *See also* internal objects
obligatory bonds, hierarchy of, 137–38, 153
obsessive-compulsive personalities: abusers with, *38*, 45–46, 170; borderline, defining, *38*; defining, *38*, 45–46, 170; enablers of, 46–47, *50*, 105; love bonds of, 42–45, 46–47, *50*, *103*; schizoid versus, 171; therapist suggestions for partner of, 105
Ogden, Thomas, 14, 16, 75; psychosis research by, 19–20, 68; schizophrenia defined by, 26–27, 68

omnipotence, dependency versus, 101
"open house" metaphor, 80, 82–83

pain: internal objects and, 109–10; love confused with, 54–55; masochism and, 51, 54, 64, 76; of self-mutilation, 29, 36; of separation-individuation process, 70–71; "traumatic bonding" through, 77, 110
paranoid borderline personalities, *39*, 92, 171
paranoid-schizoid position, 143, 144, 170
part objects, 110–11, 170
passive-aggressive personalities: abusers with, *38*, 41–42, 170–71; borderline, *38*; in business, 25–26; case study, 25–26, 42–45; defining, *38*, 41–42, 170–71; enablers of, 41, 42–45, *50*, 104–5; love bonds of, 41–45, *50*, *103*; schizoid versus, 171; therapist suggestions for partner of, 104–5
pathological liars, 19, 58–59, 93
pathological love bonds, 77, 78
pathology, 126–27, 165
Peace at Home, 62
perception, distortion of, 19–23
persecutory anxiety, 171
personality types. *See specific personality types*
perverse love bonds, 78–79
poor-me. *See* passive-aggressive personalities
primary narcissism, 69
primitive defense mechanisms: attachment versus detachment, 101–2; conjoint treatment for, 102–6; domination/control versus submission, 100–1; dual projective identification, 102; envy versus jealousy, 99–100, 168–69; impossible couples and their, 114–17; omnipotence versus dependency, 101; projective identification, 102; shame versus guilt, 99, 131, 168; theory, Klein's, 72
primitive superego, 108, 170, 171
privation, 36, *38*
procrastination, 27–28, *38*
projective identification: case study, 79–83; defining, 171, 172; introjective/projective process and, 71–72; primitive defenses, 102; psychodynamics of, 102; theories, 66, 71–72, 74–75. *See also* dual projective identification
psychoanalysis, classic, 67–68, 70
psychodynamics, *103*; aggression, 131; attachment versus detachment, 101–2; cross-cultural, 130–34, 165; dependency, 133–34; domination/control versus submission, 100–1; dual projective identification, 102; envy versus jealousy, 99–100, 168–69; love bond, 99–105, *103*; narcissist/borderline, *103*, 103–4; omnipotence versus dependency, 101; projective identification, 102; religious, 125, 126, 131, 132; shame versus guilt, 99, 131–32, 168
psychohistory, 128–30, 171
psychology. *See* ego psychology; group psychology; self psychology
"The Psychopathology of Terrorism" (Lachkar), 124
psychosis: case study, 27–28; defining, 26–27, 68; neurosis versus, 19–23; Ogden's research on, 19–20, *79*; understanding, 28–29

Quick Otto and Slow Leopold (Mason), 90

rapist, as internal/external theme, 156–57

reality testing: case study, 16–19; defining, 15–16; HFW's ability to, 56–57
reason phase, of treatment, 143, *147*, 147–48
The Red Violin, 141–42
religious groups: interracial relationships and, 127, 139; psychodynamics of, 125, 126, 131, 132; psychohistory of, 129–30
reparation, 171
reverse superego, 25–26
robber, as internal/external theme, 156–57
Roland, A, 136
Rothstein, Arnold, 155
Russian societies, 131, 159

sabotage, 10, 17–18, 35
schizoid personalities: abusers with, *39*, 47–48, 171–72; borderline, *39*; case study, 49; defining, *39*, 47–48, 171–72; enablers of, 48–49, *50*, 105; love bonds of, 48–49, *50*, *103*; narcissist versus, 47–48, 172; obsessive-compulsive versus, 171; paranoid, 143, 144, 170; passive-aggressive versus, 171; therapist suggestions for partners of, 105
schizophrenia, 26–27, 79
secondary narcissism, 69
Seinfeld, J., 10
self: false, 37, *38*, 92, 124, 132; true, 124, 132
self development: couple, phases of, 143; cross-cultural considerations of, 124, 132, 133–34, 135–36; defining, 172; Japanese concept of, 133, 135–36; paranoid-schizoid position in, 170; separation-individuation process of, 71; whole objects relation to, 173; withdrawal/detachment in, 173
self-mutilation, 29, 36
self objects, 111–12, 148, 172
self psychology: individual versus group, 133, 135–37; object relations versus, 68, 74; theories, 66, 73–74, 172
Self Psychology (Kohut), 4
separation-individuation process, 70–71. *See also* attachment; self development
Serbs, 91–92
serotonin, 24
Shakespeare, William, 1, 89
shame/blame: cross-cultural psychodynamics of, 131; darkness development stage of, 145; guilt versus, 99, 131–32, 168. *See also* borderline personalities
"silent abuser," 42
single mothers, 52–53
Sonnet 116 (Shakespeare), 1
Sperry, Len, 65–66
splitting, 172
splitting objects, 109, 169. *See also* projective identification
Stern, Isaac, 151
subjective ego, objective versus, 15–19
submission, domination/control versus, 100–1
suffocating mommy syndrome, 48, 49, 79–83
suggestions. *See* therapist suggestions
superego: defining, 172; ego versus, 13, 14, 69, 108–9; primitive, 108, 170, 171; reverse, 25–26

tatamae (public, or false, self), 124, 132
terrorism, 6, 124
themes, internal/external object, 156–57
theories: attachment, 68, 71; classic psychoanalysis, 67–69, 70; comparing, 65–66; development of, chronological, 68; ego psychology,

14–15, 69–70, *79*; internal objects, 108–9; K and −K, 75–76; mother/child bonding, 36, 69–70, 71–72, *79*, 109, 111, 168, 170; object relations, 68, 71–72, 110–11, 169; practical application of, 79–86; primitive defense mechanism, 72; projective identification, 66, 71–72, 74–75; self psychology, 66, 68, 72–73, 172
therapeutic functions, 152–57. *See also* treatment
therapeutic space, 147, 148
therapists: conjoint versus individual, 145, 149; quality of, 151–52; as self object, 148; V-Spot of, 3–4, 160–61
therapist suggestions: for borderline's partner, 104; for conjoint treatment, 75, 102–6, 153–61, 157; cross-cultural, 159–60; general, 105–6; for narcissist's partner, 103–4; for obsessive-compulsive's partner, 105; for passive-aggressive's partner, 104–5; for schizoid's partner, 105. *See also* treatment
"The Road Not Taken" (Frost), 65
The Single Woman-Married Man Syndrome (Tuch), 53
thinking: distortion of, 19–20; group, 128; linking, alpha and beta, 75–76
Tolstoy, Leo, 112
the "Tragic Man," 66
transculture, cross-culture versus, 125–26
transference, 149, 152–53
transitional objects, 68
transitional space, 147, 148
"traumatic bonding," 77, 110
treatment, 143–62; countertransference issues in, 152–53, 161; darkness phase of, 143, *144*, 144–46; ending, 150–51; enlightenment phase of, 143, *146*, 146–47; individual versus conjoint, 145, 149; of narcissists, 149; overview of, 143–44; phases of, 143, *144*, 144–48, *146*, *147*; priority of, 153–55; procedure, six-step, 148–49; reason phase of, 143, *147*, 147–48; techniques, 150–51, 157–60; by theme, 156–57; therapeutic functions of, 152–57; therapist qualities needed for, 151–52; transference issues in, 152–53. *See also* conjoint treatment; therapist suggestions
triangulation, 90
triggers, 11–13
true self, 124, 132
truth, 19, 20, 74–76, 172. *See also* pathological liars
Tuch, Richard, 53

unavailable partner/objects, 21–23

"A Valediction Forbidding Mourning" (Donne), 107
victims, enablers versus, 52
V-Spot: addictions, 23–25; artistic, 141–42; concepts, 9–29; cultural, 164–65, 167–68; defining, 1, 3, 9, 173; G-Spot versus, 3, 9, 173; healing, 10–11, 12–13; introduction to, 1–8, 9–11; locating, 10–11, 12–13; neurotic versus psychotic understanding of, 19–23; therapist's, 3–4, 160–61; triggers, 11–13. *See also* the "dance"
The V-Spot (Lachkar): influences on, 5–6; purpose of, 6–8

waiting game, 16–19, 20–21, 154–55
Walter Briehl Human Rights Organization, 6
warning signs, of emotional abuse, 62–63
When Nietzsche Wept (Yalom), 145
whole objects, 111, 173
Winfrey, Oprah, 51
Winnicott, D. W., 37, *79*, 132

withdrawal, detachment versus, 173
Wolfman case, 35
women: cross-cultural views of, 138–41; emotional tendencies of, men versus, 51; as single mothers, 52–53. *See also* emotional abuse; HFW
"Women Who Become Undone" (Oprah), 51
World War II, 138, 158

Yi, Kris, 127, 135
yoga, 10, 12, 129

~

About the Author

Joan Lachkar, Ph.D., is psychotherapist in private practice in California, is the author of *The Many Faces of Abuse: Treating the Emotional Abuse of High-Functioning Women*, *The Narcissistic/Borderline Couple: A Psychoanalytic Perspective on Marital Treatment*, and numerous publications on marital and political conflict. She is an affiliate member and instructor of the New Center for Psychoanalysis, a contributing author in the *Journal of Psychohistory*, and is on the editorial board of the *Journal of Emotional Abuse*.